ABOUT THE AUTHOR

Philip Kotler is the S. C. Johnson & Son Distinguished Professor of International Marketing at the J. L. Kellogg Graduate School of Management, Northwestern University, Evanston, Illinois. Kellogg was voted the Best Business School six times in *Business Week*'s survey of U.S. business schools. It is also rated as the Best Business School for the Teaching of Marketing, largely due to Professor Kotler's contributions during his many years there.

The first recipient of the American Marketing Association's Distinguished Marketing Educator Award, he has also been awarded the prize in Marketing Excellence from the European Association of Marketing Consultants and Sales Trainers, and was chosen Leader in Marketing Thought by the Academic Members of the AMA.

Professor Kotler has consulted for such companies as IBM, General Electric, AT&T, Honeywell, Bank of America, and Merck. He is the author of *Marketing Management*, the most widely used marketing book in graduate business schools worldwide, *The New Competition*, *Marketing Models*, *High Visibility*, *Social Marketing*, *The Marketing of Nations*, and many other works. He has traveled extensively throughout Europe, Asia, and South America, advising and lecturing to many companies.

OTHER BOOKS BY PHILIP KOTLER

Marketing Management

Principles of Marketing

Strategic Marketing for Non-Profit Organizations

Marketing Places

The Marketing of Nations

Marketing Models

Social Marketing

Marketing Professional Services

Strategic Marketing for Educational Institutions

Marketing for Health Care Organizations

High Visibility

The New Competition

Marketing for Hospitality and Tourism

Marketing for Congregations

Standing Room Only

Museum Strategies and Marketing

Praise for KOTLER ON MARKETING

"Strategy, tactics, and guidelines for improving marketing effectiveness and customer value spring to life in this must-use book."

—Bradley T. Gale, author of *Managing Customer Value*

"An unrivalled opportunity to spend quality time with one of the leading marketing thinkers in the world."

—Professor Leonard L. Berry, Author of *Discovering the Soul of Service*

"Up-to-the-minute examples of best practice. A terrific overview of the rapidly changing field of marketing strategy and tactics."

—Frederick E. Webster, Jr., C.H. Jones 3rd Century Professor of Management, Amos Tuck School, Dartmouth College

"This book is about winning profitably; optimally creating and managing demand from various customers' focused needs."

—Robert W. Galvin,
Chairman of the Executive Committee, Motorola

PHILIP KOTLER

KOTLER ON MARKETING

fP

THE FREE PRESS

This edition first published in Great Britain by Simon & Schuster UK Ltd, 2001

A CBS COMPANY

Copyright © Philip Kotler, 1999

The right of Philip Kotler to be identified as authors of this work has been
asserted in accordance with sections 77 and 78 of the Copyright, Designs
and Patents Act, 1988.

5 7 9 10 8 6

Simon & Schuster UK Ltd
Africa House
64-78 Kingsway
London WC2B 6AH

Simon & Schuster Australia
Sydney

A CIP catalogue record for this book is available from the British Library

ISBN 10: 0-6848-6047-3
ISBN 13: 978-0-6848-6047-3

Printed and bound in Great Britain by
CPI Bath

This book is dedicated to my co-authors of the international editions of *Marketing Management* and *Principles of Marketing*, who have taught me a great deal as they worked to adapt marketing management thinking to the problems and opportunities in their respective countries.

Australia

PETER CHANDLER, LINDEN BROWN, and STEWART ADAM

Monash and other Australian Universities

Canada

RONALD E. TURNER

Queen's University

France

BERNARD DUBOIS

Group HEC School of Management

Germany

FRIEDHELM W. BLIEMEL

Universitat Kaiserslautern

Italy

WALTER GEORGIO SCOTT

Universita Cattolica del Sacro Cuore

Singapore

SWEE-HOON ANG, SIEW-MENG LEONG, and CHIN TIONG TAN

National University of Singapore

United Kingdom

JOHN SAUNDERS and VERONICA WONG

Loughborough University and Warwick University

CONTENTS

PART THREE: ADMINISTRATIVE MARKETING

PART FOUR: TRANSFORMATIONAL MARKETING

PREFACE

FOR SEVERAL YEARS, Robert Wallace, the distinguished senior editor of The Free Press, urged me to write a marketing book for managers, one that would show the latest marketing thinking and not run 700 pages! He did not want me simply to condense my graduate student textbook, *Marketing Management*, but to write a completely new book. Bob had heard that I have been presenting one- and two-day marketing seminars around the world for twenty years and had even seen a copy of my seminar notebook. He said that the material in the notebook itself could constitute a new book.

I put off his requests because of my busy teaching, research, and consulting schedule. I was learning new things in consulting with AT&T, IBM, Michelin, Shell, Merck, and several banks. I was also trying to think through the revolutionary impact on the marketplace and marketing practice of the new technologies—the Internet, e-mail, fax machines, sales automation software—and new media—cable TV, videoconferencing, CDs, personal newspapers. With the marketplace changing so rapidly, it didn't seem the right time to write.

I finally realized that the marketplace would continue to undergo radical change. My rationale for postponing the book could no longer hold.

I have had a thirty-eight-year romance with marketing and continue to be intrigued. When we think that we finally understand marketing, it starts a new dance and we must follow it as best we can.

When I first came upon marketing in the early 1960s, the literature was basically descriptive. There were three approaches at the time. The *commodity* approach described the characteristics of different products and buyer behavior toward those products. The *institutional* approach described how various marketing organizations worked, such as wholesalers and retailers. The *functional* approach described how various marketing activities—advertising, sales force, pricing—perform in the marketplace.

My own training, centered in economics and decision sciences, led me to approach marketing from a *managerial* point of view. Marketing managers everywhere faced a plethora of tough decisions; they had to choose target markets carefully, develop optimal product features and benefits, establish an effective price, and decide on the proper size and allocation of the sales force and various marketing budgets. And they had to make those decisions in the face of incomplete information and ever changing market dynamics.

I felt strongly that marketing managers, in order to make better marketing decisions, needed to analyze markets and competition in *systems* terms, explicating the forces at work and their various interdependencies. That sparked my interest in developing models of markets and marketing behavior, and in 1971 I put my ideas together and published *Marketing Decision-making: A Model-building Approach*. The book ran 700 pages, starting with a picture of the simplest market consisting of one firm operating in one market selling one product and using one marketing instrument in an effort to maximize its profits. Subsequent chapters introduced added complexities, such as two or more competitors, two or more marketing instruments, two or more territories, two or more products, delayed responses, multiple goals, and higher levels of risk and uncertainty. The modeling challenge was to capture marketing effects that tended to be nonlinear, stochastic, interactive, and downright difficult.

My intention was to put marketing decision-making on a more scientific basis. In subsequent years it has been gratifying to witness substantial advances in the body of scientific literature in marketing—both explanatory and normative—contributed by a generation of talented marketing scholars bent on improving our understanding of how markets work.

Virtually all marketing theorizing before 1970 dealt with for-profit firms struggling to sell their products and services for gain. But other organizations—nonprofit and governmental—also face marketing problems, which I described in *Strategic Marketing for Nonprofit Organizations*. Colleges compete for students; museums try to attract visitors; performing arts organizations want to develop audiences; churches seek parishioners; and all of them seek funding. Individuals, too, carry out marketing activities: politicians seek votes; doctors seek patients; and artists seek celebrity. What is common to all such cases is the desire on the part of someone to attract a *response* or *resource* from someone else:

attention, interest, desire, purchase, good word-of-mouth. But to elicit those responses, one must offer something that someone else perceives to be of value, so that the other party voluntarily offers the response or resource in exchange. Thus *exchange* emerges as the core concept underlying marketing.

I also felt that marketable objects included more than *products* and *services*; one can market *people, places, ideas, experiences,* and *organizations*. My desire to understand those less routine applications of marketing led me to research and publish *High Visibility* (person marketing), *Marketing Places* and *Marketing of Nations* (place marketing), and *Social Marketing* (idea marketing), along with some published articles on experience marketing and organization marketing.

Furthermore, marketing required another broadening move, one that wouldn't assume that marketing's only task is to increase demand for some product or service. What if the current demand for a product is too strong? Shouldn't the marketer raise the price, cut advertising and promotion spending, and take other steps to bring demand more in line with supply? Those measures took on the name *demarketing,* which proved an applicable concept in many situations. What if a reform group wants to destroy the demand for a product deemed unhealthy or unsafe, such as hard drugs, tobacco, fatty foods, guns, and other questionables? Its marketing task is named *unselling.* Other marketing tasks included trying to change the image of unpopular products and trying to smooth out irregular demand. All those observations led to my recognizing that marketing's central purpose is *demand management,* the skills needed to manage the *level, timing,* and *composition* of demand.

The broadening of marketing's domain was not an easily won battle. It drew critics who preferred that marketing stick to figuring out how to sell more toothpaste, refrigerators, and computers. But my thinking has been that new perspectives enter a marketplace of ideas, and, as in any marketplace, those perspectives survive which have *use value.* I have been gratified to see the overwhelming majority of scholars and practitioners accept the legitimacy of the broadened marketing concept.

One of the main contributions of modern marketing has been to help companies see the importance of shifting their organization from being *product-centered* to becoming *market-* and *customer-centered.* Ted Levitt's classic article "Marketing Myopia," along with Peter Drucker's famous five questions that every business must ask itself, played an important role in launching the new thinking. But many years passed before many companies actually started to undergo a transformation from "inside-out" thinking to "outside-in" thinking. Even today there are still too many companies operating on a *selling product focus* instead of a *meeting needs focus*.

As great as the changes in marketing thinking have been until now, future changes in marketing thinking and practice will be even greater. Scholars today are questioning whether the core concept underlying marketing should be *exchange* or *relationships* or *networks*. Much is changing in our thinking about services marketing and business marketing. And the greatest impact is yet to come, as the forces of technology and globalization move apace. Computers and the Internet will bring about enormous behavior shifts in buying and selling. I have tried to describe and anticipate these revolutionary changes in the last chapter of this book.

My hope is that this book will enrich the marketing mindset of managers who cope with marketing problems on a daily basis. I have added "questions to consider" at the end of each chapter so that managers can reflect on each chapter's content and apply it to their company's situation. Groups of managers within a company could periodically meet to discuss each chapter and draw marketing lessons for their business.

PART ONE

STRATEGIC MARKETING

1

Building Profitable Businesses Through World-Class Marketing

There are three kinds of companies: those who make things happen; those who watch things happen; and those who wonder what's happened.—*Anonymous*

If we do not change our direction, we are likely to end up where we are headed.—*Old Chinese proverb*

A S THE WORLD spins into the next millennium, both citizens and businesses wonder what is ahead. There is not only change, but the rate of change is accelerating. A twelve-year-old girl said of her nine-year-old sister, "She is of a different generation." Her younger sister listens to different music, plays different video games, knows different movie stars, has different heroes.

Companies often fail to recognize that their marketplace changes every few years. The book *Value Migration* documents how customer requirements and competitive forces have changed significantly every few years in such industries as steel, telecommunications, health care, and entertainment.[1] Last year's winning strategy may become today's losing strategy. As someone observed, there are two kinds of companies: those who change and those who disappear.

Today's economic landscape is being shaped by two powerful forces—*technology* and *globalization*. The technological landscape today is dotted with new products that President John Kennedy in the early 1960s would

3

not have seen, such as satellites, VCRs, camcorders, photocopiers, fax machines, answering machines, digital watches, e-mail, cellular phones, and laptop computers. Technology is the ultimate shaper not only of the material substructure of society but also of human thought patterns. As Marshall McLuhan observed, "The medium is the message."[2]

One revolutionary technological force is *digitalization*, where information is being encoded in "bits," namely series of zeros and ones. The bits are massaged by computers, encoded into music and videos, and sent over phone lines at incredible speed. Nicholas Negroponte, leader of MIT's famous Media Lab, sees "bits" as replacing "atoms."[3] No longer does a software company need to manufacture a set of floppies, put them into a printed package, and ship them on a truck to various outlets, where consumers would have to go to buy them. All this work can be saved by sending the software over the Internet to be downloaded on the customer's computer.

Technology drives the second major force, globalization. McLuhan's vision of a "global village" is now a reality. A Bangkok executive who wants to buy this book can type "*www.amazon.com*" on his keyboard, enter his credit card number, and receive it in a few days thanks to Federal Express. A Cologne, Germany, florist wholesaler who is short of red roses can order and receive a planeload of red roses the next morning from Tel Aviv.

Besides technology and globalization, other forces are reshaping the economy. *Deregulation* is occurring in many economies. Protected companies, often monopolies, suddenly confront new competitors. In the United States, long distance telephone companies such as AT&T can now enter local markets; and regional Bell telephone companies have the corresponding right to enter long distance markets. And electrical utilities can now sell and ship their electricity into other communities.

Another strong force is *privatization*, where former publicly held companies and agencies have been turned over to private ownership and management, in the belief that they would be better managed and more efficient. This happened when British Airways and British Telecom were privatized. Today many public goods and services are being outsourced to private companies, including the building and management of prisons, school systems, and the like.

Yogi Berra, the legendary Yankee catcher, summed it up when he said, "The future ain't what it used to be." He might have added: "Do you feel your company is being chased by wild animals. If not, you should!" Markets are pitiless. Jack Welch, chairman of General Electric, would start his management meetings with the admonishment, "Change or die." Richard Love of Hewlett-Packard observes: "The pace of change is so rapid that the ability to change has now become a competitive advantage." The ability to change requires an ability to learn. Peter Senge and others have popularized the notion of a "learning organization."[4] Not surprisingly, companies such as Coca-Cola, General Electric, and Skandia have appointed vice presidents of knowledge, or learning, or intellectual capital. Those vice presidents have the task of designing *knowledge management systems* to enable rapid company learning about trends and developments affecting consumers, competitors, distributors, and suppliers.

As the pace of change accelerates, companies can no longer rely on their former business practices to sustain prosperity. Exhibit 1–1 compares business assumptions and practices that were practiced then with the ones being increasingly practiced now. Those in the right column are viewed as more effective contemporary approaches to profitability. Your company can almost tell how much it has adopted contemporary business practices by placing a check in each row on either the left or the right. If most of the checks are on the left, your company is locked in traditional practices.

Are There Winning Marketing Practices?

Besides winning business practices, is there a set of winning marketing practices? One frequently hears of one-liner formulas that promise marketing success. Here are nine of the more prominent one-liners:

1. Win Through Higher Quality

Everyone agrees that poor quality is bad for business. Customers who have been burned with bad quality won't return and will bad-mouth the company. But what about winning through good quality? There are four problems.

First, quality has a lot of meanings. If an automobile company claims good quality, what does it mean? Do its cars have more starting reliability? Do they accelerate faster? Do the car bodies wear better over time? Customers care about different things, so a quality claim without further definition doesn't mean much.

Second, people often can't tell a product's quality by looking at it. Consider buying a television receiver. You go into Circuit City and see a hundred different sets with the picture on and the sound blaring. You

EXHIBIT 1–1

Business Firms in Transition

Then	Now
Make everything inside the company	Buy more things outside (outsource)
Improve on one's own	Improve by benchmarking others
Go it alone	Network with other firms, collaborate
Operate with functional departments	Manage business processes with multi-discipline teams
Focus domestically	Focus globally and locally
Be product-centered	Be market- and customer-centered
Make a standard product	Make adapted and/or customized products
Focus on the product	Focus on the value chain
Practice mass marketing	Practice target marketing
Find a sustainable competitive advantage	Keep inventing new advantages
Develop new products slowly and carefully	Speed up the new product development process cycle
Use many suppliers	Use few suppliers
Manage from the top	Manage up and down and across
Operate in the marketplace	Operate also in the marketspace

look at a few popular brands that you favor. The picture quality is similar with most receivers. The casings may differ but hardly tell you anything about the set's reliability. You don't ask the salesperson to open the back of the set to inspect the quality of the components. In the end, you have at best an image of quality without any evidence.

Third, most companies are catching up to each other in quality in most markets. When that happens, quality is no longer a determinant of brand choice.

Fourth, some companies are known to have the highest quality, such as Motorola when it touts its 6 sigma quality. But are there enough customers who need that quality level and will pay for it? And what were Motorola's costs of getting to 6 sigma quality? It is possible that getting to the highest quality level costs too much.

2. Win Through Better Service

We all want good service. But customers define it in different ways. Take service in a restaurant. Some customers would like the waiter to appear quickly, take the order accurately, and deliver the food soon. Other customers would feel that this is rushing them on what otherwise should be a leisurely evening out. Every service breaks down into a list of attributes: speed, cordiality, knowledge, problem-solving, and so on. Each person places different weights at different times in different contexts on each of the service attributes. Claiming better service isn't enough.

3. Win Through Lower Prices

A low price strategy has worked for a number of companies, including the world's largest furniture retailer, IKEA; the world's largest general merchandise retailer, Wal-Mart; and one of America's most profitable airlines, Southwest. Yet low-price leaders must be careful. A lower-price firm might suddenly enter the market. Sears practiced low prices for years, until Wal-Mart beat it on prices. Low price alone is not enough to build a viable business enterprise. The Yugo automobile was low in price; it was also lowest in quality and disappeared. A measure of quality and service must also be present, so that customers feel they are buying on value, not price alone.

4. Win Through High Market Share

Generally speaking, market share leaders make more money than their lamer competitors. They enjoy scale economies and higher brand recognition. There is a "bandwagon effect," and first-time buyers have more confidence in choosing the company's products. But many high market share leaders are not that profitable. A & P was America's largest supermarket chain for many years and yet made pathetic profits. Consider the condition of such giant companies as IBM, Sears, and General Motors in the 1980s, a time when they were doing more poorly than many of their smaller competitors.

5. Win Through Adaptation and Customization

Many buyers will want the seller to modify his offering to contain special features or services they need. A business firm might want Federal Express to pick up its daily mail at 7 P.M., not 5 P.M. A hotel guest might want to rent a room for only part of the day. Such needs can represent opportunities for the seller. However, for many sellers, the cost may be too high to adapt the offering to each customer. *Mass customization* is working for some companies, but many others would find it to be an unprofitable strategy.

6. Win Through Continuous Product Improvement

Continuous product improvement is a sound strategy, especially if the company can lead the pack in product improvements. But not all product improvements are valued. How much more would customers pay if they are told about a better detergent, a sharper razor blade, a faster automobile? Some products reach the limit of their improvement possibilities, and the last improvement doesn't matter very much.

7. Win Through Product Innovation

A frequent exhortation is "Innovate or Evaporate." True, some great innovative companies, such as Sony and 3M, have earned substantial profits by introducing superb new products. But the average company has not fared well in its new product introductions. The new product failure in branded consumer packaged goods is still around 80 percent; in the industrial goods world, it is around 30 percent. A company's dilemma is that if it doesn't introduce new products, it will probably "evaporate"; if it does introduce new products, it may lose a lot of money.

8. Win Through Entering High-Growth Markets

High growth markets such as solid-state electronics, biotechnology, robotics, and telecommunications have the glamour. Some market leaders have made fortunes in those industries. But the average firm entering a high-growth market fails. One hundred new software firms start up in an area, such as computer graphics, and only a few survive. Once the market accepts some firm's brand as the standard, that firm begins to enjoy increasing volume and returns. Microsoft's Office has become the standard, and other good alternatives have been shuttled aside. An added problem is that products become obsolete very fast these fast-growing industries, and each company must invest continually to keep up. They hardly recoup their profits from their last offering before they have to invest in developing its replacement.

9. *Win Through Exceeding Customer Expectations*

One of the most popular marketing clichés today is that a winning company is one that consistently exceeds customer expectations. Meeting customer expectations will only *satisfy* customers; exceeding their expectations will *delight* them. Customers who are delighted with a supplier have a much higher probability of remaining a customer.

The problem is that when a customer's expectations are exceeded, he has higher expectations next time. The task of exceeding the higher expectations gets more difficult and more costly. Ultimately, the company must settle for just meeting the latest expectations.

Put another way, many of today's customers want the highest quality, added services, great convenience, customization, return privileges, guarantees—all at the lowest price. Clearly each company has to decide which of these many customer wants it can meet profitably.

What Constitutes a Winning Marketing Strategy?

Clearly there is no one marketing road to riches. Instead of relying on one major differentiation or thrust, a company needs to weave its own unique tapestry of marketing qualities and activities. It is not enough to do most things a little better than the competitors. Professor Michael Porter of Harvard argues that a company doesn't really have a strategy if it performs the same activities as its competitors, only a little better.[5] It is simply operationally more effective. Being *operationally excellent* is not the same as having a robust strategy. Operational excellence might help the firm win for a while, but other firms will soon catch up or pass up the firm.

Porter sees a business as having a robust strategy when it has strong points of difference from competitors' strategies. Thus Dell Computer developed a robust strategy by choosing to sell computers over the telephone instead of through retailers. It developed a mastery of direct and database marketing and could convince customers of its superior value and service. Then Dell created a subsequent strategy breakthrough by adding the Internet as a sales channel. Today Dell is selling more than $3 million dollars' worth of computers daily on the Internet.

Other companies have created unique strategies. Ikea created a new way to make and sell furniture that stood in stark contrast to typical furniture retailers. The Saturn division of General Motors sells cars in an entirely different way from the typical auto manufacturer. Enterprise Rent-A-Car carved out a unique niche in the rental car market by renting older cars in cheaper locations and tying in with referrals from insurance companies.

But don't these successful new strategies get imitated very quickly, only to settle into being ordinary? Yes, imitators come along, as Southwest Airlines and IKEA have learned. However, it is one thing to copy some aspects of a new strategy, but quite another for an imitator to copy all aspects of the *strategic architecture*. The great strategies consist of a unique configuration of many reinforcing activities that defy easy imitation. The imitator not only has to incur great costs in trying to duplicate all the activities of the leader, but at best he ends up as only a pale imitation with average returns.

What Marketing Challenges Do Most Companies Face?

I have asked many managers in my seminars to describe how they see today's customers. Here are their answers:

- Customers are growing more sophisticated and price sensitive
- They are short of time and want more convenience
- They see growing product parity among the suppliers
- They are less manufacturer brand sensitive and are more accepting of reseller brands and generics
- They have high service expectations
- They have decreasing supplier loyalty

Then I ask how well their marketing tools are working, and they tell me:

- Their products are not much different from competitors' products
- They are giving away a lot of costly service and add-ons to get the sale
- Their pricing is readily matched by competitors
- Advertising is getting more expensive and less effective
- They are spending too much on sales promotion
- Sales force costs are rising

EXHIBIT 1–2

Questions Posed By Marketers

---

1. How can we spot and choose the right market segment(s) to serve?

2. How can we differentiate our offering from competitive offerings?

3. How should we respond to customers who press us for a lower price?

4. How can we compete against lower-cost, lower-price competitors from here and abroad?

5. How far can we go in customizing our offering for each customer?

6. What are the major ways in which we can grow our business?

7. How can we build stronger brands?

8. How can we reduce the cost of customer acquisition?

9. How can we keep our customers loyal for a longer period?

10. How can we tell which customers are more important?

11. How can we measure the payback from advertising, sales promotion, and public relations?

12. How can we improve sales force productivity?

13. How can we establish multiple channels and yet manage channel conflict?

14. How can we get the other company departments to be more customer-oriented?

All this means that companies are facing weighty challenges in trying to improve their performance in the marketplace. I asked marketing managers to list the main questions they are facing in setting marketing strategy and tactics. Exhibit 1–2 lists fourteen of the major questions. I hope to examine all of these questions in the book.

Marketing issues, of course, will vary among companies in their importance. Each business sector copes with different forces. *Branded goods manufacturers* have their set of concerns:

- Shrinking margins
- Rising sales and promotion costs
- Growing retail power and shrinking shelf space

- Competition from store brands and generics
- Increased niche attacks

Store-based retailers have their worries:

- Shrinking margins
- Category killers
- Competition from catalogs, mail order, and other forms of nonstore shopping

As for industrial-based firms, they differ greatly among themselves in their characteristics, success factors, and the role played by their marketing departments. The Appendix at the end of the book conveys those differences for ten different types of business-to-business marketing firms.

Toward a Newer Marketing

It is no wonder that many CEOs complain that their marketing isn't working. They see their company spending more on marketing and accomplishing less. One reason is that they are spending more on the same old type of marketing that they have in the past. *Neanderthal marketing* consists of the following practices:

- Equating marketing with selling
- Emphasizing customer acquisition rather than customer care
- Trying to make a profit on each transaction rather than trying to profit by managing customer lifetime value
- Pricing based on marking up cost rather than target pricing
- Planning each communication tool separately rather than integrating marketing communication tools
- Selling the product rather than trying to understand and meet the customer's real needs

The old marketing thinking is, fortunately, now giving way to newer ways of thinking. Smart marketing companies are improving their customer knowledge, customer connection technologies, and understanding of customer economics.[6] They are inviting customers to co-design the product. They are ready to make flexible market offerings. They are using more targeted media and integrating their marketing communications to deliver a consistent message through every customer contact. They are utilizing more technologies such as video-conferencing, sales automation, software, Internet web pages, and Intranets and Extranets. They are reachable seven days a week, twenty-four hours a day at their 1-800 customer telephone number or by e-mail. They are better able to identify the more profitable customers and to set up different levels of service. They see their distribution channels as being partners, not adversaries. In sum, they have found ways to deliver superior value to their customers.

The premium will go to those companies that invent new ways to create, communicate, and deliver value to their target markets. We can call them Marketing Visionaries. Such companies should be honored in a Marketing Hall of Fame. I submit Exhibit 1–3 as a list of the kinds of companies that deserve to be included on the basis of their creative marketing breakthroughs.

Marketing in the Year 2005

We will consider all of these things in the pages that follow. For now, we must recognize that marketing will be much different in the first decade of the twenty-first century.

Here I will add my thoughts about where marketing is headed in the new millennium. I will do this by "looking back into the future." It is the year 2005. Here are the principal developments in the evolving marketplace/marketspace.

There has been a substantial disintermediation of wholesalers and retailers owing to electronic commerce. Virtually all products are now available without going to a store! The customer can access pictures of any product on the Internet, read the specs, shop among online vendors for the best prices and terms, and click order and payment over the Internet. Expensively printed catalogs have disappeared. Business-to-business purchasing over the Internet has increased even faster than online consumer buying. Business purchasing agents shop for their routine items on the Internet, either advertising their needs and waiting for bidders, or simply surfing in their "bookmarked" web sites.

Store-based retailers find store traffic highly diminished. In response, more entrepreneurial retailers are building entertainment and theater into their stores. Many bookstores, food stores, and clothing stores now include coffee bars and feature lecturers and performances. Essentially these stores are "marketing an experience" rather than marketing a product assortment.

EXHIBIT 1–3

Marketing Visionaries

Leader	Company
1. Anita Roddick	The Body Shop
2. Fred Smith	Federal Express
3. Steve Jobs	Apple Computer
4. Bill Gates	Microsoft
5. Michael Dell	Dell Computer
6. Ray Kroc	McDonald's
7. Walt Disney	Disney Corporation
8. Sam Walton	Wal-Mart
9. Tom Monaghan	Domino's Pizza
10. Akio Morita	Sony
11. Nicholas Hayek	Swatch Watch Co.
12. John W. Nordstrom	Nordstrom
13. Gilbert Trigano	Club Mediterranee
14. Ted Turner	CNN
15. Frank Perdue	Perdue Chicken
16. Richard Branson	Virgin Air
17. Soichiro Honda	Honda
18. Simon Marks	Marks & Spencer
19. Luciano Benetton	Benetton
20. Charles Lazarus	Toys 'R' Us
21. Les Wexner	The Limited
22. Colonel Sanders	Kentucky Fried Chicken
23. Ingvar Kamprad	IKEA
24. Bernie Marcus	Home Depot
25. Charles Schwab	Charles Schwab & Co.
26. Herb Kelleher	Southwest Airlines
27. Paul Orfalea	Kinko's
28. Jeff Bezos	Amazon
29. Jim McCann	1-800-FLOWERS
30. Phil Knight	Nike

Most companies have built proprietary customer databases containing rich information on individual customer preferences and requirements. They use this information to "mass-customize" their offerings to individuals. An increasing number of companies present online product platforms on which customers design their desired products. Many automobile, computer, appliance, and food companies invite customers to visit their web pages and design the market offering (product, service, systems, programs) by filling in choices on a form. The modified product is then visually displayed on the screen.

Businesses are doing a better job of retaining their customers through finding imaginative ways to exceed customer expectations. As a result, competitors have found it increasingly difficult to acquire new customers. Consequently, most companies are spending time figuring out how to sell more products and services to their existing customers.

Companies are focusing on building customer share rather than market share. Many have figured out new ways to increase cross-selling and up-selling. Companies are gaining segment and customer insight from their *data warehouses* by applying newer and more effective *data mining* techniques.

Companies have finally managed to get their accounting departments to generate real numbers on profitability by segment, individual customer, product, channel, and geographical unit. Companies are now focusing attention on their most profitable customers, products, and channels. They are formulating reward packages for their more profitable customers.

Companies have switched from a transaction perspective to a customer-loyalty–building perspective. Many have moved to *customer lifetime supply* thinking, whereby they offer to deliver a regularly consumed product (e.g., coffee, soft drinks) on a regular basis at a lower price per unit. They can afford to make less profit on each sale because of the long-term purchase contract.

Most companies now outsource over 60 percent of their activities and requirements. A few outsource 100 percent, making them virtual companies owning very few assets and therefore earning extraordinary rates of return. Outsourcing firms are enjoying a booming business. In the case of equipment manufacturers, most prefer to work with single supply partners who design and supply overall systems (an automobile braking system, a seating system, etc.) in partnership with the branded manufacturer. Most companies today are networked companies, relying heavily on strategic alliances with other companies.

Many field salespeople are franchisees rather than company employees. The company equips them with the latest sales automation tools, including a capacity to develop individualized multimedia presentations and to develop customized market offerings and contracts. Most buyers are showing a distinct preference for meeting salespeople on their computer screens rather than in the office. An increasing amount of personal selling is occurring over electronic media, where the buyer and seller see each on their computer screens in real time. Salespeople are traveling less, and airlines are shrinking in size. The most effective salespeople are well-informed, trustworthy, likable, and good listeners.

Mass TV advertising has greatly diminished as a result of 500 viewing channels. Printed newspapers and magazines have greatly diminished in number. On the other hand, marketers can now reach their target markets more effectively by advertising through online specialized magazines and news groups.

Companies are unable to sustain competitive advantages (outside of patents, copyrights, superior locations, proprietary information, etc.). Competitors are quick to copy any advantage through benchmarking, reverse engineering, and leapfrogging. Companies believe that their only sustainable advantage lies in an ability to learn faster and change faster.

Now we are back in 1999. But I trust the preceding 2005 scenario will provoke companies to deliberate more strategically on their future. Successful companies will be the few who can keep their marketing changing as fast as their marketplace.

Questions to Consider

Here are some questions that you might consider in judging how your company and its marketing practices are meeting the principal issues in the marketplace.

1. How have technology, globalization, and deregulation affected your business in the last five years?
2. In using Exhibit 1–1 on business firms in transition, did your business appear basically in the "then" column or the "now" column? Which "now" practices would make more sense for your company to adopt?
3. Has your company been basing its marketing strategy largely on one of the nine one-liner strategies? Which one? Has it worked? What do you think is needed now?
4. List the main marketing issues facing your business. What do you regard as your most creative marketing responses to those issues?
5. What do you think of the marketing predictions for the year 2005? What are your predictions for your industry? What are you doing to prepare for them?

2

Using Marketing to Understand, Create, Communicate, and Deliver Value

One illusion is that you can industrialize a country by building factories. You don't. You industrialize it by building markets. —*Paul G. Hoffman*

Customers are increasingly choosing vendors on the basis of long-term value, not long-term history.—*Anonymous*

Quality is when our customers come back and our products don't.—*Siemens quality motto*

HAVING EXAMINED CURRENT marketing issues and responses, we are now ready to examine the role that marketing can play in helping companies grow their top line. If companies focus only on their costs, they will never grow to greatness. "Without a top line, there will be no bottom line."

Companies need growth if they are to attract talent, create job advancement opportunities, satisfy their stakeholders, and compete more effectively. Wayne Calloway, former PepsiCo CEO, stated the case for growth eloquently:

Growth is pure oxygen. It creates a vital, enthusiastic corporation where people see genuine opportunity. They take bigger chances. They work harder and smarter. In that way, growth is more than our single most important financial driver; it's an essential part of our corporate culture. It's why so many talented leaders want to work for PepsiCo rather than lots of other fine corporations.

At the same time, one must be cautious about making growth itself an objective. The company's objective must be "profitable growth." In too many companies, managers are urged to grow their sales and profits faster than the industry average. As a result, they pursue every possible market and customer, which tends to blur their target market and image and to dilute their resources.

Marketing has the main responsibility for achieving profitable revenue growth for the company. Marketing must identify, evaluate, and select market opportunities and lay down strategies for achieving eminence if not dominance in target markets. But marketing has many images, good and bad, accurate and inaccurate, within the company and within the general public. Therefore in this chapter we shall address the following questions:

- What are the most serious misconceptions about marketing?
- Is sound marketing only about "finding and filling needs"?
- How broad a market can a company profitably serve?
- What are the main steps in the marketing management process?

Serious Misconceptions About Marketing

There is a high degree of misunderstanding of what marketing is and what it can do for a company. In fact, some CEOs place unrealistic expectations on their chief marketing officer. No wonder the average duration of a marketing director may be sixteen to eighteen months!

How CEOs View Marketing

Many CEOs are appalled by their companies' high failure rate of new products, rising advertising and selling costs, flat or falling market shares, declining gross margins, and other signs of weak market performance. They often single out their marketing/sales group as the culprit. Here are the results of interviews with CEOs:

- In 1993, Coopers & Lybrand surveyed the CEOs of one hundred companies. Many saw their marketing departments as "ill-focused and overindulged."

- In 1993 McKinsey & Company released a report saying that many CEOs saw their marketing departments as "unimaginative, generating few new ideas, no longer delivering."
- In 1994 Booz, Allen & Hamilton issued a report warning that CEOs thought "brand managers were failing to get to grips with commercial realities."

Some CEOs clearly ought to be disappointed in their marketing people. Others, however, may misunderstand what marketing does or is capable of doing, or may have developed unreasonable expectations.

Two Mistaken Views of Marketing

Here are two commonly held, but mistaken, views of marketing:

MARKETING IS SELLING. The view that marketing and selling are the same is the most common type of confusion, held not only by many members of the public but also by many business people. Selling, of course, is part of marketing, but marketing includes much more than selling. Peter Drucker observed that "the aim of marketing is to make selling superfluous." What Drucker meant is that marketing's task is to discover unmet needs and to prepare satisfying solutions. When marketing is very successful, people like the new product, word-of-mouth spreads fast, and little selling is necessary.

Marketing cannot be equivalent to selling because it starts long before the company has a product. Marketing is the homework that managers undertake to assess needs, measure their extent and intensity, and determine whether a profitable opportunity exists. Selling occurs only after a product is manufactured. Marketing continues throughout the product's life, trying to find new customers, improve product appeal and performance, learn from product sales results, and manage repeat sales.

Marketers criticize their senior management for not seeing marketing expenditures as an investment, not a cost, and for emphasizing short-term results, not focusing on the long term, and also for being too risk-averse.

MARKETING IS MAINLY A DEPARTMENT. Another limited view of marketing is that it is essentially just another company department. True, companies do have marketing departments where much of the marketing thinking and work take place. Yet if marketing attitudes and work were located only in this department, the company would stumble badly. A company could have the best marketing/sales department in its industry and still fail in the marketplace. David Packard, cofounder of Hewlett-Packard, wisely said: "Marketing is far too important to be left only to the marketing department." Any department can treat customers well or badly, and this will affect their further interest in the company. A customer may phone the company and find it difficult to get information or reach the right party. The product that is ordered may arrive in a defective condition because manufacturing standards were loose or the product was packed poorly. The product might arrive later than promised because of faulty inventory information. The invoice may puzzle the customer because the accounting department added unexplained charges. All those glitches can happen when other departments are not focused on satisfying the customer.

Some have suggested that the lack of customer-mindedness in other departments may partly result from the marketing department's existence! The other departments might think the marketing department's job is to "manufacture and satisfy customers" while they take care of their own operations. Could departmental attitudes be better if the company had no marketing department? For example, Marks & Spencer, one of Britain's best retailers, did no advertising and had no marketing department and yet attracted hordes of loyal shoppers, largely because everyone at Marks & Spencer thought of the customer first.

Progressive companies seek to get all their departments to be customer-oriented, if not customer-driven. A company can assess which of its departments are really customer-oriented by deciding which of the statements in Exhibit 2–1 are true in its own case. For example, a truly customer-oriented R&D department would have its people occasionally meet customers, work closely with other departments on new projects, benchmark competitors' products, solicit customer reactions to proposed new product designs, and continually improve the product based on customer feedback. Such an R&D department would contribute strongly to a company's marketing performance. Exhibit 2–1 shows signs of customer-orientation for other departments in the company.

Finding and Filling Needs

In highly competitive markets, all departments must focus on winning customer preference. Jack Welch, General Electric's celebrated CEO, tells his employees: "Companies can't give job security. Only customers can!" He makes his employees highly aware of their impact, irrespective of their department, on customer satisfaction and retention. The implication: If you are not thinking customer, you are not thinking.

EXHIBIT 2–1

Assessing Which Company Departments Are Customer-Minded

R&D

- They spend time meeting customers and listening to their problems.
- They welcome the involvement of marketing, manufacturing, and other departments in each new project.
- They benchmark competitors' products and seek "best of class" solutions.
- They solicit customer reactions and suggestions as the project progresses.
- They continuously improve and refine the product on the basis of market feedback.

Purchasing

- They proactively search for the best suppliers rather than choose only from those who solicit their business.
- They build long-term relations with fewer but more reliable high-quality suppliers.
- They don't compromise quality for price savings.

Manufacturing

- They invite customers to visit and tour their plants.
- They visit customer plants to see how customers use the company's products.
- They willingly work overtime when it is important to meet promised delivery schedules.
- They continuously search for ways to produce goods faster and/or at lower cost.
- They continuously improve product quality, aiming for zero defects.
- They meet customer requirements for "customization" where this can be done profitably.

Marketing

- They study customer needs and wants in well-defined market segments.
- They allocate marketing effort in relation to the long-run profit potential of the targeted segments.
- They develop winning offers for each target segment.
- They measure company image and customer satisfaction on a continuous basis.
- They continuously gather and evaluate ideas for new products, product improvements, and services to meet customers' needs.
- They influence all company departments and employees to be customer-centered in their thinking and practice.

EXHIBIT 2–1 *(continued)*

Sales

- They have specialized knowledge of the customer's industry.
- They strive to give the customer "the best solution."
- They make only promises that they can keep.
- They feed back customers' needs and ideas to those in charge of product development.
- They serve the same customers for a long period of time.

Logistics

- They set a high standard for service delivery time and meet this standard consistently.
- They operate a knowledgeable and friendly customer service department that can answer questions, handle complaints, and resolve problems in a satisfactory and timely manner.

Accounting

- They prepare periodic "profitability" reports by product, market segment, geographic areas (regions, sales territories), order sizes, channels, and individual customers.
- They prepare invoices tailored to customer needs and answer customer queries courteously and quickly.

Finance

- They understand and support marketing expenditures (e.g., image advertising) that represent marketing investments that produce long-term customer preference and loyalty.
- They tailor the financial package to the customers' financial requirements.
- They make quick decisions on customer creditworthiness.

Public Relations

- They disseminate favorable news about the company and they "damage control" unfavorable news.
- They act as an internal customer and public advocate for better company policies and practices.

Other Customer Contact Personnel

- They are competent, courteous, cheerful, credible, reliable, and responsive.

We need to distinguish three levels of marketing performance, which can be called responsive marketing, anticipative marketing, and need-shaping marketing.

RESPONSIVE MARKETING. Marketing has been defined as the task of "finding and filling needs." This is a commendable form of marketing when there exists a clear need and when some company has identified it and prepared an affordable solution. Recognizing that women want to spend less time cooking and cleaning led to the invention of the modern washing machine, dryer, dishwasher, and microwave oven. Today many smokers who want to stop smoking can find various treatments. Much of today's marketing is responsive marketing.

ANTICIPATIVE MARKETING. It is another feat to recognize an emerging or latent need. As the quality of water deteriorated in many places, Evian, Perrier, and a number of other companies anticipated a growing market for bottled drinking water. As pharmaceutical companies recognized the growing stress in modern urban society, several started research on antistress drugs. Anticipative marketing is more risky than responsive marketing; companies may come into the market too early or too late, or may even be totally wrong about thinking that such a market would develop.

NEED-SHAPING MARKETING. The boldest level of marketing occurs when a company introduces a product or service that nobody asked for and often could not even conceive of. No one in the 1950s asked for a Sony Walkman, a Sony Betamax, or a Sony $3\frac{1}{2}$-inch disc. Yet Sony, under its brilliant founder and chairman, Akio Morita, introduced those and many other new products that since have become everyday staples. Morita summarized his marketing philosophy in these words: "I don't serve markets. I create them."[1]

Perhaps the difference between responsive marketers and those who anticipate or shape needs is best summarized in the difference between a *market-driven company* and a *market-driving company*. Most companies are at best market-driven, which itself is an advance over being product-driven. Market-driven companies focus on researching current customers to identify their problems, gather new ideas, and to test proposed product improvements and marketing mix changes. Their efforts typically result in incremental improvements, not radical innovations.

Market-driving companies, on the other hand, raise our sights and our civilization. Such companies create new markets or refine categories or change the rules of the game. They generate significantly new products, services, business formats; establish new price points; develop new channels; raise service to an unbelievable level. Among market-driving firms are CNN, Club Med, Federal Express, The Body Shop, IKEA, Benetton, and Charles Schwab. And certain well-established firms also exhibit a market-driving orientation, such as DuPont, Sony, Gillette, Hewlett-Packard, Tetra Pak, and 3M.

How Broad a Market Can a Company Profitably Serve?

One of the key decisions a company must make is how homogeneously to treat the market. At one extreme is *mass marketing*, where the company offers a standard product or service to the whole market. Thus the Coca-Cola Company wants its famous drink to be within an "arm's reach of everyone." And Kodak assumes that its famous yellow box of film will satisfy anyone who plans to take photos.

At a less grandiose level are companies that practice *target marketing*. They design products/services for one or more specific segments rather than for the whole market. Daimler-Benz aims to sell its Mercedes automobiles not to the whole market but to affluent buyers who want a well-engineered, luxurious automobile. Procter & Gamble designed its Head and Shoulders shampoo specifically for persons who need to control a dandruff problem.

The lowest molecular level of marketing, *customer-level marketing*, is practiced by companies that focus and adapt their offerings and/or communications to each individual customer. A custom homebuilder, for example, sits down with each customer to design the home that he or she wants. And BMW, the auto company, offers a website on which a potential buyer can design the individual features he or she desires in a BMW.

Each level of marketing presents a host of opportunities and risks. We shall examine the workings and implications of each below.

Mass Marketing

The Industrial Revolution ushered in the ability of industries to mass-produce, mass-distribute, and mass-advertise common products such as soaps, toothpaste, beverages, and foods. Although many of those products were originally sold in bulk, an increasing number of them became packaged and carried brand names. Manufacturers used mass advertising to presell customers to request their brands so that retailers would have to stock their brands. Manufacturers also offered direct incentives (e.g., trade promotion) to retailers to carry and prominently display their highly advertised brands. Thus by heavily advertising their brands ("pull") and motivating resellers to carry and display their brands ("push"), leading brand manufacturers secured a strong position in the stores and in the minds of shoppers.

Today some critics are predicting the demise of mass marketing. They say that the mass market is disintegrating into smaller and more numerous customer segments, each with more specific tastes and requirements, calling for more targeted marketing. They say that today's marketing budgets cannot support the high costs of introducing and advertising a mass brand, especially if it is only a "me-too" brand. Furthermore, they note that growing media fragmentation makes it more costly to deliver a message efficiently to a mass audience. Forty years ago, most Americans read *Life* magazine and watched a few top-rated prime time programs on one of three television networks. Today's consumers can watch (or zap) more than fifty channels and can read any of ten thousand magazines.

The predicted demise of mass marketing is somewhat premature. In the former Soviet Union, where citizens were deprived of quality goods for seventy years, the conversion from planned to free market economies has created a golden opportunity for mass marketers. Such companies as McDonald's, Nike, and Procter & Gamble are rushing in with their mass-produced products and are attracting numerous consumers eager to buy their well-known brands.

In addition, a specific form of mass marketing called *mass selling* is showing explosive growth around the world. Mass-selling organizations—Avon, Amway, Mary Kay, and Tupperware—are competing with store-based retailers using an army of self-employed distributors, who sell their company's goods—cosmetics, costume jewelry, etc.—door-to-door, office-to-office, or through home-based parties. The distributors, usually homemakers looking to earn some extra money, buy a small kit of sample products, receive a modicum of sales training, and approach friends, neighbors, and strangers in search of sales. They earn a commission on what they sell and a further commission on the sales of any distributors that they personally recruit. Mary Kay, at year's end, rewards her highest performing distributors with pink Cadillacs and other assorted prizes at a highly charged and emotional annual convention.

Mass selling is growing rapidly in many parts of the world—e.g., Indonesia, India, China—as promising an opportunity to millions of people to earn some extra money and even become rich. Mass selling has been abused by some companies, which exaggerate the potential incomes and/or make shoddy products that no one will buy from the distributors. Called "pyramid selling schemes," they are to be distinguished from bona fide and well-established mass-selling organizations practicing what is variously called "network marketing" or "multilevel marketing."[2]

Target Marketing

In the path-breaking article "Product Differentiation and Market Segmentation as Alternative Marketing Strategies," published in 1956, Wendell Smith contrasted the firm that offered product variety ("product differentiation") with the firm that designed products for specific market segments ("market segmentation").[3] Market segmentation held that every market consisted of groups (segments) of customers with somewhat different needs and wants. Toothpaste buyers, for example, differ as to whether they primarily seek anticavity protection, better breath, or whiter teeth. Not surprisingly, different toothpaste brands have appeared promoting one benefit or another, hoping to become the toothpaste brand of choice of the targeted segment.

Eighty years ago General Motors passed Ford to become the largest U.S. automaker as a result of recognizing the key importance of segmentation. Whereas good old Henry Ford would "give the customer any color as long as it was black," GM adopted the strategy of designing and offering a car "for every purse, purpose, and personality." Between 1920 and 1923, Ford's share of the market slid from 55 percent to 12 percent.

In deciding to do target marketing, a company can slice the market into finer and finer "segments." In fact, we can distinguish three levels of market deconstruction: the *brand segment level*, the *niche level*, and the *market cell level*.

SEGMENTS. Many markets can be broken down into a number of broad segments. *Benefit segmentation* means grouping people who are seeking a similar benefit; for example, there are buyers who seek a low price, others who seek high product quality, and still others who seek excellent service. *Demographic segmentation* means grouping people who share a common demographic makeup: affluent senior citizens, young low-income minorities, and so on. *Occasion segmentation* means grouping people according to product use occasions; for example, airline passengers flying for business, pleasure, or emergency reasons. *Usage level segmentation* means grouping people into whether they are heavy, medium, light users or nonusers of the product. *Lifestyle segmentation* means grouping people by lifestyles, such as "furs and station wagon suburbanites," or "shotgun and pickup truck macho males."

Clearly, any market can be segmented in several ways. The marketer hopes to recognize a substantial unmet need that might represent a profitable market opportunity. In identifying a set of segments, the marketer has two choices. The marketer can focus on one segment (*single segment marketing*), or two or more, each receiving a different and appropriate offering (*multisegment marketing*).

Single segment marketing offers three advantages:

1. The company can more easily identify the individual buyers in the segment, meet them, run focus groups, and design very focused and appealing offerings.
2. The company will face fewer competitors in a well-defined segment and know better who they are.
3. The company will enjoy a good chance to become the "supplier of choice" to the segment and earn the largest market share and margin.

On the other hand, the single segment marketer runs the risk that the segment will become less populated as consumer wants shift, or will attract too many competitors, thus reducing every competitor's profits. Those risks have led more companies to prefer multisegment marketing, knowing that even if one segment's profit potential weakens, the firm's fortunes can be sustained by the other segments. Furthermore, multisegment marketing permits the company to enjoy certain economies of scale and scope, thus giving the company a cost advantage in each segment in which it competes.

NICHES. Niches typically describe smaller sets of customers who have more narrowly defined needs or unique combinations of needs. Thus a sports car market segment may be further refined into several buyer niches: a niche that wants very expensive, powerful racing-type cars (such as Ferraris or Lamborghinis); a niche that wants less expensive, less racer-like cars but powerful ones nevertheless (such as Porsches); those who want a more conventional-looking car with a sportslike performance (such as BMWs); and a niche that wants a less expensive car that looks like a sports car but it doesn't perform that way (such as Ford Mustangs).

Focusing on serving the customers in a niche has several advantages, including the opportunity to know each customer more personally, to face far fewer competitors (zero, one, or possibly two), and to earn a high margin, since the customers are quite willing to pay more because the niching company is so expert in meeting their needs. Of course, the nicher faces the same risks as the single segment marketer if the niche should weaken. The company has to watch out that the niche doesn't become a pothole. If worried, the company should pursue a *multiniche* strategy rather than a single niche strategy.

In many markets today, niches are the norm. Blattberg and Deighton say that "niches too small to be served profitably today will become viable as marketing efficiency improves."[4] Companies may have to choose niches or be hurt by nichers. And there is strong evidence that there are riches in niches.[5] Hermann Simon, in his book *Hidden Champions*, documents the surprising number of German companies that are barely known to the public but who have global market shares exceeding 50 percent in their respective niches and strong profits.[6] Here are some examples:

- Tetra has 80 percent of the world tropical fish market.
- Hohner has 85 percent of the world harmonica market.
- Becher has 50 percent of the world's very large umbrella market.
- Steiner Optical has 80 percent of the world's military fieldglasses market.

These hidden champions tend to be found in stable markets, are typically family-owned or closely held, and are long-lived. Their success can be explained as follows:

1. They are strongly dedicated to their customers and offer superior performance, responsive service, and punctual delivery (rather than low price).
2. Their top management stays in direct and regular contact with key customers.
3. They emphasize continuous innovation directed at improving customer value.

Hidden champions combine high product focus with geographic diversity and establish the leading reputation in the targeted niche.

MARKET CELLS. Companies may want to identify even smaller groups of customers who share some characteristics that provide a market opportunity; they can be called *market cells*. Today many companies build *customer databases* containing information about their customers' demographics, past purchases, preferences, and other characteristics. American Express and other credit card companies have tons of customer profile data, as do catalog mail-order firms, telephone companies, public utility companies, banks, and insurance companies. Those companies have a *data warehouse* waiting to be analyzed. Companies like IBM, Andersen Consulting, and EDS, offer a service called *data mining*, which uses high-powered analytical and statistical techniques to unearth interesting patterns and findings about customers. Here is an example:

> A leading clothing catalog company with over 2,000,000 customers invited IBM to mine its data and help it discover customer groupings. Instead of coming up with the usual 5 segments, or 50 niches, the IBM researchers identified 5,000 market cells. IBM found, for example, that 850 customers of the catalog company had purchased a blue shirt and a red tie! Now the reason this is interesting is that these buyers would probably be more interested in buying (say) a navy blue jacket than the average customer of the catalog company. It may pay for the catalog company to send a letter to just these 850 customers offering a very special price on a navy blue jacket. If the company is correct, this market cell's response rate could be as high as 10%.

Customer-level Marketing

Before the Industrial Revolution, craftsmen would make individually ordered items for their customers. Tailors did "custom-tailoring," and shoemakers made separate shoes for each customer. As the Industrial Revolution advanced, manufacturers increasingly produced for stock and used branding and advertising to stimulate customers to seek out their products. The economies of large-scale production favored product standardization. Prices came down, and customers accepted fairly standard products in order to enjoy the cost saving.

With the advent of the computer, database marketing, and flexible factories, the cost of offering more customized products and communications has declined, not to the level of producing a standard product but at least not much higher. We are witnessing the reemergence of customized marketing, not as the dominant marketing form, but as one showing increased growth and promise. Today we can order a specially made bicycle, a customized pair of jeans, a one-of-a-kind woman's swimsuit, and so on.

A distinction can be drawn between *customized marketing* and *mass customized marketing*. Customized marketing takes place when the seller prepares a new product from scratch for the buyer, as is done by a custom tailor or metal-forming job shop. Mass customization takes place when the company has established basic modules that can be combined in different ways for each customer.[7] Thus Dell Computer is able to deliver to each customer a customer-specified computer loaded with customer-specified hardware and software. BMW can mass-customize its cars, in that most of the car is ready except for options requested by different customers. Mass customization also occurs when a service institution makes adjustments in its offerings to meet a specific customer's requirements. Thus the Ritz-Carlton hotel chain keeps information in its database about each customer's desires in the way of room size, floor level, smoking or nonsmoking, fruit or flowers in the room, extra pillows, and so on. Another use of mass customization is where a bank sends out birthday cards or individualized offerings to each customer.

The Main Steps in the Marketing Management Process

Marketers have a mindset, just as lawyers, accountants, bankers, engineers, and scientists have their specific mindsets. Marketers see the marketing management process as consisting of five basic steps that can be represented as:

$$R \rightarrow STP \rightarrow MM \rightarrow I \rightarrow C$$

Where:

R = Research (i.e., market research)
STP = Segmentation, targeting, and positioning
MM = Marketing mix (popularly known as the four P's, i.e., product, price, place, and promotion)
I = Implementation
C = Control (getting feedback, evaluating results, and revising or improving STP strategy and MM tactics)

Effective marketing starts with research, R. Research into a market will reveal different segments, S, consisting of buyers with different needs. The company would be wise to target, T, only those segments which it could satisfy in a superior way. For each target segment, the company will have to position, P, its offering so that target customers could appreciate how the company's offering differs from competitors' offerings. STP represents the company's strategic marketing thinking.

Now the company develops its tactical marketing mix, MM, consisting of the mix of product, price, place, and promotion decisions. The company then implements, I, the marketing mix. Finally, the company uses control measures, C, to monitor and evaluate results and improve its STP strategy and MM tactics.

Research

Research is the starting point for marketing. Without research, a company enters a market like a blind man. The story is told about a Hong Kong shoe manufacturer who wonders whether a market exists for his shoes on a remote South Pacific island. He sends an *order taker* to the island who, upon a cursory examination, wires back: "The people here don't wear shoes. There is no market." Not convinced, the Hong Kong shoe manufacturer sends a *salesman* to the island. This salesman wires back: "The people here don't wear shoes. There is a tremendous market." Afraid that this salesman is being carried away by the sight of so many shoeless feet, the Hong Kong manufacturer sends a third person, this time a *marketer*. This marketing professional interviews the tribal chief and several of the natives, and finally wires back:

> The people here don't wear shoes. However they have bad feet. I have shown the chief how shoes would help his people avoid foot problems. He is enthusiastic. He estimates that 70 percent of his people will buy the shoes at the price of $10 a pair. We probably can sell 5,000 pairs of shoes in the first year. Our cost of bringing the shoes to the island and setting up distribution would amount to $6 a pair. We will clear $20,000 in the first year, which, given our investment, will give us a rate of return on our investment (ROI) of 20 percent, which exceeds our normal ROI of 15 percent. This is not to mention the high value of our future earnings by entering this market. I recommend that we go ahead.

As this example shows, good marketing involves careful research into the market opportunity and the preparation of financial estimates based on the proposed strategy indicating whether the returns would meet the company's financial objectives.

Research will lead a company to recognize that the buyers in any market normally differ in their needs, perceptions, and preferences. Women will need shoes different from men's; heavy people will require shoes different from thin people's. When fashion enters the shoe market, preferences will widen much more as a result of differences in income, education, and tastes.

Segmentation, Targeting, and Positioning—Strategic Marketing

Since the research is likely to uncover several customer segments, management must decide which segments to pursue. It should target those segments to which it can bring superior "firepower." By checking its competencies against the success requirements in each segment, it can choose the target segments more wisely.

The company must then *position* the company's offering so that target customers know the key benefit(s) embodied in the offering. For example, Volvo has positioned its automobile as the world's *safest car*. It reinforces that positioning through its car design, tests, advertising, and so on. Positioning is the effort to implant the offering's key benefit(s) and differentiation in the *customers' minds*.

In addition to the key benefit, sellers will present additional reasons to potential buyers as to why they should buy their brand. A brand is not only single-positioned on one central attribute or benefit, but carries fuller positioning. The full positioning of the brand is called the brand's *value proposition*. It is the answer to the customer's question, "Why should I buy your brand?" Volvo's value positioning includes not only its safety but its roominess, durability, and styling, along with a price that seems fair in terms of this mix of benefits.

Marketing Mix—Tactical Marketing

The company's marketers must then move into the *tactical marketing stage*, to set the tools of the marketing mix (MM) that will support and deliver the product's positioning. The tools are known as the four Ps:

- *Product:* The market offering itself, specifically a tangible product, packaging, and a set of services that the buyer would acquire through the purchase
- *Price:* The price of the product along with other charges that are made for delivery, warranty, and so on
- *Place (or distribution):* The arrangements to make the product readily available and accessible to the target market
- *Promotion:* The communication activities, such as advertising, sales

promotion, direct mail, and publicity to inform, persuade, or remind the target market about the product's availability and benefits

Implementation

The company, having engaged in strategic and tactical planning, must now produce the designated product, price it, distribute it, and promote it. This stage is called implementation. All the company's departments go into action: R&D, purchasing, manufacturing, marketing and sales, human resources, logistics, finance, and accounting.

In this stage, all kinds of implementation problems can occur. R&D may not find it easy to create the required product. A coffee company, for example, wanted to develop a "rich, strong, robust tasting" coffee. The product development department took many months to find a coffee blend that would lead test consumers to say that the coffee taste matched the description. During implementation, the manufacturing department may claim that the coffee blend cannot be manufactured on a large scale, or only at excessive cost. Purchasing may report that the price of the particular coffee beans is too volatile to allow the target price always to be charged.

Implementation problems often occur within the sales and marketing department. Thomas Bonoma argued that most marketing strategies are okay, but that marketing often fails at the implementation stage.[8] Failures include failing to "presell" the company's sales force on the product's specialness or its price; executing the advertising concept in a poor way; not delivering service at the promised level; and so on. More recently, Frank Cespedes highlighted many implementation problems resulting from poor linkages among *product management, field sales,* and *customer service*. He stressed the need for *concurrent marketing*, namely smoother and tighter linkages among these critical, customer-related functions.[9]

Marketing implementation requires even further linkages. Lanning sees a brand's value proposition as a promise to deliver a certain *resulting experience*.[10] Yet many customers don't receive this experience because of the market's limited control of the *value delivery system*. This is echoed by Knox and Maklan, who claim that many companies fail to align *brand value* with *customer value*.[11] Their brand managers focus on developing the value proposition, whereas whether customers actually receive the value proposition depends on the marketer's ability to influence the company's core processes, such as manufacturing and supply, asset management, and company reputation management.

Control

The final step in the marketing process is control. Successful companies are learning companies. They collect feedback from the marketplace, audit and evaluate results, and make corrections designed to improve their performance. A company that is failing to achieve its goals might learn that the fault lies with one of the four-P elements of the marketing mix, or even more fundamentally with segmentation, targeting, or positioning. Good marketing works on the cybernetic principle of steering the boat by constantly monitoring its position in relation to its destination. The art and science of marketing control is taken up in Chapter 10.

Questions to Consider

Here are some questions that will help you assess the role of marketing and marketing effectiveness in your company.

1. How would you define marketing in your company? How is it seen by the other departments in the company?
2. How customer-minded is each of the other departments in your company? Use Exhibit 2–1 as a checklist. What are the weakest departments? What can be done to get each of these departments to be more customer-minded?
3. Does your business unit operate on the mass market level, the segment level, the niche level, or the individual customer level? Is this still the right level given the current and future marketplace?
4. List those circumstances where your marketing strategy and plans were sound but there were unanticipated problems of implementation. What implementation problems tend to occur and what can be done to avoid them?

3

Identifying Market Opportunities and Developing Targeted Value Offerings

Marketing's job is to convert societal needs into profitable opportunities.—*Anonymous*

Vision is the art of seeing things invisible.—*Jonathan Swift*

Adversity is opportunity in disguise.—*Old saying*

The best way to predict the future is to invent it.—*Dennis Gabor*

OPPORTUNITIES ABOUND, and alert marketers can sense them. Suppose you live in a country where furniture is well-made but expensive. Lower-income households, and particularly young singles and marrieds, often buy their furniture on credit and have a hard time paying their bills. Is there an opportunity in this situation? Yes. Wherever there is a need, there is an opportunity. An alert marketer can address the situation in two ways. He can arrange to produce lower-quality, lower-cost, lower-price furniture. Or he can figure out a way to produce good quality furniture at a substantially lower cost and price. The latter solution is preferable to the former. And that is precisely what one of the most able Swedish entrepreneurs did, namely Ingvar Kamprad, the founder of IKEA, today the world's largest furniture retail chain. Here is the story:

As a young person in Sweden after the Second World War, Kamprad observed that many young families had a hard time buying Swedish furniture because of its high price. The price was high due to its high quality and the high margins charged by furniture retailers who did not actively compete with each other. Young people had to bear high interest payments or buy poorly made imported furniture. Kamprad saw a way to offer good-quality furniture at substantially lower prices. His cost-reducing strategy consisted of combining five sources of savings: (1) His retail company would buy or order large volumes of furniture to get lower price; (2) The furniture would be designed in "knockdown" form and therefore shipped flat from the manufacturers to his stores at a much lower transportation cost; (3) Customers would see the assembled furniture in show-room settings, make their selection, locate the specific furniture items in the warehouse (self-service), pay for them, and drive them home, thus avoiding delivery costs; (4) Customers would assemble the furniture, thus saving the manufacturers and stores further cost; and (5) Ikea stores would work on a low markup and high volume, in contrast to the typical Swedish furniture stores with their high markups and low volume. All this permitted IKEA to undercut its competitors by 20 percent and still make a large profit.[1]

Marketing is the *art of finding, developing, and profiting from opportunities*. If the marketing department doesn't see any opportunities, it is time to fire the marketing department! If the marketing managers can-not imagine new products, services, programs, and systems, then what are they being paid for?

In this chapter, we shall examine the following issues:

- What is a marketing opportunity?
- What are the main company sources for ideas on new opportunities?
- How can a company organize itself internally to find more promising opportunities?
- What are the main possible company growth paths?
- How can a company evaluate and choose among a set of opportunities?
- How can a company improve its success rate in launching new products and services?

What Is a Marketing Opportunity?

We define a *marketing opportunity* as an *area of buyer need and interest in which there is a high probability that a company can perform profitably by satisfying that need*. The *attractiveness* of the market opportunity depends on several factors: the number of potential buyers, their purchasing power, their eagerness to buy, and so on. A marketing opportunity exists when a marketer identifies a group of sufficient size whose needs are going unsatisfied. Ray Kroc's genius in creating McDonald's lay in noticing that a lot of people desired fast food service, low cost, tasty food, and a consistent expectation of what the food would taste like. No one offered those features before McDonald's appeared on the scene.

What Are the Main Sources of Market Opportunities?

There are three situations that give rise to market opportunities:

1. Supplying something in short supply
2. Supplying an existing product or service in a new or superior way
3. Supplying a new product or service

Supplying Something in Short Supply

When something is in short supply, when buyers are queuing up to buy it, a marketing opportunity exists. This situation requires the least amount of marketing talent, since the opportunity will be visible to everyone. In wartime, food, equipment, and spare parts are in short supply, and it doesn't take a genius to notice this. Manufacturers can take full advantage of the situation, including charging high prices, unless there is an enforced price control program. Shortages also ensue following disasters like earthquakes, tornadoes, and floods, but they tend to be temporary, and the market opportunities are short-lived.

Nations that operated under communism created forced savings to finance rapid industrial expansion, leaving consumers with goods shortages and services of poor quality and variety. In an open market economy, those shortages would have been quickly corrected by the inflow of capital. However, capital was not permitted to flow in to remedy the consumer shortages. Today, however, McDonald's, Nike, the Gap, and other global retailers have quickly moved into former communist countries and eliminated the shortages and queues.

Supplying an Existing Product or Service in a New or Superior Way

Companies use several methods for finding ideas to improve an existing product or service. Here we shall examine three methods: the *problem detection method*, the *ideal method*, and the *consumption chain method*.

PROBLEM DETECTION METHOD. There are many common goods and services which people accept in their present form with less than full satisfaction. Marketers can learn a lot by using the *problem detection method*, namely asking people who use the product or service if they have any disappointments or suggestions for improvement. Here are examples of what they might say:

My car uses too much gas.
My toaster is hard to clean.
I dislike the bank's long waiting lines.
My PC battery runs out after three hours.
Sometimes I can't find my TV remote control.

Each statement suggests a market opportunity. For example, the last statement led Magnavox to add a button on its TV sets which the owner can press, causing the remote control unit to buzz wherever it happens to be lost in the home. It should be noted that the problem detection method tends to produce product/service *improvements* rather than product/service *innovations*.

THE IDEAL METHOD. Here the marketer interviews a set of consumers and asks them to imagine an ideal version of the product or service that they are consuming. In a number of cases the wishes may turn out to be fairly easy to satisfy. Exhibit 3–1 presents a list of wishes that have come up in different situations and describes the solutions that some alert marketers provided.

A set of wishes may contain seemingly contradictory elements. For example, suppose someone said: "I wish that some company would make cookies which are delicious to eat but have no fat and much fewer calories." The normal consensus is that this is not possible. Consumers will have to choose between tasty high-fat cookies and much less tasty low-fat cookies. Procter & Gamble, however, looked hard at this challenge and spent several years researching a fat substance called Olestra. It turns out that Olestra's molecules are too big to be absorbed as fat in the body, and yet Olestra offers all the taste benefit expected in high-fat cookies. P&G has received approval from the Federal Food and Drug Administration to market Olestra. P&G may realize a bonanza by selling Olestra to makers of cookies, snack foods, french fries, and ice cream.

Interestingly, P&G has used the idea of resolving contradictions in guiding its search for many new products. Exhibit 3–2 lists some contradictions that P&G resolved, along with some other company examples.

CONSUMPTION CHAIN METHOD. Here the marketer interviews consumers to chart their steps in acquiring, using, and disposing of a product. The

EXHIBIT 3–1

Listening to Consumer Wishes

> "I wish that I could buy a new car without having to haggle over the price with a high-pressured sleazy salesman nor end up with a 'lemon' which the dealer won't take back."

Now, this seems like a strong set of wishes to satisfy. Yet Saturn (a new division of General Motors) was established to meet this customer's wishes. Many customers must have had the same wish, given the large number of Saturn buyers and their high loyalty to Saturn.

> "I wish that I could buy a used car with confidence and not worry that it won't perform as described by the used car salesman."

This wish is now a reality thanks to the formation of a new breed of dealers in used cars (now renamed "pre-owned cars") such as Car Max and AutoNation.

> "I wish that I could find a movie theater which offered a lot of movie choices and provided a restaurant instead of just a popcorn and candy stand, and where I didn't have to worry about someone tall sitting in front of me."

This wish is now satisfied by large multi-screen theaters featuring restaurant service and having stadium-type seating.

> "I wish that I could fly to another city at about half the cost, and have confidence that the plane would be comfortable and reliable. I would be happy to go without food service and reserved seats."

This wish must have been heard by Southwest Airlines, today America's most profitable airline.

---

marketer maps this "consumption chain" and then considers at each step whether the company can introduce some new products, services, or benefits. Exhibit 3–3 shows a sample set of questions that may be asked.

Professor Sandra Vandermerwe has provided several illustrations using a similar idea, which she calls mapping the *Customer Activity Cycle*.[2] Suppose IBM wants to provide excellent information products and services to the banking industry. IBM's challenge is to learn how a bank goes about deciding, shaping, and managing its information system. At some point a bank will consider whether it needs to make an

EXHIBIT 3–2

Products that Successfully Resolved Contradictions

- A shortening product that doesn't include animal fat but cooks and tastes like shortenings that do. *Crisco*.

- A deodorant that is strong enough for a man, but mild enough for a woman's skin. *Secret*.

- A potato chip that doesn't get stale or broken when the package is opened. *Pringles*.

- A feminine pad offering maximum protection but having the comfort of a thin pad. *Always Ultra Thins*.

- Khaki pants that won't wrinkle. *Dockers*.

- A fabric that has the comfort and breathability of cotton but is waterproof. *Goretex*.

- An automobile with the passenger capacity of a sedan and the handling of a sports car. *BMW*.

information system improvement. It would want to understand its information technology (IT) options. The bank then needs to think of how to integrate its current and new system. Then it may be ready to choose a vendor. This is followed by installation and setup, then training, and then maintenance and repair if needed. Some time later, the bank will review and further update its IT system.

Given the customer activity cycle, IBM's challenge is to prove to the bank that it could be a superior partner in providing products, services, programs, and systems. Exhibit 3–4 displays the entire customer activity cycle and adds boxes to each step showing what IBM can do to add value.

The customer activity cycle suggests that IBM should consult the bank on the bank's strategic options, provide systems and software integration, offer to remove the old equipment, offer a training program and a preventative maintenance program, and so on. The main point is that the marketer, here IBM, should not just focus on selling superior *purchase value* to the bank. IBM must also take responsibility for selling superior *use value*. IBM should view this not as a one-time *transaction* but as a continuing *relationship* aimed at generating superior customer value at every point.

EXHIBIT 3–3

Using the Consumption Chain to Find New Opportunities

---

1. How do people become aware of their need for your product or service?

2. How do consumers find your offering?

3. How do consumers make their final selections?

4. How do customers order and purchase your product or service?

5. How is your product or service delivered?

6. What happens when your product or service is delivered?

7. How is your product installed?

8. How is your product or service paid for?

9. How is your product stored?

10. How is your product moved around?

11. What is the customer really using your product for?

12. What do customers need help with when they use your product?

13. What about returns or exchanges?

14. How is your product repaired or serviced?

15. What happens when your product is disposed of or no longer used?

Source: Ian C. MacMillan and Riat Gunther McGrath, "Discovering New Points of Differentiation," *Harvard Business Review*, July–August 1997, pp. 133–45.

Supplying a New Product or Service

The previous methods depend upon studying how buyers buy and surveying their expressed needs. But consumers are somewhat limited in imagining new products and services that might emerge from technological or creative breakthroughs. Consumers did not propose "Walkmans," "videocassette recorders," or "videocameras." Indeed, those would have been hard to imagine. Nor did customers ask for cellophane, nylon, orlon, teflon, lycra, kevlar, and other DuPont breakthrough products; those came out of laboratory research.

Now we shall consider what companies can do to identify product improvements and brand-new product and service ideas.

EXHIBIT 3–4

Customer Activity Cycle: IBM Bank Customer (Simplified)

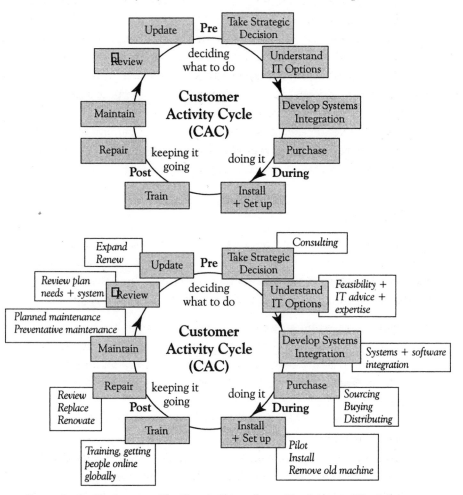

Source: Sandra Vandermerwe, *The Eleventh Commandment: Transforming to 'Own' Customers* (London: Wiley, 1996), pp. 117 and 121.

How Can a Company Organize Itself to Find More Promising Opportunities?

Companies draw upon a number of sources for new ideas. For example, they hope that their salespeople will hear about customer needs and bring the information back to the company. Yet there are three problems. First, salespeople are so busy that they tend not to use their time to report back new product/service ideas. Second, they normally would not know to whom to give such ideas, other than their sales manager. Third, salespeople are rarely given any financial reward for bringing ideas back to the company.

Companies also hope to see new product ideas emerge from their research and development (R&D) group. There are, however, two problems. First, the R&D people usually work on assigned problems rather than on their own ideas. Second, when R&D does propose a new idea, it may turn out to be inappropriate from a profit standpoint.

We would like to propose two models companies can use to develop more and better ideas for new products/services. They are *the idea manager model* and the *strategic breakthrough model*.

The Idea Manager Model

A company that wants new product and service ideas needs to install a system that directs the flow of new ideas to a central point where such ideas can be collected, reviewed, and evaluated. Otherwise, good ideas sputter in various departments and die. Essentially, a company must:

1. Appoint a respected senior person to be the company's idea manager
2. Create a multidiscipline committee consisting of a scientist, an engineer, a purchasing person, a manufacturing person, a salesperson, a marketer, and a finance person, to meet regularly and evaluate proposed new products and services
3. Set up a toll-free number for anyone who wants to send a new idea to the idea manager
4. Encourage all company stakeholders—employees, suppliers, distributors, dealers—to send their ideas to the idea manager
5. Set up a formal recognition program to reward those who contribute the best new ideas during the year

As this system becomes established in a company, ideas will flow in more freely. No longer will good ideas die because of having no place to go or no senior product advocate. When the members of the idea management committee meet each week, they will have plenty of ideas to review. Some ideas will turn out to be inappropriate or infeasible, and the idea manager will communicate this finding back to those who supplied the ideas. Other ideas will have a small profit potential and will receive later consideration. A few ideas will seem to have strong promise. They will be assigned to committee members to investigate and report back on at the next meeting.

When the members of the committee meet again, they will discard some of the promising ideas as less promising than they thought. Other promising ideas will appear even more promising, and the committee will set up a budget for further research. One promising idea may receive $50,000 for marketing research; another idea may receive $250,000 for setting up a prototype.

The results of financing the most promising ideas will be reported back to the committee at subsequent meetings. In the case of disappointing results, the committee will "kill" the project. Ideas will have to pass through successive screens, and receive a "go" or "no-go" decision at each juncture. This organizational approach is very similar to that used by the 3M company, one of the most innovative U.S. companies.

The idea manager approach should yield two favorable results. First, it should create an innovation-oriented company culture as a result of the ease of knowing to whom to send good ideas and the existence of rewards. Second, it should yield a larger number of ideas among which will be found some especially good ones. Generally speaking, the greater the number of ideas generated, the greater likelihood that a few great ones will show up.

The Strategic Breakthrough Model

Companies often find themselves in a stalemated situation where it appears that they cannot reach their projected sales goals. Consider the situation illustrated in Exhibit 3–5. The company has set a high sales goal to be reached by the fifth year. It has projected the various sources of sales over the five-year period. Its current products in its current markets (given the same market share) supply the base level, which grows for a while and then declines because of the product life cycle. Sales would be higher if the company could increase its market share. More sales can come from introducing the company's current products into new markets (geographical and segmental). Additional sales will come from launching new products. Finally, the company could acquire new companies or brands. Yet all those strategy additions may not add up to management's desired sales performance goal. Either the company will have to reduce its sales (and profit) goal or find "breakthrough" ideas to fill the remaining strategic gap.

That was the situation facing Jack Welch, CEO of General Electric,

EXHIBIT 3–5

Strategic Gap Model

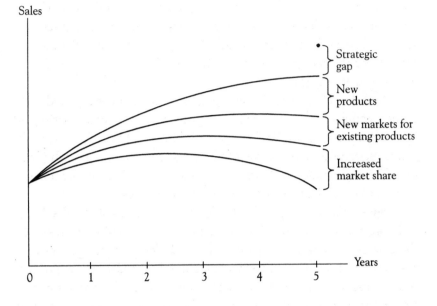

some years ago. It appeared that GE would not be able to reach its five-year sales and profit goals. At that point Welch asked each GE division to find one or two "breakthrough" ideas that would significantly raise the businesses' sales and profit performance. He wanted more than *improvement thinking;* he wanted *breakthrough thinking.*

This author was hired to work with one of the divisions, GE Medical Systems in Milwaukee, and to lead senior managers in their search for breakthrough ideas. The division produced expensive medical equipment such as CAT scanners, costing $500,000–$1,000,000. Hospitals were finding it increasingly difficult to afford expensive medical equipment. There was a political movement to discourage all but a few hospitals in a community from buying expensive medical equipment. GE Medical Systems management had to figure out how to sell more CAT scanners in the face of tighter hospital budgets.

The strategic breakthrough model worked as follows. GE Medical Systems scheduled an all-day "breakthrough" session involving twenty senior managers. The twenty managers formed four teams, each with a different mandate. The respective team mandates were:

- Find new customers and segments
- Find new sales strategies
- Find new pricing and equipment financing solutions
- Find new product features

The teams met in separate rooms in the morning to brainstorm, and in the early afternoon reconvened to present their ideas to the whole group. About twelve ideas emerged. Then the managers began to critique each idea. One by one, ideas were dropped as inappropriate or infeasible. But before the managers were fully discouraged, two ideas not only survived but appeared very promising. Those two ideas were subsequently launched with great success.

The strategic breakthrough model is especially useful when a company is drifting and badly needs some innovative, discontinuous thinking. The breakthrough session puts pressure on senior management to leave behind their normal assumptions and day-to-day concerns and to think collectively and creatively about significant new initiatives.

What Are the Possible Company Growth Paths?

Marketing, as we have seen, bears the main responsibility for growing the company's top line. Marketing's main thrust and skill is *demand management*, namely to influence the level, timing, and composition of demand in the pursuit of the company's objectives.

Marketers spend most of their time trying to build the level of demand. Under some circumstances, such as when there is overdemand, marketers may try to reduce demand or change its timing or composition.[3]

Let us focus on the challenge of building demand. One starting point is to see demand-building as consisting of three processes: *getting customers*, *keeping customers*, and *growing customers*. Each process in turn involves a number of steps, which will be treated in Chapter 7 of this book.

Another view of the possible paths for building demand is supplied by an extended version of the framework proposed by Igor Ansoff, shown in Exhibit 3–6.[4] Each of the nine cells suggests a different demand expansion path.

To the list shown in Exhibit 3–6 can be added two additional growth paths not so apparent from the matrix. They are (1) innovating new value delivery systems and (2) invading new market spaces.

The following companies have achieved outstanding growth by establishing a new delivery system for an existing product or service:

EXHIBIT 3–6

Nine Ways to Build Demand

	Products		
	Existing	*Modified*	*New*
	Sell more of our existing products to our existing types of customers. (Market penetration)	Modify our current products and sell more of them to our existing customers. (Product modification)	Design new products that will appeal to our existing customers. (New product development)
Markets	Enter and sell our products in other geographical areas. (Geographical expansion)	Offer and sell modified products to new geographical markets.	Design new products for prospects in new geographic areas.
	Sell our existing products to new types of customers. (Segment invasion)	Offer and sell modified products to new types of customers.	Design new products to sell to new types of customers. (Diversification)

- Michael Dell, as a twenty-four-year-old student at the University of Texas, recognized early that personal computers could be sold by mail and telephone. He felt that there were enough buyers who would have confidence to order a Dell computer over the phone, especially if backed by a money-back guarantee. Additional confidence occurred later when Dell's ads began to show that Dell customers reported the highest satisfaction among all buyers of different brands of computers. More recently, Michael Dell took another innovative distribution step by selling computers over the Internet to both businesses and consumers. He reports daily Internet sales averaging more than $3 million.
- First Direct is a British bank without any buildings or branches. But it stands ready to serve its customers' banking needs night or day, seven days a week. Transactions and information are available on the phone and eventually will be available through the computer.

- Jeffrey Bezos established in 1994 a website called *www.amazon.com*, which lists more than 2.5 million book titles that are easy to order and priced lower than at most bookstores. Amazon has added such innovative features as suggesting other books that might interest a customer based on his or her ordering pattern, notifying customers of new books published by their favorite author, and featuring book reviews by professional critics as well as readers.[5]

The other path for growth involves an existing company spreading into new industry spaces. Examples include Disney, Merck, Honda, and Nike.

- Walt Disney started out as an animated film producer. Not content just to make cartoons, he and his company moved into licensing his characters for merchandised goods, entered the broadcasting industry, and built theme parks, and more recently the company is developing vacation and resort property. Disney's portfolio evolution is shown in Exhibit 3–7.
- The giant pharmaceutical firm Merck is not content only to develop and sell ethical pharmaceuticals. In 1993 Merck purchased Medco, a mail-order pharmaceutical distributor, for $6.6 billion. It formed a joint venture with DuPont to establish more basic research. It formed another joint venture with Johnson & Johnson to bring some of its ethical products into the over-the-counter market. It has alliances with biotech firms, and it operates Merck Generics as well.
- The giant Japanese company Honda likes to boast that it can fit six Hondas into a two-car garage. When people can't figure this out, they are reminded by Honda that in addition to cars, it makes motorcycles, lawnmowers, marine engines, snow blowers, and snowmobiles. Honda's core product is engines, and it has distinctive core competencies in making engines. Then it enters different industries requiring engines and makes the end product.
- The shoe company Nike started out designing high-performance shoes for serious athletes. Later it hired famous athletes who touted Nike shoes. Subsequently it added sports clothing to its line. More recently it supplied sports apparel to teams such as the Dallas Cowboys. Nike's latest move is to produce Nike events such as soccer matches and golf tournaments.

All these cases illustrate the opportunities facing a company that is willing to move into adjacent or different industries.

EXHIBIT 3–7
Disney's Portfolio Evolution

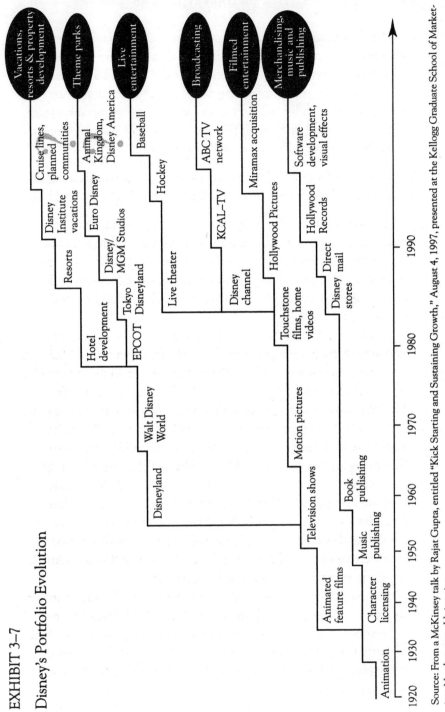

Source: From a McKinsey talk by Rajat Gupta, entitled "Kick Starting and Sustaining Growth," August 4, 1997, presented at the Kellogg Graduate School of Marketing, Northwestern University.

How Can a Company Evaluate and Choose Among a Set of Opportunities?

Companies that are fortunate enough to recognize abundant marketing opportunities have a new problem, namely, to decide which opportunities are the most worthwhile to pursue. They want to pick apples, not lemons. Most companies set up criteria to guide their search and choice of worthwhile projects. For example, the Gould Corporation established the following acceptance criteria to evaluate new product development opportunities:

- The product would be ready to be launched within five years.
- The product would have a market potential of at least $50 million and a 15 percent growth rate.
- The product would provide at least a 30 percent return on sales and 40 percent on investment.
- The product would be capable of achieving technical or market leadership.

Those criteria helped Gould screen out some otherwise interesting ideas and to focus on ones that best fitted its business scope and investment criteria.

Within the set of acceptable ideas, the company will want to measure the potential profit against the potential risk. The story is told of a company president who was considering a new product proposal that might bring in $50 million of lifetime profits. He countered with the question: "If we are wrong, how much might we lose?" His new product development manager said the downside risk would be a loss of $10 million. The CEO immediately rejected the proposal because of the downside risk. However, he should have raised one more question before making a snap decision: "What is the probability that we would lose $10 million?" If the probability was 10 percent, then he should probably go ahead with the project. If the probability was, say, 50 percent he might decide not to gamble.

Estimating the overall probability of a successful launch usually consists of making three separate probability estimates:

Overall probability of success	=	Probability of technical completion	×	Probability of commercialization given technical completion	×	Probability of economic success given commercialization

For example, if the three probabilities are estimated as .50, .65, and .74 respectively, the company would conclude that the overall probability of success is .24. The company then has to judge whether the profit potential is high enough to warrant developing the product given the low overall probability of success.

How Can a Company Improve Its Success Rate in Launching New Products and Services?

It is one thing to find good-looking opportunities; it is another to be capable of turning them into successfully commercialized products. New product failure rates are as high as 80–90 percent in mass consumer packaged goods and as high as 20–30 percent in industrial goods.

Why the difference? New brands of fast-moving consumer goods are often very similar to existing brands, are launched with much advertising that has an uncertain effect, and must dislodge consumers from well-established shopping habits favoring their current brands. Industrial goods companies tend to launch new products when a need can be documented, where they can pretest their product with a group of interested companies, and where they have a ready list of names of likely prospects.

So many things can go wrong in developing and launching a new product:

- The CEO may have initiated the project as a pet idea without any evidence confirming the idea's viability.
- The original product concept may have been modified by each successive department, until it hardly resembled the original winning idea.
- Different departments may have forced cost savings and sales trade-offs which diluted the final product's appeal to the buyers.
- The company failed to get good quality market coverage because of a failure to attract enough qualified distribution outlets.
- The company failed to buy enough advertising to gain sufficient awareness and trial.
- The company priced the product too high.
- The company invested so much in developing the new product that it launched it in the hope of recovering sunk costs.

In order to develop a picture of the factors common to successfully commercialized products, Madique and Zirger asked several electronics companies to identify their greatest product successes and to supply information for each case.[6] They found several factors common to these successfully launched products, including:

- Successful products all had a very high estimate of the profit return. The researchers found that pre-project profit estimates tend to be overoptimistic. Therefore if the profit estimate is very high, even when that level wasn't reached, the return could still be quite good.
- Successful companies spend an adequate amount to publicize the product's existence. Some companies make the mistake of spending little on publicity thinking that they have invented a "better mouse-trap" and the world will come beating a path to their doors.
- Winning products are usually the first ones introduced, not the later entries.
- Product development is in the hands of a multidisciplinary team that works well together.
- The CEO is very supportive of new product ideas and programs.

Questions to Consider

Mark Twain once complained: "I was seldom able to see an opportunity until it had ceased to be one." It is the fate of most companies to see a competitor come out with something new that they should have thought of. Worse, the idea may have been kicking around in their organization without ever surfacing at a level where it could have been seized and launched. Good ideas are in the air, and what separates the masters from the plodders is how well organized they are to capture and evaluate ideas, and then to develop and launch them successfully. Most companies lack an innovative culture, and yet innovation is the best defense in a hypercompetitive marketplace where few competitive advantages last very long. While innovation is risky, noninnovation can be fatal.

Here are some things for your business unit to think about:

1. Describe five major opportunities facing your business. Assess each opportunity in terms of its potential profit and probability of success.
2. List several problems that customers have with your product or service. Suggest a solution in each case.
3. How would customers ideally like to acquire and use your product or service? What opportunities does this suggest?
4. Map the normal customer activity cycle that customers go through

in acquiring, using, and disposing of your product. What opportunities are suggested by points in the customer activity cycle?

5. How well organized is your company for stimulating and collecting new product and service ideas? Give your company one of the following grades:

Poor:	The company has no organized way to stimulate and collect ideas.
Fair:	The company depends on getting ideas from salespeople and R&D.
Good:	The company has appointed a person to stimulate and collect ideas, but the system needs further development.
Excellent:	The company has a well-working idea management system that produces many useful ideas.

6. Does your business prepare a strategic gap analysis? When a gap exists, what does the business do about it? Lower the goal? Set up breakthrough sessions?

4

Developing Value Propositions and Building Brand Equity

The value decade is upon us. If you can't sell a top-quality product at the world's lowest price, you're going to be out of the game . . . the best way to hold your customers is to constantly figure out how to give them more for less.—*Jack Welch, Chairman, General Electric*

GERTRUDE STEIN'S FAMOUS remark, "A rose is a rose is a rose," would never be uttered by a marketer. The perception of an object is highly influenced by its context. For example, Evian is able to sell water for $15 an ounce. We are not alluding to Evian's bottled water, which commands a price of about 25 cents an ounce. Evian also produces a moisturizer in a small-cartridge spray tube, which sells for $15. It contains water, but to the user it provides a refreshing spray on the face on a hot day.

Similarly, most people couldn't tell the difference, in a blindfold test, between Coca-Cola and President's Choice Cola (a store brand of Loblaw's Supermarket in Toronto). Yet they pay substantially more for Coca-Cola when they see the brand name. When Coca-Cola undertook to reformulate its drink in 1985, there was a national outcry: "How dare them change the taste of our national drink!" Certain brands are sacred to the consumers. Interbrand estimates that Coca-Cola's brand name is worth $35 billion, much more than all of its factories.

This is not to say that the art of marketing is to choose a good brand name, advertise it widely, and make a fortune. Many steps are involved

EXHIBIT 4–1

Main Steps in Developing a Strong Brand

Develop the value proposition

1. Choose a *broad positioning* for the product.

2. Choose a *specific positioning* for the product.

3. Choose a *value positioning* for the product.

4. Develop the *total value proposition* for the product.

Build the brand

1. Choose a *brand name*.

2. Develop *rich associations and promises* for the brand name.

3. Manage all the customers' *brand contacts* so that they meet or exceed the customers' expectations associated with the brand.

---

in developing a strong brand. They are listed in Exhibit 4–1 under two main headings: *developing the value proposition* and *building the brand*.

Developing the Value Proposition

No company can be good at everything. First, companies have limited funds and must decide where to concentrate them. Second, choosing to be good at one thing may reduce the possibility of being good at something else. For example, if a company chooses to mass-produce a standard product to achieve the lowest cost, it is not free to respond to many customer requests for modifications.

Choosing a Broad Positioning

What are the broad positioning alternatives? Professor Michael Porter, in his *Competitive Strategy*, proposed three broad alternatives: the business unit should focus on being the *product differentiator, the low cost leader,* or the *nicher*.[1] He warned firms that if they tried to be good in all three ways, but not superior in any way, they would lose out to firms that would be suone way. The middle way is a trap. Firms normally don't have ......ugh money to be good in all ways. In addition, each positioning strategy calls for a different organizational culture and management system.

However, critics point out that some firms have managed to be superior at both product differentiation and low cost. Procter & Gamble is not only a great marketing firm doing superior product differentiation, but it is also very lean in its manufacturing cost structure. Toyota not only produces the highest-quality automobile but produces it at the lowest unit cost.

Subsequently, two consultants, Michael Treacy and Fred Wiersema, proposed an alternative three-way framework, which they called *value disciplines*.[2] Within its industry, a firm could be the *product leader*, the *operationally excellent firm*, or the *customer intimate firm*. This framework is based on the notion that in every market there are three types of customers. Some customers favor the firm that is advancing the technological frontier (product leadership). Another customer group does not need the latest products but wants highly reliable and dependable performance (operational excellence). A final customer group prefers the firm that is most responsive and flexible in meeting their individual needs (customer intimacy).

Treacy and Wiersema observed that it is difficult for a firm to be best in all three ways, or even in two ways. Most firms do not have sufficient funds to be best at everything. Furthermore, the three value disciplines require different managerial systems and attitudes that often conflict. Operationally excellent companies like McDonald's or Federal Express operate highly efficient systems that are difficult to alter. A customer asking McDonald's to cook the hamburger longer or a customer asking Federal Express to pick up its mail later would cause their systems to slow down. Operationally excellent firms operate like machines, and that is both their strength and their weakness. If they tried to be customer intimate and made many changes to satisfy individual customers, they would not be able to perform at their promised level of efficiency.

Similarly, operationally excellent firms find it hard to be product leaders. Introducing new products on a frequent basis disrupts the smooth functioning of the system. Each value discipline requires different management systems, processes, organization, and culture. The authors suggest, however, that business units within the same company can each practice a different value discipline. For example, General Electric's major appliance division pursues operational excellence, its engineered plastics division pursues customer intimacy, and its jet engine division pursues product leadership.

Treacy and Wiersema propose that a business should follow four rules for success:

1. Become best at one of the three value disciplines.
2. Achieve an adequate performance level in the other two disciplines.
3. Keep improving one's superior position in the chosen discipline so as not to lose out to a competitor.
4. Keep becoming more adequate in the other two disciplines, since competitors keep raising customers' expectations about what is adequate.

Broad positioning frameworks provide a useful starting point for positioning. However, they conceal a wealth of other positioning possibilities.

Choosing a Specific Positioning

Companies need to go beyond a broad positioning to express a more concrete benefit and reason to buy. Many companies advertise a *single major benefit positioning*, drawing from such possibilities as:

- Best quality
- Best performance
- Most reliable
- Most durable
- Safest
- Fastest
- Best value for the money
- Least expensive
- Most prestigious
- Best designed or styled
- Easiest to use
- Most convenient

Thus in the automobile market, Mercedes owns the "most prestigious" position; BMW owns the "best (driving) performance" position; Hyundai owns the "least expensive" position; and Volvo owns the "safest" position.

Volvo's case is interesting in that Volvo recognized that in every country of the world, some car buyers make safety their highest priority. In discovering this global niche, Volvo is able to sell its cars all over the world. Volvo has added a *second benefit positioning* of their automobile, namely the claim that it is one of the most durable cars. They use that second positioning in countries like Mexico, where the buyer is concerned more with buying a long-lasting car than with safety.

Some companies even practice *triple benefit positioning*. SmithKline

Beecham promotes its Aqua-Fresh toothpaste as offering three benefits: anticavity protection, better breath, and whiter teeth. The toothpaste exudes from the tube in three colors, each suggesting and delivering a different benefit. Beecham wants its Aqua-Fresh brand to "counter-segment," that is, to attract three segments instead of one.

In searching for a specific positioning, the business unit should consider the following possible sources:

- *Attribute positioning:* The company positions itself on some attribute or feature. A beer company asserts that it is the *oldest* beer maker; a hotel describes itself as the city's *tallest* hotel. Positioning by a feature is normally a weak choice since no benefit is explicitly claimed.
- *Benefit positioning:* The product promises a benefit. Tide claims that it cleans better, Volvo claims that its cars are safer. Marketers primarily work with benefit positioning.
- *Use/application positioning:* The product is positioned as the best in a certain application. Nike might describe one of its shoes as the best to wear for racing and another as the best to wear for playing basketball.
- *User positioning:* The product is positioned in terms of a target user group. Apple Computer describes its computers and software as the best for graphic designers; Sun Microsystems describes its work-station computers as the best for design engineers.
- *Competitor positioning:* The product suggests its superiority or difference from a competitor's product. Avis described itself as a company "that tries harder" (than Hertz, by implication); 7 UP called itself the Uncola.
- *Category positioning:* The company may describe itself as the category leader. Kodak means film; Xerox means copy machines.
- *Quality/price positioning:* The product is positioned at a certain quality and price level. Chanel No. 5 is positioned as a very high-quality, high-price perfume; Taco Bell represents its tacos as giving the most value for the money.

Companies must avoid the following errors in positioning their brand:

- *Underpositioning:* Failing to present a strong central benefit or reason to buy this brand
- *Overpositioning:* Adopting such a narrow positioning that some potential customers may overlook the brand
- *Confused positioning:* Claiming two or more benefits that contradict each other

- *Irrelevant positioning:* Claiming a benefit which few prospects care about
- *Doubtful positioning:* Claiming a benefit that people will doubt the brand or company can actually deliver

Choosing a Value Positioning

We have discussed the selection of one or more specific benefits that the brand will advertise, without mentioning anything about how the brand will be priced. But buyers think in terms of value for the money: what they get for what they pay. The seller must value-position the brand. We can distinguish five value positions.

More for More

Companies can always be found that specialize in making the most upscale version of the product and charging a high price to cover their higher costs. Called luxury goods, such products claim to be better in quality, craftsmanship, durability, performance, or style. Examples include Mercedes automobiles, Mont Blanc writing instruments, and Gucci apparel. The product is not only fine in itself, it is delivering prestige to the buyer. It becomes an emblem of a higher lifestyle, a more exclusive status. Often the price far exceeds the actual increment of quality.

"More for more" positioning can thrive as long as there are affluent buyers who are not shy about conspicuous consumption or who feel that they should support the efforts of high-quality-conscious producers. In almost every category of product or service, one or more sellers will be found who offer the "best." One can find very expensive restaurants, hotels, coffees, brandies, and so on. One is surprised occasionally at the entry of a new competitor who sets an unusually high price, such as a kitchen stove for $30,000 or a new brand of scotch whisky for $500. Häagen-Dazs came in as a premium ice cream brand at a price never before charged for ice cream; Starbucks came in as an expensive coffee where coffee could always be had for much less; some Cuban cigar brands command an unbelievably high price. In general, a company should be alert to the possibility of introducing a "much more for much more" brand in any underdeveloped product or service category.

Yet more-for-more brands are vulnerable: They often invite imitators who claim the same quality but are priced lower. And luxury goods are at risk during economic downturns when buyers become more cautious in their spending.

More for the Same

Companies have been able to attack a "more for more" brand by introducing a brand claiming comparable quality and performance but priced much lower. The Toyota company introduced its new Lexus automobile with "more for the same" value positioning. Its headline read: "Perhaps the First Time in History That Trading a $72,000 Car for a $36,000 Car Could Be Considered Trading Up." It demonstrated the high quality of its new Lexus in several ways: through the raving newspaper and car magazine reviews of car journalists; through a widely distributed videotape showing the Mercedes and Lexus side by side and the superior qualities of the Lexus; and through evidence that Lexus dealerships were providing a better buying experience than Mercedes dealerships. Mercedes car owners in many American cities ended up making their next car purchase a Lexus. Since that time the Lexus repurchase rate has been 60 percent, twice that of the average car brand repurchase rate.

The Same for Less

It seems that everyone is happy when they can buy a typical product or brand at less than the normal price. Everything—Arrow shirts, Goodyear tires, Panasonic TV sets—seems to be available at a lower price at some store or discount shop. Not long ago many people would buy their electronic equipment by phoning 47th Street Photo in New York City, placing their orders, and giving their credit card numbers; the prices couldn't be beaten. Today many shoppers are able to shop the Internet for lowest prices of cars, computers, books, and other goods.

Discount stores don't claim to have superior products, but they can offer ordinary brands at deep savings, based on superior purchasing power. The success of many personal computer manufacturers is based on cloning the original leading brands, such as IBM or Apple, and selling the unknown clone brands at 20–30 percent less.

Less for Much Less

Some people complain that some manufacturers or service providers provide more than they require but they still have to pay the higher price. One cannot say to a hotel, "take out the TV set and charge me less," or tell an airline, "skip the food and charge me less." People buy a videocassette recorder (VCR) that enables them to play a videotape and record TV programs, but most people don't use or know how to use the recording feature. There would be a market for cheaper VCRs offering fewer features.

Therefore sellers have an opportunity to enter a market with a "less for much less" offering. There is a hotel in Tokyo that rents not a room but a berth for substantially less than the normal hotel price. Aldi's, a German supermarket chain, operates smaller supermarkets carrying fewer items, most not shelved but still in boxes, where customers must bring their own shopping bags; it offers its customers "less for much less." Southwest Airlines, the most profitable U.S. air carrier, charges much less by not serving food, not assigning seats, not using travel agents, and not transferring luggage to other carriers.

More for Less

Of course, the winning value positioning would be to offer prospects and customers "more for less." This is the attraction of highly successful *category killer* stores. Toys 'R' Us, for example, offers the largest selection of toys for the lowest prices; and Sportmart offers the largest selection of sports equipment and sports clothing for the lowest prices. Mass merchandisers make a similar claim: walking into a Wal-Mart store, one meets a friendly greeter, sees a whole array of attractively laid-out, well-known branded goods, finds everyday low prices, and generous return policies, and leaves thinking of Wal-Mart as a place where he or she can get more for less.

All said, each brand must adopt a value positioning strategy designed for its target market. "More for more" will draw one target market; "less for much less" will draw another. The only value positioning that will inevitably fail is "less for more." Here the customer ultimately feels cheated, tells others, and the brand soon disappears from the market.

Developing the Total Value Proposition

Ultimately, each company must be able to answer the customer's question: "Why should I buy from you?" Now Volvo's answer, for example, is not limited to the car's safety and durability. It will also mention other benefits and features the car provides: guarantees, a hotline, and so forth. We call this set of benefits and features the brand's *total offering*. Now the prospect will also want to assess his *total costs* of acquiring, using, storing, and disposing of the product. The seller's price is only one of the costs; others are the effort, time, and psychic costs. Then the prospect examines the difference (or ratio) of the total offering to the total cost for each competitive

EXHIBIT 4–2

Measuring Customer Preference

Customer Satisfaction Requirements	Importance of Requirement[a]	Manufacturer Performance[b]			
		Kodak	Xerox	Canon	Ideal
High-quality Copies	10	8	7	8	10
Uptime of the Copier	9	9	7	7	10
Quality of Service	8	8	7	4	10
Responsiveness to Problems	8	6	8	4	10
Pricing and Terms	8	6	8	7	10
Ease of Use	7	9	8	7	10

[a] Importance Requirements rated from 1 (very unimportant) to 10 (very important).
[b] Manufacturer Performance rated from 0 (disastrous) to 10 (outstanding).

$CSI_{(Perfect)} = (10 \times 10) + (9 \times 10) + (8 \times 10) + (8 \times 10) + (8 \times 10) + (7 \times 10) = 500$ (Maximum score)

$$CSI_{(Kodak)} = \frac{(10 \times 8) + (9 \times 9) + (8 \times 8) + (8 \times 6) + (8 \times 6) + (7 \times 9)}{500} = \frac{384}{500} \times 100 = 77$$

$$CSI_{(Xerox)} = \frac{(10 \times 7) + (9 \times 7) + (8 \times 7) + (8 \times 8) + (8 \times 8) + (7 \times 8)}{500} = \frac{373}{500} \times 100 = 75$$

$$CSI_{(Canon)} = \frac{(10 \times 8) + (9 \times 7) + (8 \times 4) + (8 \times 4) + (8 \times 7) + (7 \times 7)}{500} = \frac{312}{500} \times 100 = 62$$

Source: Roger J. Best, *Market-Based Management* (Upper Saddle River, NJ: Prentice-Hall, 1997), p. 12.

offering he is considering. We believe the prospect will choose the supplier who appears to offer the most attractive *total value proposition*.

We provide an illustration of this buyer choice process in Exhibit 4–2. Suppose the purchasing agent of a large company needs to buy ten copy machines and is reviewing the offerings of three vendors. We believe a buyer will base his final choice on four types of information. First, he will clarify what his company wants as benefits and features of the chosen copy machine. Assume that the particular buyer is seeking the six attributes shown in Exhibit 4–2. Second, the buyer will assign different importance weights to the six attributes. Suppose the buyer assigns up to ten points to express the importance he attaches to each attribute. Third, the buyer will consider a limited number of vendors: Suppose they are Kodak, Xerox, and Canon. Fourth, he will have an image of how capable each vendor is of delivering each benefit. Looking at the Kodak column in Exhibit 4–2, we see that the buyer assigns Kodak an 8 on "high quality copies," a 9 on "uptime of the copier," and so on. The numbers in the Kodak column represent the buyer's image of Kodak's standing on the six attributes. We might also say that Kodak's column of numbers represents the buyer's perception of Kodak's total offering.

Which company will the buyer choose if the price and other costs are the same for all three vendors? The buyer will choose the vendor who will offer the most of what he seeks. One way to get at this is to imagine a fourth vendor who is perfect in every way; he stands at a 10 in everything the buyer wants (see the last column of Exhibit 4–2). Certainly the buyer would buy from the perfect vendor if he existed. A perfect vendor would get a score of 500 points (simply multiply the importance weights by the respective ideal points). Applying the same multiplication of importance weights to the other vendors, we find that Kodak gets 384 points (or 77 percent of a perfect vendor), Xerox gets 373 points (75 percent), and Canon 312 points (62 percent). Since a perfect vendor doesn't exist, the buyer's next best choice is Kodak, who satisfies him at 77 percent of his ideal requirements.

If we drop the assumption that the buyer faces the same prices and costs, we would assume that the buyer will assess the total cost of each copy machine, subtract it from the total offering, and select the brand that offers the greatest difference (or ratio) of total offering to total cost.

Thus we conclude that all the homework to find a core positioning, a value positioning, and a total value proposition ends up allowing a company to describe why its total offering is superior to a competitor's total offering.

The next step is to use these results to build a strong brand identity that delivers a picture of the value that the potential customer could expect to receive.

Building the Brand

The art of marketing is largely the art of brand building. When something is not a brand, it will be probably be viewed as a commodity. Then price is what counts. When price is the only thing that counts, the only winner is the low-cost producer.

But having just a brand name is not enough. What does the brand name mean? What associations, performances, and expectations does it evoke? What degree of preference does it create? If it is only a brand name, then it fails as a brand.

Choosing a Brand Name

A brand name must first be chosen, and then its various meanings and promises must be built up through brand identity work. In choosing a brand name, it must be consistent with the value positioning of the brand. A "more for more" offering must carry a brand name suggestive of high quality, or at least not suggesting something of low quality. Recently the photos of two beautiful women were shown to a group of men who were asked which was the more beautiful woman. The vote was equally split. Then the researcher wrote that the first woman's name was Elizabeth and the second woman's name was Gertrude. Now the vote was 80 percent in favor of Elizabeth. Names do make a difference.

In naming a product or service, the company faces many possibilities: it could choose the name of a person (Honda, Calvin Klein), location (American Airlines, Kentucky Fried Chicken), quality (Safeway stores, Duracell batteries), lifestyle (Weight Watchers, Healthy Choice), or an artificial name (Exxon, Kodak). Among the desirable qualities of a brand name are the following:

1. *It should suggest something about the product's benefits.* Examples: Beautyrest mattress, Craftsman tools, Accutron watch.
2. *It should suggest product qualities such as action or color.* Examples: Sunkist oranges, Spic and Span cleanser, Firebird automobile.
3. *It should be easy to pronounce, recognize, and remember; short names help.* Examples: Tide, Crest, Puffs.
4. *It should be distinctive.* Examples: Mustang, Kodak, Exxon.
5. *It should not carry poor meanings in other countries and languages.* Example: *Nova* is a poor name for a car to be sold in Spanish-speaking countries; it means "doesn't go."

Building Positive Associations

The best known brand names carry associations. For example, here is a list of words that people say they associate with McDonald's:

Golden Arches	Kids	Quality
Big Mac	Fun	Happy Meal
Ronald McDonald	Consistency	Value meal
High calories	Paper waste	Charity

A company should ask three questions about the associations:

1. Which associations are positive and which are negative?

The most positive associations are fun, quality, happy meal, and value meal. There are two negative associations: high calories and paper waste. Those alert McDonald's to the possible need for action, such as offering a lean hamburger alternative and/or salad bar and using less paper for keeping the hamburgers warm.

2. How strong is each association?

McDonald's would like all positive associations to be strong. For example, charity is a positive association, but not many people may be aware of McDonald's high level of charitable giving. McDonald's might therefore let more people know about its generous gifts to charity.

3. Are any associations unique to McDonald's?

If a competitor's brand name evoked all the same associations, McDonald's wouldn't benefit from differentiation. Two associations are unique to McDonald's, namely Golden Arches and Ronald McDonald.

In trying to build a rich set of positive associations for a brand, the brand builder should consider five dimensions that can communicate meaning:[3]

Attributes. A strong brand should trigger in the buyer's mind certain attributes. Thus the Mercedes automobile triggers a picture of a well-engineered car that is durable, rugged, and expensive. If a car brand does not trigger any attributes, then it would be a weak brand.

Benefits. A strong brand should suggest benefits, not just features. Thus the Mercedes triggers the idea of a well-performing car that is enjoyable to drive and prestigious to own.

Company values. A strong brand should connote values that the company holds dear. Thus Mercedes is proud of its engineers and engineering innovations and is very organized and efficient in its operations. The fact that it is a German company adds more pictures in the buyer's mind about the character and culture of the brand.

Personality. A strong brand should exhibit some personality traits. Thus if Mercedes were a person, we would think of someone who is of middle age, serious, well-organized, and somewhat authoritarian. If Mercedes were an animal, we might think of a lion and its implied personality.

Users. A strong brand should suggest the kinds of people who buy the brand. Thus we would expect Mercedes to draw buyers who are older, affluent, and professional.

In summary, brands are strong when their very name connotes positive attributes, benefits, company values, personality, and users in the buyer's mind. The brand builder's job is to create a brand identity that builds on those dimensions.

Tools for Building the Brand Identity

Brand builders use a set of tools to strengthen and project the brand image. Strong brands typically exhibit an *owned word*, a *slogan*, a *color*, a *symbol*, and a set of *stories*.

Owned Word

A strong brand name, when mentioned to people in the target market, should trigger another word, preferably a favorable one. Here is a list of brands that own a word:

Company	Word
Volvo	"Safety"
BMW	"Driving performance"
Mercedes	"Engineering"
Federal Express	"Overnight"
Apple computer	"Graphics"
Lotus	"Spreadsheets"
Kodak	"Film"

Slogan

Many companies have successfully added a slogan or tag line to their company or brand name, which is repeated in every ad they issue. The effect of using the same slogan over and over again is almost hypnotic and subliminal in the brand image it creates. Here are some well-known brand slogans, which many people on the street would be able to recall or recognize:

British Airways: "The World's Favorite Airline"
AT&T: "The Right Choice"
Budweiser: "The King of Beers"
Ford: "Quality Is Our Number One Job"
General Electric: "We Bring Good Things to Life"
Miele: "Forever Better"

It is not always easy to develop a catchy slogan that works well in the customer's mind. Philips, the giant Dutch lighting and electronics company, changed its slogan several times and still needs something better. Its original slogan was "From Sand to Chips," suggesting that Philips used sand to both develop their lightbulbs (glass is made from sand) and to develop advanced computer chips (sand is silicon). But that went over the heads of many consumers and offered no benefit idea, but simply a description of what Philips made as a company. So Philips changed its slogan to "Philips Invents for You." But this led some wags to say: "Who asked them to?" Then Philips adapted a new slogan: "Let's Make Things Better." But now some wags say: "I didn't know things were so bad." So the search for a strong slogan for Philips goes on.

Colors

It helps for a company or a brand to use a consistent set of colors to aid in the brand's recognition. Caterpillar paints all of its construction equipment yellow. Yellow is also the corporate color of Kodak film. IBM uses blue in its publications, and, not surprisingly, IBM is called "Big Blue."

Symbols and Logos

Companies would be wise to adopt a symbol or logo to use in their communications. Many companies hire a well-known spokesperson, hoping that his or her qualities transfer to the brand. Nike uses Michael Jordan, who has worldwide recognition and likableness, to advertise its shoes. Chanel No. 5 used Catherine Deneuve, one of the world's most beautiful women, as its symbol. Candice Bergen, the actress, advertises Sprint telecommunications. Sporting goods manufacturers sign contracts with top athletes to serve as their symbols, even naming the equipment after them.

Spokespeople, of course, do not come cheap. In addition, they can get involved in a scandal. Although Hertz paid heavy dollars for O. J. Simpson to advertise its car rental service, it dropped him like a hot potato when O. J. was caught fleeing from Los Angeles when his wife was found murdered.

A less expensive approach is to develop a character, animated or otherwise, to etch the brand's image into the consumer's mind. The advertising agency Leo Burnett has successfully created a number of memorable animated characters, including the Jolly Green Giant, Tony the Tiger, and Charley the Tuna. The same agency also created the Marlboro Man, who is not animated, but is neither an expensive actor nor the same person all the time.

Still another approach is to choose an object to represent a company or brand. The Travelers insurance company uses an umbrella, suggesting that buying insurance is equivalent to having an umbrella available in case it rains. The Prudential insurance company features the Rock of Gibraltar, suggesting that buying its insurance is equivalent to "owning a piece of the Rock," which of course, is solid and dependable. Companies have also developed various logos, or abstract designs, which have become very familiar to people. Even the way the brand name is written can make a difference in its recognition and memorability.

A Set of Stories

Some brands will be associated with stories, which are a benefit if favorable and interesting, about the company or brand. The stories might relate to the founder(s) and the struggle to create the company. One thinks of the role that Henry Ford played in founding his company, or Alfred Sloan in engineering the success of General Motors.

One widespread story is that Coca-Cola was founded by two people who did everything to keep the formula a secret from others, locking it in a safe every night. Ben & Jerry's is a famous brand of ice cream whose founders, Ben Cohen and Jerry Greenfield, are very likable and give 7 percent of their profits to charity. Similarly, The Body Shop, now with more than 1,100 stores, has many stories told about its founder, Anita Roddick, who has strong views about social and political causes, that add personality to her company.

Nordstrom, one of America's most successful department stores, with the highest customer loyalty rating, abounds in stories that circulate among its customers and others. We hear about the man who came into Nordstrom with an automobile tire, asking for his money back. Nordstrom gave him back his money. The only catch is that Nordstrom doesn't sell tires. Now that's service. If you buy shoes at Nordstrom, and your feet aren't exactly the same size, the salesperson fits you with one shoe from one size and another shoe from another size, but only charges you for one pair. If you arrive to buy an advertised blue cashmere sweater and they are sold out, the sales clerk is likely to offer to find the same or a similar sweater at a competitor's store and send it to you.[4]

We hear other stories of exemplary customer-oriented behavior. The Ritz-Carlton bellboy who found that an important guest left for the airport without his briefcase and took it upon himself to rush to the airport, only to arrive late, but then took the next plane and found the guest and gave him the briefcase. The Federal Express driver who, when his truck broke down, hailed a cab and carried as many packages as he could to the airport to get them there in time. Such stories serve to ex-emplify and deepen consumers' appreciation of the brand.

A brand implies a relationship between a product and a customer. It connotes a set of qualities and services that the customer can expect. Brand loyalty is built by meeting the customer's expectations, or even better, exceeding them, which delivers "customer delight."

Evaluating a Brand's Effectiveness

Young & Rubicam (Y&R), one of the world's largest advertising agencies, suggests that successful brands have two qualities: *brand vitality* and *brand stature*. Each in turn is made up of two qualities. A brand has brand vitality when it is (1) differentiated in the consumer's mind from other brands and (2) when the differentiation is relevant to the consumer's needs. The brand has stature when it commands (1) high esteem and (2) high familiarity in its target market. Using those dimensions, Y&R draws certain conclusions in evaluating a brand:

1. A brand that has high familiarity but low esteem is a troubled brand. The brand's quality or features need to be improved before advertis-ing it. Heavy advertising can actually accelerate the demise of a low esteemed-brand.
2. A brand that has high likability but low familiarity is a prime candi-date for a heavy advertising campaign.
3. A brand with high vitality but low stature is another prime candidate for strong advertising.
4. A brand whose differentiation and relevance are slipping will start losing esteem and then familiarity.

Much of a brand manager's work is to build the brand image. But the brand manager's work must not stop there. The brand manager needs to make sure that the *brand experience* matches the *brand image*. Much can go wrong. A fine brand of canned soup described in a full-page color ad may be found in a dented and dusty condition on the bottom shelf in a supermarket. The ad describing a gracious hotel chain may be belied by the behavior of a surly concierge. The well-honed image of a small ap-pliance manufacturer is belied when the customer receives a damaged appliance because of careless packaging by the shipping clerk.

Brand building therefore calls for more than brand image building. It calls for managing every *brand contact* that the customer might have with the brand. Since all company employees, distributors, and dealers can affect the brand experience, the brand challenge is to manage the quality of all brand contacts. Jan Carlzon, former CEO of Scandinavian Airlines (SAS), expressed this well in his book, *Moments of Truth*.[5] When he managed SAS, he saw his challenge as making sure that the airline's five million passengers a year who met an average of five SAS employees—this made 25,000,000 brand contacts—on each occasion experienced a positive moment of truth. Each of his employees must deliver the right brand impression to every passenger he or she meets.

Questions to Consider

Here is a chance to assess your value proposition and brand strength. Answer the following questions for one of your business units or product lines.

1. Rate your business on each of the three value disciplines from 0 to 100. Are you above 80 in at least one value discipline? And are you at least 50 in each of the other two value disciplines? If so, you are in an excellent position to succeed. Otherwise, you'd better start changing now.
2. What is your specific positioning?
3. What is included in your total offering?
4. What are the specific costs that your buyers consider or incur when thinking about whether to buy your product?
5. Based on your answer to questions 3 and 4 above, state your total value proposition.
6. Using Exhibit 4–2, list the attributes, importance weights, competitors, and their standings as they might be seen by an average buyer or a particular buyer.
7. List a word that your brand might own. List other word associations that might arise. Which are favorable and unfavorable? How extensively mentioned is each association? Which associations are unique to your brand? What actions do your answers to these questions suggest?
8. Do you have a slogan? Is it working? What would be a better slogan?
9. What symbols support the brand? What improvements might be made?
10. What stories do people know or tell about your company? Do certain stories deserve more circulation?

PART TWO

TACTICAL MARKETING

5

Developing and Using
Market Intelligence

Time spent in reconnaissance is seldom wasted.—*Sun Tzu, fourth century* B.C.

It is a capital mistake to theorize before one has data.—*Sir Arthur Conan Doyle*

TODAY'S MARKETING IS becoming a battle based more on ownership of information than on ownership of other resources. Competitors can copy each other's equipment, products, and procedures, but they cannot duplicate the company's information and intellectual capital. The company's information content may constitute its chief competitive advantage.

Several companies have recently recognized this by appointing vice presidents of knowledge, learning, or intellectual capital. Every company contains more information than any manager can possibly know. The information is scattered in countless databases, plans, records, and heads of many longtime managers. The company must somehow bring order into its information gold mine so that its managers can more easily find answers to questions and make informed decisions.

Companies must also develop efficient routines for finding new information. Information costs time and money to acquire, maintain, and distribute. Marketing researchers have developed sophisticated techniques for acquiring new information, as well as for managing existing information. Here we shall discuss three questions:

- What kinds of information do companies need in order to make better marketing decisions?
- What are the principal ways in which relevant information can be gathered?
- What are the best ways to manage company information so that high-quality information is easily and quickly available to company decision-makers?

Types of Useful Information

Companies can make two errors with respect to information. They can gather too much information or too little. The solution is to develop a model of those forces in the company's macroenvironment and task environment that primarily drive its sales, costs, and profits. Different company managers can be asked what decisions they normally make and what they would need to know in order to make more informed decisions. The resulting information template must be a cross between what managers need to know and what is economically feasible. Exhibit 5–1 lists questions that a cross-section of marketing managers might be asked in order to determine what information the company should gather.

The inquiry into the information needs of managers will reveal the types of information that bear most on their decision-making. Exhibit 5–2 lists the three main types of information that most companies require. Here we shall comment on the role played by each type of information.

Macro-environment

Countless market opportunities emerge out of the ever changing macroenvironment. Companies must be skillful at trend-spotting. Recently an investor noticed a strong trend among office workers toward wearing more casual clothes. He sold short on companies manufacturing formal clothes. When the same investor noticed more banking by computers, he sold short in banks that were saddled with many branches and much real estate. Every new trend led him to invest in one set of companies and disinvest in another.

Whereas an investor can easily move money in and out of the stock market, a company must take a longer perspective on which businesses to enter or build and which to disinvest or divest. Yet both—investors and companies—must pay continuous attention to what is happening in each of the five main components of the macro-environment.

EXHIBIT 5–1

Questions to Guide Manager Information Gathering Needs

1. What types of information do you regularly get?

2. What types of special studies do you periodically request?

3. What types of information would you like to get that you are not getting now?

4. What information would you want daily? Weekly? Monthly? Yearly?

5. What magazines and trade reports would you like to see routed to you on a regular basis?

6. What specific topics would you like to be kept informed of?

7. What types of data-analysis programs would you like to use?

8. What would be the four most helpful improvements in the company's marketing information system?

EXHIBIT 5–2

Types of Information Needed

Macro-environment

Demographic trends
Economic trends
Lifestyle trends
Technological trends
Political/regulatory trends

Task Environment

Consumer information
Collaborator information
Competitor information

Company Environment

Company sales and market shares
Company orders and back orders
Company costs
Customer profitability by customer, product, segment, channel, order size, and geography
Other information

DEMOGRAPHIC TRENDS. One of the most useful things about demographic trends is their predictability. Given any age-distributed population and fairly stable birth rates, marriage rates, and mortality rates, one can fairly accurately project the age composition of the population several years ahead. If a particular age group is rapidly growing in size—as senior citizens are today—businesses can shift to products and services that are highly consumed by the senior population, such as health care and leisure activity.

Another useful form of demographic data is migration data. Some places lose population, and "hot spots" gain population. Since consumption of many items is closely related to population size, age, education, and ethnic, racial, and religious characteristics, this information is critical. Here are two examples:

> Restaurants need to monitor the changing food preferences of their clientele. In the 1970s young adult customers ate a lot of red meat; in the 1980s they showed more interest in chicken and fish dishes; in the early 1990s their interest grew in healthful menus of low-calorie, low-cholesterol, and vegetarian dishes; by the mid-1990s, Generation Xers were favoring finger food (nachos, fried onion rings) and showed less interest than the Baby Boomers (born between 1946 and 1964) in healthful foods. Clearly restaurant chains must monitor such changing food preferences. Even the mighty McDonald's cannot depend on the hamburger as its sole offering, so it has added chicken dishes and has experimented with pizza and a salad bar.

> Companies must track the changing ethnic makeup of the U.S. population. White (non-Hispanic) Americans will become a minority by the year 2050. The African-American population is expected to double from 32 million in 1992 to 62 million in 2050; during the same period, the Hispanic population is expected to grow 3.5 times from 24 million to 88 million; and the Asian and Pacific population is expected to grow three times from 13 million to 41 million. Several companies are capitalizing on these trends. Banc One of Columbus, Ohio, has appointed a Vice President of Hispanic Marketing whose task is to tap into the burgeoning Latino market. Banc One recently printed checks bearing the picture of the slain popular Latino singer Selena. Goya, a New Jersey food company, focuses almost exclusively on the Latino market, selling over more than seven hundred authentic-tasting Mexican entrées and appetizers to Spanish-owned mom-and-pop stores. Avon, the world's largest direct selling company, has hired thousands of African-American sales consultants who sell its products to other African-Americans; Black Enterprise magazine honored Avon as one of "The 25 Best Places for Blacks to Work."

Everything said applies to the importance of studying the population characteristics of each country, not just the United States. As companies expand globally, they will be drawn to countries with large populations, stable governments, and good purchasing power. Demographics must be the starting point in their country-by-country assessments.

ECONOMIC TRENDS. A population alone does not constitute a market. The people must also be ready, willing, and able to buy. And purchasing power is almost always unequally distributed both among consumers and among customer firms.

In the case of consumers, companies distinguish between upper, middle, and lower income classes. Some companies—such as Coca-Cola and Hershey's—serve all three groups; their products are low-cost and have broad appeal. Most consumer companies, however, design for just one or design something different for each income group. Ferrari designs its cars for the superrich, and Hyundai designs its cars for lower-income buyers. General Motors makes several car brands to meet the needs of people with different "purses, purposes, and personalities."

When the middle class is large in a country, many manufacturers will design for the middle class. In recent years, U.S. income distribution has grown more unequal, with an increasing percentage of poor people and rich people. That has led manufacturers and retailers to focus on a "Tiffany strategy" or a "Wal-Mart strategy," or both in some cases. They are finding it less attractive to focus on the middle class when the growth is at the two extremes.

Companies continuously monitor the economy and pay close attention to economic forecasts. If the news is bad, consumers and companies will reduce their spending, and this operates as a self-fulfilling prophecy in making the situation worse. Conversely, if consumers and companies are optimistic, they spend more liberally, and this produces further good news.

Companies regularly monitor specific indicators of economic health, such as employment levels, interest rates, consumer debt levels, inventory levels, industrial production, and housing starts. They base their business plans for the coming year on current expectations about the economy.

LIFESTYLES. People within the same income class can pursue quite different lifestyles. One wealthy person may maintain a jet set lifestyle marked by a Ferrari, a Rolex watch, Valentino suits, and lots of travel. Another with the same wealth might have a conservative lifestyle marked by hard work, high savings, and careful spending.

Lifestyles are manifested in people's *activities*, *interests*, and *opinions*. Names are given to certain lifestyles, such as Hippies, Yuppies, Traditionalists. A formal classification of lifestyles has emerged from *geodemographic analysis*. Claritas Inc. has developed PRIZM (Potential Rating Index by Zip Markets), which classifies more than 500,000 U.S. residential neighborhoods into sixty-two distinct lifestyle groupings called PRIZM clusters.[1] The clusters take into consideration thirty-nine factors grouped into five broad categories: (1) education and affluence, (2) family life cycle, (3) urbanization, (4) race and ethnicity, and (5) mobility. The clusters carry descriptive titles such as *Blue Blood Estates*, *Winner's Circle*, *Hometown Retired*, *Shotguns and Pickups*, and *Back Country Folks*. Here are three PRIZM clusters:

American Dreams: This segment represents the emerging, upscale, ethnic, big-city mosaic. People in this segment are likely to buy imported cars, *Elle* magazine, Mueslix cereal, tennis weekends, and designer jeans. Their annual median household income is $46,000.

Rural Industrial: This cluster includes young families in heartland offices and factories. Their lifestyle is typified by trucks, *True Story* magazine, Shake 'n Bake, fishing trips, and tropical fish. Annual median household income is $22,900.

Cashmere and Country Club: These aging baby boomers live the good life in the suburbs. They're likely to buy Mercedes, *Golf Digest*, salt substitutes, European getaways, and high-end TVs. Annual median household income is $68,600.

Marketers use PRIZM to answer such questions as: Which clusters (neighborhoods or ZIP codes) contain our best prospects? Which locations provide our best geographical opportunities? Which promotional media and appeals reach our prospects best? Direct marketers, such as Spiegel, use geoclustering information to decide where to mail their catalogs. The Helene Curtis Company, in marketing its Suave shampoo, uses PRIZM to identify neighborhoods with high concentrations of young working women; such women respond best to advertising messages that Suave is inexpensive, yet will make their hair "look like a million." Barnes & Noble, the bookstore chain, locates its stores where there are concentrations of *money and brain people*, because they buy a lot of books.

Marketers try to spot lifestyle changes. The market research firm of Yankelovich periodically surveys people's attitudes and behavior in regard to health and exercise, food habits and preferences, religious involvement, and so on. A particular Yankelovich Monitor report might indicate, for example, that people are eating more red meat again, good news for some marketers and bad news for others.

An influential futurist today is Faith Popcorn, who wrote *The Popcorn Report* and subsequently *Clicking*.[2] Exhibit 5–3 shows ten trends that Popcorn has identified.

TECHNOLOGY. All companies face technological disruption, if not obsolescence. The abacus is replaced by the adding machine, which is replaced by the hand calculator which is replaced by the computer. The 78 rpm music record is replaced by the 33, which is replaced by the audio tape and then the CD. The hernia operation by incision is replaced by the hernia operation by laparoscopy.

Such changes have a severe impact on existing market leaders who are heavily invested in the current technology. Current technology is usually challenged by new firms, which see innovation as their main hope of gaining a market foothold. In principle, the market leader should also innovate, even practice "self-cannibalization." The way to beat your competitors is to attack yourself first. Probably the best practitioners of self-cannibalization are such Japanese companies as Sony, Casio, and Canon. Casio, for example, introduced a digital watch that included a small calculator; then it introduced a new version with a capacity to carry fifty phone numbers in the watches' memory; another version later carried one hundred phone numbers; still a later version included world time. Competitors find it hard to keep up with Casio's rapid self-cannibalization pace.

Sony practices self-cannibalization with abandon. Akio Morita, its former chairman, would sometimes establish three teams after launching a new product such as the Walkman. The first team's mandate was to design short-run improvements to make in the next Walkman; the second team was to design medium-term improvements for the Walkman; and the third team was to try to obsolete the Walkman.

Companies need to imagine possible paths of technological evolution. When recognizing alternative paths, companies must place a bet on which technology will win. Market research often won't be of much help.

That means companies run a risk when they innovate and also when they don't innovate. Product leadership is won by a few companies that have learned how to innovate successfully and continuously, companies such as 3M, Merck, Sony, and Gillette. These companies have *routinized* the process of innovation, with a Go-NoGo system which supports potential winners while cutting short the life of potential losers.

EXHIBIT 5–3

Faith Popcorn's Ten Lifestyle Trends

1. *Cashing out:* Cashing out is the impulse to change one's life to a slower but more rewarding pace. It is manifested by career persons who suddenly quit their hectic urban jobs and turn up in Vermont or Montana running a small newspaper, managing a bed-and-breakfast establishment, or joining a band. They don't think the office stress is worth it. There is a nostalgic return to small-town values with clean air, safe schools, and plain-speaking neighbors.

2. *Cocooning:* Cocooning is the impulse to stay inside when the outside gets too tough and scary. More people are turning their homes into nests. They are becoming "couch potatoes," glued to the TV, watching movies, ordering goods from catalogs, redecorating their homes, and using their answering machines to filter out the outside world. In reaction to increased crime and other social problems, Armored Cocoon people are burrowing in, building bunkers. Self-preservation is the underlying theme. Also manifest are Wandering Cocoons, people eating in their cars and phoning from their cars. Socialized Cocooning describes the forming of a small group of friends who frequently get together for conversation, for "saloning."

3. *Down-aging:* Down-aging is the tendency to act and feel younger than one's age. The sexy heroes today are Cher (over forty-five), Paul Newman (over sixty-five), Elizabeth Taylor (over sixty). Older people are spending more on youthful clothes, hair coloring, and facial plastic surgery. They are engaging in more playful behavior, willing to act in ways not normally found in their age group. They buy adult toys, attend adult camps, and sign up for adventurous vacations.

4. *Egonomics:* Egonomics is people's desire to develop an individuality so that they are seen and treated as different from anyone else. It is not egomania but simply the wish to individualize oneself through one's possessions and experiences. People are increasingly subscribing to narrow-interest magazines; joining small groups with a narrow mission; and buying customized clothing, cars, and cosmetics. Egonomics provides marketers with a competitive opportunity to succeed by offering customized goods, services, and experiences.

5. *Fantasy adventure:* Fantasy adventure meets people's growing needs for emotional escapes to offset their daily routines. People express this need through vacations, eating exotic foods, going to Disneyland and other fantasy parks, redecorating their homes with a Santa Fe look, and so on. For marketers, the desire for adventure is an opportunity to create new fantasy products and services or to add fantasy touches to their current products and services.

6. *99 Lives:* 99 Lives is the desperate state of people who must juggle many roles and responsibilities — think of SuperMom, who has a full-time career, must manage the home and the children, do the shopping, and so on. People feel time-poor and attempt to save time by using fax machines and car phones,

eating at fast food restaurants, and so on. Marketers can address this need by creating *cluster marketing enterprises* — all-in-one service stops, such as "Video Town Laundrette," which includes laundry facilities, a tanning room, an exercise bike, copying and fax machines, and 6,000 video titles to rent.

7. *S.O.S. (Save Our Society):* S.O.S. is the drive of a growing number of people to make society more socially responsible along the three critical Es: Environment, Education, and Ethics. These individuals are joining groups to promote more social responsibility on the part of companies and other citizens. Marketers are urging their own companies to practice more socially responsible marketing, along the lines of The Body Shop, Ben & Jerry's, Levi Strauss, and other socially concerned companies.

8. *Small indulgences:* Stressed-out consumers need occasional emotional fixes. They might not be able to afford a BMW car but might buy a BMW motorcycle. They might eat healthfully during the week and then indulge themselves with a pint of superpremium Häagen-Dazs ice cream on the weekend. They won't take a two-week vacation to Europe but instead a three-day minicruise in the Caribbean. Marketers should be aware of the deprivations many consumers feel and the opportunity to offer them small indulgences for an emotional lift.

9. *Staying alive:* Staying alive is about people's drive to live longer and better lives. They now know that their lifestyle can kill them—eating the wrong foods, smoking, breathing bad air, using hard drugs. People are ready to take responsibility for their own health and choose better foods, exercise more regularly, and relax more often. Marketers can meet this need by designing healthier products and services for consumers.

10. *The vigilante consumer:* Vigilante consumers are those who will no longer tolerate shoddy products and inept service. They want companies to be more human. They want automobile companies to take back "lemons" and fully refund their money. They subscribe to the *National Boycott News* and *Consumer Reports,* join MADD (Mothers Against Drunk Driving), and look for lists of good companies and bad companies. Marketers must be the conscience of their company in bringing about higher standards in the goods and services they provide.

Source: This summary is drawn from various pages of Faith Popcorn's *The Popcorn Report* (New York: Harper Business, 1992).

Other companies thrive by playing the role of *fast follower*. They monitor competitors' new products and services and quickly copy them at much less risk and expense. Their principal risk is that of always coming in second and never gaining the leading market share. The market pioneer typically wins and keeps market leadership, although the rule is not without many exceptions. Steven Schnaars analyzed twenty-eight industries where the imitators surpassed the innovators.[3] The key point is that fast followers may win; but *slow followers* rarely win.

POLITICS/REGULATIONS. Companies also need to monitor developments in politics, legislation, and regulations that might help or hurt their business. A pharmaceutical company can be affected by a powerful senator who proposes new regulatory legislation or by a new head of the Food and Drug Administration who favors stronger enforcement than his predecessor. Developments in the political sphere can change company fortunes overnight. Most companies closely monitor political, regulatory, and enforcement developments. Many also try to gain influence in the political process. They make donations to political parties and legislators; they sponsor paid lobbyists; and they run ads and underwrite feature articles advancing their position.

The Task Environment

Companies need continuous information about the key actors with whom they interact in the marketplace. The key actors are subsumed under three broad Cs, namely consumers, collaborators, and competitors.

Consumers

Consumers are persons and organizations who buy products to use or to incorporate within another product. They do not acquire products for the purpose of resale. Serving and satisfying consumers, of course, is the *raison d'être* of marketing strategy. Doing it well requires knowing many things about the target consumers. The main questions are summarized in the following seven-Os framework:

Who are the consumers?	Occupants
What do they need and want?	Objects
Why objectives are they trying to satisfy?	Objectives
Who participates in the buying decision?	Organizations
How do consumers make their buying decisions?	Operations
When do consumers seem ready to buy?	Occasions
Where do consumers prefer to buy?	Outlets

A company depends upon its marketing researchers and salespeople to provide reliable answers to these questions. The answers lead to a model of the main factors driving consumer behavior. The model is then used as a platform for market strategy construction. Of course, consumers change through time, and the company must periodically revalidate the model.

Collaborators

Collaborators covers all those actors in the task environment who assist the company in carrying out its operations and achieving its objectives with consumers. They include *middlemen, suppliers, marketing agencies,* and *logistics agencies*.

MIDDLEMEN. Middlemen are persons and organizations standing between producers and consumers, such as *distributors, dealers, agents,* and *brokers*. Distributors and dealers buy goods and then resell them; they are called *resellers*. Distributors (who also go by the name wholesalers in many trades) buy large quantities and resell them to dealers (also called retailers). In contrast, agents and brokers don't take possession of goods but receive a commission for finding customers.

Producers can sell direct to consumers or sell through middlemen. Producers use middlemen when the latter are more efficient and experienced in reaching the target consumers. Eliminating middlemen does not eliminate the work of distribution. The producer must decide whether middlemen can do the work more efficiently. Sometimes middlemen lose their relative efficiency and the producer moves into direct marketing. Today we are witnessing a substantial increase in the direct marketing of banking and insurance services.

In deciding to use middlemen, the producer must view them as both customers and partners. The producer needs to understand their needs, objectives, and operations and must offer trade terms and reseller support that will win middlemen's enthusiasm and loyalty. As long as the resellers enjoy comparatively good earnings and a good relationship with the producer, they will continue to carry and promote his goods. Some producers insist on going to the next step, treating the resellers as partners who jointly search for ways to improve the product and the process of efficient distribution. Milliken & Company, for example, calls its resellers "Partners for Profits" and makes an effort to supply various tools that will help them succeed.

SUPPLIERS. Marketers focus their attention on the demand side of the business, not the supply side. Yet the supply side often frustrates the marketers. How do you sell automobiles that aren't made well? How do you sell office furniture when you have to tell the customer it won't be available for six months?

The quality and cooperativeness of a company's suppliers will have a large impact on the company's success. Suppliers who ship low-quality goods, deliver late, are hard to reach, or are subject to strikes are the bane of a company's existence. Yet many companies end up with such suppliers because they accept the lowest bidders and fail to develop long-lasting and satisfying relationships with suppliers. Such producers are "penny-wise and pound-foolish." "Cheap" suppliers are often the most costly.

Good suppliers are not that abundant and often are tied up by competitors or lack capacity to serve a new customer. The term *reverse marketing* describes attempts by a company to persuade reluctant suppliers to be the company's suppliers.[4] Thus, a construction equipment manufacturer might locate a Swedish hydraulic pump manufacturer and may have to offer very generous terms to attract the Swedish firm as a supplier.

Most producers are moving toward working with fewer but better suppliers. Such companies as Ford, Motorola, and Allied Signal have cut their number of suppliers anywhere from 20 to 80 percent. These companies want each chosen supplier to supply a larger component system. They also want the chosen supplier to achieve continuous quality and performance improvement, while lowering the supply price each year by a given percentage. The companies work closely with their suppliers during product development. Chrysler, for example, is exemplary in forming strong relationships with suppliers and treating them as partners who jointly search for production and logistics improvements.[5]

Whirlpool illustrates an enlightened procedure for dealing with suppliers. Before designing a new washing machine, Whirlpool's engineers, marketers, and purchasing people specify the quality and budget levels for steel parts, motors, and other components. Purchasing will search for suppliers who would make the "best strategic partners," those who can deliver the best combination of quality, technology, service, and price. The chosen suppliers will participate with Whirlpool in further design and efficiency studies. The aim is to view the company and its suppliers as a "value delivery system," which can hope to outperform competitors in meeting target customer requirements.

Companies need to stay up to date with their suppliers' capacities, performance, and problems. By managing an early warning system to detect quality or supply problems, the company can avoid the embarrassment of failing to meet its marketing commitments.

MARKETING AGENCIES. Companies work with various marketing agencies—advertising agencies, sales promotion firms, direct mail firms, public relations firms—to accomplish their objectives. Those agencies are highly variable in their performance. A company can suffer or prosper by its choice of agencies. Companies need to set up an evaluation system and periodically validate that their marketing agencies are performing at the desired level.

LOGISTICS AGENCIES. Companies rely on various logistics agencies—transportation companies, warehouses, and expediters—to source their inputs and distribute their outputs efficiently. Logistics costs amount to 10 to 15 percent of many companies' costs. Companies can effect substantial savings by improving logistics arrangements and suppliers.

Competitors

Companies need accurate information about their competitors. The company's most immediate competitor is the one most like itself: The competitor would sell to the same target market and use the same marketing mix. The competitor is a dominant competitor if it wins a disproportionate number of proposals when both companies bid for the business. But if the competitor loses most of the bids in joint bidding, then the competitor is a subordinate competitor. The company has to worry mostly about a competitor who wins most of the bids.

Companies must keep an eye on more distant competitors, who potentially may be more dangerous. A company is more likely to be buried by a new technology than by its existing competitors. An integrated steel mill such as U.S. Steel must not only worry about other integrated steel mills, such as Bethlehem, but also about competition coming from minimills like Nucor, aluminum plants such as Reynolds, and engineered plastics manufacturers such as GE. All those materials are replacing steel in several applications. Some observers believe that the main threat to any company comes from not its current competitors but its potential competitors.

What does a company need to know about its competitors? It needs to know their *objectives, strategies, strengths and weaknesses*, and *response patterns*. Exhibit 5–4 lists some questions that companies need to answer about their competitors.

How can a company go about collecting the *competitive intelligence*

EXHIBIT 5–4

Questions About Each Competitor

Objectives

- Is the competitor basically pursuing current profitability? market share growth? technological leadership?
- Is the competitor interested in making aggressive inroads or more interested in coexistence?

Strategies

- How is the competitor trying to win: Lower prices? Higher quality? Better service? Lower costs?
- Are the competitor's actions basically short-run or long-run oriented?

Strengths and weaknesses

- What are the competitor's superior strengths relative to us?
- What are the competitor's chief weaknesses that we can exploit?

Response patterns

- How will the competitor respond if we raise our price? lower our price?
- How will the competitor respond if we aggressively increase our promotion budget or sales force size?

---

suggested by the questions in Exhibit 5–4? Companies collect competitive intelligence in a number of ways:

1. They scan newspapers, magazines, and other print material for information about their competitors. They study the competitors' ads, packaging, and speeches. They usually hire clipping services for the purpose.
2. They study the competitors' web pages on the Internet, which might include detailed product and pricing information, new product information, company policies and values, extensive job listings, company organizational structure, and information about business locations, offices, distributors, and service centers.
3. They hire people away from a particular competitor to help the company know the competitor's mindset and likely initiatives and reactions.
4. They survey their salespeople and middlemen for their impressions and experiences with a particular competitor.

5. They benchmark the competitor's performance by talking to customers, resellers, suppliers, and consultants. They may "mystery-shop" a competitor's offering. They also buy and reverse-engineer the competitor's products.

The main problem is that competitive information is usually scattered throughout the company. In response, some companies have established a competitive intelligence office, which consolidates competitor information and advises on what might be expected in a competitive engagement. Alternatively, some companies assign managers to be experts on particular competitors and to advise others needing information.

Company Environment

Companies are repositories of rich internal records that include data on orders, sales, prices, costs, inventory levels, receivables, payables, and other entities. Managers use this information to prepare sales forecasts, budgets, profit and loss statements, balance sheets, cash flow statements, and so on.

Of great importance is the *customer database* with its detailed information on each customer's past transactions, characteristics, and response profile. But too often customer-specific information is only in the salesperson's head or laptop. When the salesperson leaves or retires, the information may be lost. In response, many companies have adopted sophisticated *sales automation systems* whereby the information in the salesperson's computer is downloaded daily and retained in the company's central computer.

Companies also organize a *product database*, which their salespeople can download to review product features, benefits, and persuasive arguments. In sophisticated systems, the salesperson can demonstrate the product to the customer on the laptop screen and can even design in customer-desired modifications. The salesperson can price the product on the spot and can even print out a customized contract if the customer is ready to buy.[6]

Methods of Gathering Information

Given the types of information that companies need, the question arises as to how to collect this information efficiently. Information carries both a cost and a value. A company can spend too much on *information acquisition*, leading to comments like, "We are drowning in information and starved of knowledge." There are vast differences between *data, information, knowledge,* and *wisdom.* Unless the data are processed into information, which is turned into knowledge, which becomes market wisdom, much of it is wasted.

Marketing researchers distinguish three information gathering approaches, which differ in cost and value. In ascending order of cost, they are *observation*, *secondary data*, and *primary data*.

Observation

Company managers can learn a great deal through observation. The Japanese have a saying: "Watch not the person's mouth but his feet." Toyota's marketing researchers in the 1970s stood near supermarkets in large parking lots and watched how customers loaded their groceries into the trunks of their cars. Based on what they saw, they redesigned Toyota's trunk to provide more room and easier sliding of packages. In another case, the CEO of a large Japanese pharmaceutical company signed himself into a hospital as a patient in order to observe how the physicians and nurses treated their patients.

Software firms can learn a great deal by observing how its *lead users* use and modify their software; that provides clues for improving the software in the next launch.[7] Company personnel can learn a great deal by visiting competitor's stores, observing buyers in action, and engaging in casual conversation. While observation is not usually capable of providing strong or systematic evidence, it certainly can be suggestive and useful in exploratory research.

Secondary Data

Secondary data are existing data collected for another purpose. Researchers usually start by examining secondary data to see whether their problem can be partly or wholly solved without collecting costly primary data. One can obtain data from myriad government publications, encyclopedias, and periodicals or can even buy commercial data from such companies as A. C. Nielsen, Information Resources, Simmons, or Dun & Bradstreet.

Primary Data

When the needed data do not exist or are dated, inaccurate, incomplete, or unreliable, the researcher will have to gather primary data at a higher cost. Here a choice must be made between *one-on-one interviewing*, *focus group research*, *mail or phone surveys*, and *experimental design*.

ONE-ON-ONE INTERVIEWING. There are situations where a company will need to arrange somewhat extensive interviews with individuals. Market researchers often gather in this way information pertaining to a proposed project or problem. The interviewer typically presents a set of questions of both open and closed form. Individual interviewing is expensive because of the cost of setting up and carrying out single interviews and because the interviewees sometimes require payment, as might be the case in interviewing such professionals as physicians, lawyers, and consulting engineers.

FOCUS GROUP RESEARCH. A focus group is a gathering of six to ten people who are invited to spend a few hours with a skilled moderator to discuss a product, service, organization, or other marketing entity. The participants are normally paid a small sum for participating in the focus group. The moderator needs to be objective, knowledgeable on the issue, and versed in group dynamics. The moderator encourages free and easy discussion, hoping that the group dynamics will reveal deep feelings and thoughts. At the same time, the moderator "focuses" the discussion. The discussion, recorded through note-taking or on audio or videotape, can be subsequently studied by managers to understand consumer beliefs, attitudes, and behavior.

The author observed a group of middle-income consumers as they discussed whether they would buy a new small car which a few minutes earlier they sat in and tried out. These comments emerged: It is too small; it seems unsafe in an accident; it is priced too high; it is good only for short shopping trips; and women would like it more than men. Those remarks caused great concern about the automobile's design.

Focus groups are an excellent way to explore new ideas and consumer opinions and feelings. However, researchers must avoid generalizing the findings to the whole target market, since the sample size is too small and the sample is not randomly drawn.

MAIL AND TELEPHONE SURVEYS. While observation and focus groups are best suited for exploratory research, surveys are best suited for descriptive research. Companies undertake surveys to learn about people's knowledge, beliefs, preferences, and satisfaction, and to measure these magnitudes in the target population. If the survey is properly conducted and the response level is high, the results of a sample can fairly well reflect the population parameters within a predetermined degree of error. Unfortunately, those conditions are rarely met in sampling human populations. The sources of possible bias include poorly drafted questions, poorly trained or dishonest interviewers, and respondents who fail to answer accurately or honestly. Of great concern is the progressively lower response rate of those who are randomly chosen to be sampled. Researchers are normally pleased if they get a 30 percent response rate with mailed surveys, and telephone surveys that produce a 60 percent response rate please their sponsors. Today many people resist answering surveys because they are busier than ever or are suspicious that the survey is a front for a disguised sales effort. In any event, a low survey response rate, particularly if the respondents differ significantly from the nonrespondents, can yield highly unreliable measures. To guard against this, companies should engage only highly accredited market research firms with strong technical skills in the art of survey research.

EXPERIMENTS. The most scientifically valid research is experimental research. It calls for selecting matched groups of subjects, exposing them to different treatments, controlling extraneous variables, and checking whether observed response differences are statistically significant. To the extent that extraneous factors are eliminated or controlled, the observed effects can be related to the variations in the treatments. The purpose of experimental research is to capture cause-and-effect relationships by eliminating competing explanations of the observed differences.

As an example, DuPont wanted to test the effect of varying its paint advertising expenditure as a percentage of sales. Suppose DuPont typically spent 5 percent of its sales on advertising. As an alternative, DuPont selects several comparable cities and spends 7½ percent in some, 5 percent in others, and 2½ percent in still others. If sales don't rise when 7½ percent is spent in some cities, or if sales fall significantly when 2½ percent is spent in other cities, then 5 percent sounds like the right advertising expenditure level.

Managing the Information System

Given the great importance of reliable marketing information and the fact that it is normally scattered throughout the company, the case can be made that the company should establish a *marketing information center* (MIC). It would be staffed with personnel skilled in *defining information needs, preparing research instruments, collecting and classifying information, evaluating its quality,* and *circulating it* to proper decision-makers.[8]

The staff should also manage a *marketing decision support system,* which is a coordinated collection of data, systems, tools, and techniques with supporting software and hardware by which a business gathers and interprets relevant information from the environment and turns it into a basis for marketing action. The MIC staff can analyze data using sophisticated *statistical models* such as *multiple regression*, *discriminant analysis*, *factor analysis*, *cluster analysis*, and *conjoint analysis*.[9] The staff can also apply sophisticated *decision models* for segmenting markets, setting prices and advertising budgets, analyzing media, and planning sales force activity. Today several companies are using the models described in Exhibit 5–5.

Questions to Consider

Given the exploding volume of data, the growing ubiquity of high-speed computers, and the urgent need of companies to reengineer their marketing, we can expect rapid progress in what is called *marketing engineering*. Marketers in the past relied mostly on *conceptual models* of how marketing tools impacted demand, but today it is getting increasingly possible to measure and model system effects more accurately. Several tools and examples are described in the recent book by Lilien and Rangaswamy.[10]

As part of the Marketing Information Center, some companies have established a *War Gaming Room*, which is a way of monitoring real-time developments in the marketplace and making real-time decisions. Global financial institutions and airlines, in particular, need to make real-time decisions. The War Gaming Room's functions are described in some detail by consultant Bradley Gale.[11]

The future of marketing information collection, distribution, and retrieval is promising given the rapid approach toward a "net-centric economy." Thanks to computers and the Internet, companies are able to establish an Intranet for more rapid circulation of information within the company; an Extranet for exchanging data and ideas between the company and its customers, suppliers, and distributors; and the Internet itself for finding and retrieving countless bits of information that might be available on the World Wide Web. All this promises a new age of information-based marketing strategy.

Here we ask you to consider a few questions about the state of your marketing intelligence system.

1. Is there a management information center (MIC) in your company which collects, organizes, and disseminates information to the man-

EXHIBIT 5–5

Some Well-known Marketing Decision Models

BRANDAID: A flexible marketing-mix model focused on consumer packaged goods whose elements are a manufacturer, competitors, retailers, consumers, and the general environment. The model contains submodels for advertising, pricing, and competition. The model is calibrated with a creative blending of judgment, historical analysis, tracking, field experimentation, and adaptive control.[1]

CALLPLAN: A model to help salespeople determine the number of calls to make per period to each prospect and current client. The model takes into account travel time as well as selling time. The model was tested at United Airlines with an experimental group that managed to increase its sales over a matched control group by eight percentage points.[2]

DETAILER: A model to help salespeople determine which customers to call on and which products to represent on each call. This model was largely developed for pharmaceutical detail people calling on physicians where they could represent no more than three products on a call. In two applications, the model yielded strong profit improvements.[3]

GEOLINE: A model for designing sales and service territories that satisfies three principles: the territories equalize sales workloads; each territory consists of adjacent areas; and the territories are compact. Several successful applications were reported.[4]

MEDIAC: A model to help an advertiser buy media for a year. The media planning model includes market segment delineation, sales potential estimation, diminishing marginal returns, forgetting, timing issues, and competitor media schedules.[5]

PROMOTER evaluates sales promotions by determining baseline sales (what sales would have been without promotion) and measuring the increase over baseline associated with the promotion.[6]

ADCAD recommends the type of ad (humorous, slice of life, and so on) to use given the marketing goals and characteristics of the product, target market, and competitive situation.[7]

COVERSTORY examines a mass of syndicated sales data and writes an English-language memo reporting the highlights.[8]

---

[1]John D. C. Little, "BRANDAID: A Marketing Mix Model, Part I: Structure; Part II: Implementation," *Operations Research*, 23 (1975): 628–73.

[2]Leonard M. Lodish, "CALLPLAN: An Interactive Salesman's Call Planning System," *Management Science*, December 1971, pp. 3–24.

[3]David B. Montgomery, Alvin J. Silk, and C. E. Zaragoza, "A Multiple-Product Sales Force Allocation Model," *Management Science*, December 1971, pp. 3–24.

[4]S.W. Hess and S.A. Samuels, "Experiences with a Sales Districting Model: Criteria and Implementation," *Management Science*, December 1971, pp. 41–54.

[5]John D. C. Little and Leonard M. Lodish, "A Media Planning Calculus," *Operations Research*, January–February 1969, pp. 1–35.

[6]Magid M. Abraham and Leonard M. Lodish, "PROMOTER: An Automated Promotion Evaluation System," *Marketing Science*, Spring 1987, pp. 101–23.

[7]Raymond R. Burke, Arvind Rangaswamy, Jerry Wind, and Jehoshua Eliashberg, "A Knowledge-based System for Advertising Design," *Marketing Science*, 9, no. 3 (1990): 212–29.

[8]John D. C. Little, "Cover Story: An Expert System to Find the News in Scanner Data," Sloan School, MIT Working Paper, 1988.

agers needing this information? What can be done to improve the quality and availability of up-to-date and accurate information?

2. Does your company do enough forecasting in regard to demographics, economic trends, lifestyles, technological trends, and political/regulatory trends? Does your company lead or follow in recognizing new opportunities arising from the changing environment?

3. Does the company correctly anticipate problems arising from relations with your consumers, resellers, and suppliers? If not, what measures can be used to serve as an early warning system?

4. How can you improve the collection and organization of data concerning your present and future competitors?

5. Are you satisfied that the marketing research people are delivering usable information? Do they have enough funds to do their job? What improvements can you suggest?

6. Does your company use any sophisticated decision models? If not, why not?

6

Designing the Marketing Mix

A product is not a product unless it sells. Otherwise it is merely a museum piece.—*Ted Levitt*

Having a competitive advantage is like having a gun in a knife fight.—*Anonymous*

MANY YEARS AGO Professor Neil Borden at the Harvard Business School identified a number of company activities that can influence the buyer.[1] Any company should be able to prepare its own long list. For example, a pharmaceutical company can influence physician prescribing behavior by making sales calls, giving free samples, writing journal articles, placing journal ads, and sponsoring medical conferences. Borden suggested that all those activities constitute a "marketing mix" and should be planned in concert for maximum impact. Companies should determine the cost-effectiveness of different marketing mix tools and should formulate the most profit-maximizing marketing mix.

Although many activities constitute the marketing mix, scholars have sought a classification that will make it easier to see the forest among all the trees. Professor Jerome McCarthy, in the early 1960s, proposed a marketing mix consisting of four Ps: *product, price, place,* and *promotion.* Each P covers several activities in turn (see p. 96). In more recent times, further elaborations or transformations have been proposed.

In this chapter we shall first look at the current state of four-P thinking. Then we shall proceed to examine each P in some detail.

94

Four-P Thinking Today

The four-P framework calls upon marketers to decide on the product and its characteristics, set the price, decide how to distribute their product, and choose methods for promoting their product. Some critics feel that the four Ps omit or underemphasize certain important activities. For example:

1. *Where are services? Just because they don't begin with a P doesn't justify omitting them.* The answer is that services such as taxi rides and haircuts are products too. They are called *service products*. And services accompanying a product, such as delivery, installation, and training, are also components of the product. Some scholars and practitioners prefer the word "offerings" to "product." Offerings would convey a more general meaning.
2. *Where is packaging? Isn't packaging one of the key competitive elements in consumer marketing?* Marketers would answer that packaging is also part of the product and doesn't need to be listed as a fifth P.
3. *Where is personal selling? Isn't the sales force of key importance in business marketing?* Marketers treat the sales force as a tool in the promotion P. Their argument is that promotional tools are numerous and often can substitute for each other. For example, a direct-mail sales letter could be described as a "salesman with wings."

All said, many activities that might appear to be left out of the four-P marketing mix are subsumed under one of the four (see Exhibit 6–1). This author, however, has suggested the addition of two more Ps that are becoming more important, especially in global marketing.[2] They are:

- *Politics.* Political activity can greatly influence sales. If laws are passed banning cigarette advertising, this hurts cigarette sales. If laws require steel companies to install pollution control equipment, this will increase the sale of pollution control equipment. Therefore marketers may want to use lobbying and political activity to affect market demand.
- *Public opinion.* The public moves through new moods and attitudes that can affect their interest in certain products and services. At different times, the U.S. public turned away from beef consumption, milk consumption, and other activities. Companies selling beef and milk do not stand idly by. They finance campaigns to influence people to feel safer in buying and consuming their products.

EXHIBIT 6–1

The Four-P Framework

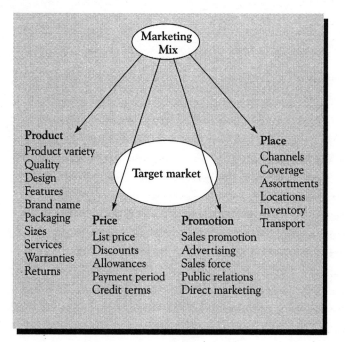

The issue is not whether there should be four, six, or ten Ps so much as what framework is most helpful in designing marketing strategy. Just as economists use two principal concepts for their framework of analysis, namely *demand* and *supply*, the marketer sees the four Ps as a filing cabinet of tools that could guide their marketing planning.

Now there is another criticism, this one quite valid, holding that the four-P concept takes a seller's view of the market, not buyer's view. A buyer, considering an offering, may not see it in the seller's way. Each of the four Ps might be better described as the four Cs from the buyer's point of view:[3]

Four Ps	Four Cs
Product	Customer value
Price	Cost to the Customer
Place	Convenience
Promotion	Communication

Thus while marketers see themselves as selling a product, customers see themselves as buying value or a solution to a problem. And customers are interested in more than the price; they are interested in their total costs of obtaining, using, and disposing of a product. Customers want the product and service to be as conveniently available as possible. Finally, customers don't want promotion; they want two-way communication. Marketers would do well to first think through the customer's four Cs and then build the four Ps on that platform. With these qualifications, we are now ready to look more closely at each P.

Product

The basis of any business is a product or offering. A company aims to make the product or offering different and better in some way that will cause the target market to favor it and even pay a price premium.

But products differ in the degree to which they can be differentiated. At one extreme are the so-called commodities, such as basic chemicals, metals, fruit and vegetables, salt, and so on. Marketing talent is most tested with the so-called commodity products. But it is not always wise to assume that they are commodities. A commodity is simply a product waiting to be differentiated. Consider the following examples of successful "commodity" differentiation:

- *Perdue Chicken:* Frank Perdue decided some years ago to breed chickens in such a way that he could guarantee their tenderness. "It takes a tough man to breed a tender chicken," he would say in his TV ads. Today Perdue branded chicken has a 30 percent market share on the East Coast and sells at a 10 percent premium over unbranded chicken. Perdue's conclusion: "If you can differentiate a dead chicken, you can differentiate anything."
- *Colombian coffee.* Whenever a coffee manufacturer or retailer wants to advertise good coffee, it advertises that it used Colombian coffee. At one time Colombian coffee beans may have been among the best; but coffee beans from Brazil, Argentina, and other places are probably on a par. Nevertheless, the idea still persists, aided by advertising, that Colombian coffee is still the best coffee in the world. Other "commodities" that are differentiated in the mind and earn a premium are Hawaiian pineapples, Idaho potatoes, and Wisconsin cheese.
- *Marlboro Cigarettes.* The flavors of most well-known brands of cigarettes are pretty similar. Many cigarette smokers would not be able to identify the brand of cigarette they are smoking in a blindfold test. This suggests that differentiation often exists in the mind, not in the

physical product, which seems to be confirmed by the fact that one brand, Marlboro, enjoys a 30 percent market share worldwide. The chief difference seems to be based on the long-lived advertising campaign identifying the brand with rugged cowboys. By overlaying cigarettes with a strong universally appreciated image, Philip Morris established Marlboros as the world's leading cigarette brand.

- *Absolut Vodka.* By legal definition, all vodka is the same. In a blindfold test, most people would not be able to identify the brand of vodka they drank. Yet one of the world's leading selling brands is Absolut, a brand that comes from Sweden, not from Russia, where vodka consumption is highest. How did Absolut build such a preference for its version of a "commodity"? Primarily through a brilliant advertising campaign where every few months a new Absolut ad appears, created by a different artist showing the famous Absolut bottle lurking somewhere in the picture. Lovers of art and culture want to serve their evening dinner guests with vodka poured from an Absolut bottle. What Absolut did was to enlist the power of "marketing aesthetics."[4]
- *DuPont dacron, nylon, orlon.* DuPont deserves credit for creating brilliant new fibers displaying different properties. In each case it gives them memorable names. After they go off patent, competitors introduce their own version of the fibers, which are essentially similar and typically priced lower. But they cannot give them the brand name DuPont created. And customers still prefer to order dacron, nylon, orlon, etc., even though equivalent and cheaper fibers are available.

The conclusion is that "commodities" can be differentiated in real or psychological terms. Sometimes a slight real difference can be created (as in Perdue chicken), sometimes the place of origin provides a difference (as with Colombian coffee), sometimes an image can be grafted on the commodity (Marlboro cigarettes or Absolut vodka), and sometimes the exclusive use of the name provides the differentiation (DuPont's fibers). Professor Theodore Levitt observed: "There is no such thing as a commodity. All goods and services are differentiable."

At the other extreme of commodities are products that are highly differentiable in physical terms, such as vehicles, heavy equipment, and buildings. Such products have many degrees of design freedom. In the case of an automobile, it can be differentiated by size, style, horsepower, seating arrangements materials, and hundreds of other features. Consequently automobile manufacturers can compete on the basis of claiming that their product greatly differs from competitors' products. Besides, they can add a layer of psychological differentiation, such as prestige (Mercedes), sports driving superiority (Porsche), or safety (Volvo).

In general, product marketers understand that the challenge is to create *relevant* and *distinctive* product differentiation. The differentiation may be based on:

- physical differences (e.g., features, performance, conformance, durability, reliability, design, style, packaging)
- availability differences (e.g., available from stores or orderable by phone, mail, fax, Internet)
- service differences (e.g., delivery, installation, training, consulting, maintenance, repair)
- price differences (e.g., very high price, high price, medium price, low price, very low price)
- image differences (e.g., symbols, atmosphere, events, media)

Two effective physical differentiators are features and design. *New features* offer a quick and visible way to demonstrate an added benefit; furthermore many new features are patent-protectable. *Design* can visibly differentiate a product or packaging. Although a competitor may be able to copy the design, the originator will enjoy at least a short-term lead.

Any successful differentiation will tend to draw imitators. When imitators introduce their versions of the product, often at a lower price, it puts pressure on the innovator. The innovator faces three choices:

- Lower the price to protect market share and accept lower profits
- Maintain the price and lose some market share and profits
- Find a new basis to differentiate the product and maintain the current price

Of the three choices, the third offers the best hope of maximizing long-run profitability. It requires the firm to recognize that it cannot rely on its current advantage. It must constantly search for the *next advantage*. The hope of finding one "long-lasting, sustainable advantage" in a hypercompetitive marketplace is largely a pipe dream.

Price

Price differs from the other three marketing mix elements in that it produces *revenue*; the other elements create *costs*. Consequently companies work hard to lift their prices as high as their level of differentiation will support. At the same time, firms recognize that they must consider the price's impact on volume. The firm seeks the revenue level (price times volume) that, when the costs are subtracted, results in the largest profits.

Companies try to estimate the profit impact of a higher price. One company president told the author that if he could only charge an extra dollar for every unit, his profits would increase by some million dollars. Here are some estimates of the impact of a 1 percent price increase on profits, assuming volume remains the same:[5]

Coca-Cola	6.4%
Fuji Photo	16.7%
Nestlé	17.5%
Ford	26.0%
Philips	28.7%
Typical U.S. Co.	12.0%

It is important, of course, to distinguish between list price and realized price. Discounting is so rampant today that hardly any buyer pays list price. The buyer may receive a price-off, a rebate, a free service thrown in, or a gift, all of which drains the realized price. Most companies do a poor job of measuring and controlling the "cascading" or "diluting" effect of such pricing allowances.[6] Companies that think certain customers are profitable may be surprised when ABC *accounting* (Activity Based Costing) is applied.[7] A large customer who is getting a lot of price-offs and service favors may turn out to be unprofitable.

In setting their prices, many companies add a "markup" to their estimated costs. That is known as *cost-based pricing*. In the food business, producers and retailers apply certain standard markups to each product category, at least as a starting point. In the management consulting business, consulting firms normally set their fees at $2\frac{1}{2}$ times the consultant's cost, figuring that this will cover their total costs and leave an attractive profit margin.

Alternatively, some companies practice *value-based pricing*. They estimate the most that the buyer would pay for the offering. They don't charge that price, because the buyer may resist buying. They charge something less—the value price—to leave the buyer with some "consumer surplus." The seller hopes that its costs are much lower than the value price, in which case the seller enjoys a good profit. If the seller's costs are close to or exceed the value price, the seller probably would never make the offer.

DuPont is a prime practitioner of value pricing. For example, suppose DuPont invents an improved hose that carriers a strong chemical from one process to another. The old hose needs to be replaced yearly, requiring the customer firm to close its factory one day each year. Suppose that costs the customer $10,000. Now assume that the new hose had the advantage of lasting three years before needing replacement. DuPont knows that if the customer still chooses the old hose, it would cost the customer $30,000 in three years plus the cost of three hoses, whereas the improved hose would cost the customer only $10,000 over a three-year period plus the price charged for the improved hose. Now DuPont estimates the price at which the customer would be indifferent between (1) buying an old hose each year and shutting down the factory each year for one day and (2) buying an improved hose once every three years. DuPont would then set a price for the new hose somewhat below the indifference price to provide the customer with an incentive to switch to the improved hose. The size of the offered customer incentive to switch is higher, the more anxious DuPont is to win early customers for the improved hose and the greater the likelihood that competition will come out with the same improvement. Notice that DuPont sets the price without regard to its cost of developing and producing the improved hose; presumably its costs are sufficiently below the price it can charge.

Value pricing appears in other contexts. People pay more for orchestra seats than for balcony seats; for Saturday night performances than weekday performances; for the services of more skillful doctors or consultants.

Smart marketers will bundle their product with additional benefits and price the total offering. They may create different bundled offerings, giving the customer a choice. Exhibit 6–2 shows how DuPont offers a certain chemical built into two different value packages, each priced differently. There is a "less-for-less" package and a "more-for-more" package. If a customer wants only some of the "more-for-more" package, DuPont will prepare a third value package and price it according to the prices listed at the right. Thus if the customer wants only the higher purity level and the total system, the value package will cost $102.50 a pound. DuPont believes in flexible bundling and pricing, and customers appreciate the opportunity to pick and choose.

Yet companies wish to motivate customers to take as much of the total available package as possible. That is accomplished by offering a special price to the customer for the whole offering that is less than the sum of the separate prices. A bank, for example, maintains a schedule of separate charges for a checking account, savings account, home mortgage, auto loans, and safe deposit boxes. The banker, in an effort to cross-sell more bank services to the customer, might offer a special price

EXHIBIT 6–2

DuPont Offers Different Value Bundles

Attribute	Low Level	High Level	
Quality	Impurities less than ten parts per million	Impurities less than one part per million	$1.70
Delivery	Within two weeks	Within one week	.15
System	Supply chemical only	Supply total system	.80
Innovation	Little R&D support	High-Level R&D support	2.00
Retraining	Train on initial purchases	Retrain on request	.40
Service	Through home office	Locally available	.25
	Price= $100 a pound	$100/lb. + $5.30 = $105.30 a pound	

if the customer will take the whole set of services. Banks call that "relationship pricing," or "pricing the relationship."

Smart companies will create not just one product offering but a range of offerings at different price points. They will create a *product line*. For example, the Marriott hotel chain created the hospitality product line shown in Exhibit 6–3. Its original offering was that of a good-quality hotel at an above-average price, called Marriott Hotels. Then it created a set of more expensive hotels called Marriott Marquis Hotels. Because Marriott enjoyed a good name, it kept the name Marriott and added a qualifier to suggest even more prestige. Later Marriott launched a successful chain of motels, which it called Courtyard, and added the phrase in smaller letters, "by Marriott." When Marriott later launched a still less expensive motel chain, it chose the name Fairfield Inn and didn't display Marriott's name. Now the four hotel systems are pegged at different price points, something like $280, $180, $80, and $50. Each hotel system offers a different set of physical and service features. The establishment of a wide-ranging hotel product line means that Marriott doesn't lose out if there is a shift from one type of hotel to another as a result of a recession or changes in travelers' preference. It has built a "safety net" that will keep travelers somewhere within its system.

EXHIBIT 6–3

Marriott's Product Line of Hotels by Price/Performance

		Quality			
		Superior	*Good*	*Standard*	*Economy*
Price	High	Marriott Marquis			
	Above Average		Marriott		
	Average			Courtyard	
	Low				Fairfield Inn

Place (or Distribution)

Every seller must decide how to make its goods available to the target market. The two choices are to sell the goods directly or to sell them through middlemen. Within a given industry both distribution choices can be found. Consider the following examples:

Cosmetics. Most cosmetic companies—Revlon, Estée Lauder, Lancôme—sell their products to retailers who in turn sell them to consumers. When Avon tried to do the same, it couldn't persuade retailers to give it shelf space. So Avon resorted to direct distribution, hiring "Avon ladies" to sell Avon products door to door. Avon built its own sales force of more than a million representatives and enjoyed great success as a practitioner of *direct selling*. Other companies subsequently adopted Avon's model, adding such other features as *party selling* (Mary Kay and Tupperware) and *multilevel marketing* (Amway).

Personal computers. Most personal computer manufacturers, such as IBM, Hewlett-Packard, and Compaq, sell their PCs through retailers. That gives them quick national distribution at a lower cost than the alternative. Michael Dell reckoned that a substantial number of potential consumers would be willing to order their personal computers over the phone without seeing them. Dell Computer grew its market share at such a rate that retailer-based manufacturers were forced to rethink their distribution strategy. Dell, Gateway, and other direct marketers enjoyed lower costs, charged lower prices, offered greater customization, and were available to customers by phone seven days a week, twenty-four hours a day. Compaq, IBM, and others began to flirt with the delicate strategy known as *dual distribution*, whereby they would sell both through retailers and directly. Their retailers, of course, would complain and threaten to drop the brand. Those companies had to convince the manufacturers that they were either selling different computers through the direct channels or at least charging the same prices as retail.[8]

Even when a company chooses to sell direct, it has a further choice to make. Many insurance companies, for example, sell direct through their own field sales agents. The first-year cost of selling an auto insurance policy through its agent may be $250, and it can be as high as $1,100 to sell a life insurance policy. The insurance company may not break even for a few years, hoping the new customers will stay with the company and not defect in the first few years. However, other insurance companies, such as Insurance Direct, have started to sell insurance over the phone and/or the Internet at a considerably lower selling cost. That has led agent-based insurance companies to flirt with the idea of adding telemarketing as a second channel, or even abandoning agents altogether. But it is very difficult to run two competing channels, even if they are both direct channels. Companies find it hard to win its field sales force's approval for adding a telemarketing operation that competes for sales with its field sales force.

In the consumer market, there is an intense battle taking place among retailers (e.g., small versus large retailers, large retailers versus other large retailers). In addition, a growing battle is now emerging between *home-based shopping* and *store-based shopping*. Today's consumers are able to order more goods in more ways from the home instead of having to drive, park, and stand in line in a store. Today's consumers can order from home clothes, electronics, appliances, furniture, and countless other goods through any of six channels:

- Catalogs sent to the home
- Direct mail offers sent to the home
- Home shopping programs on TV
- Offers described in newspapers, magazines, or over radio or TV
- Telemarketing calls to the home
- Internet-placed orders

As people get more time-pressured, their at-home purchasing will grow more rapidly than store-based purchasing. In fact, store-based purchasing is growing only at about 2 percent a year, while some channels catering to home-based buying are growing at a double-digit rate. Retailers, therefore, are challenged to bring customers back into the stores. But if the stores charge higher prices, if the parking is difficult, if the service is poor, if the stores are generally uninteresting, they will be fighting a losing battle. Creative retailers, on the other hand, are fighting the battle by enhancing the shopping experience, adding fun, entertainment, or other customer delights to attract and please customers. Here are some examples:

- *Barnes & Noble bookstores.* Barnes & Noble represents a reinvention of the bookstore.[9] Not only do their stores carry a very large number of books, but they provide chairs and tables, maintain a coffee and pastry section, stay open from 9 A.M. to 11 P.M. seven days a week, and schedule talks by authors and other presentations. Not surprisingly, people flow in and out of Barnes & Noble bookstores throughout the day, and many make it a destination after their evening dinner. In many ways, Barnes & Noble has become a community center.
- *NikeTown.* How can people be attracted to a store selling athletic shoes and clothing? NikeTown found the answer in its three-story Michigan Avenue store in Chicago. Visitors enter and face a giant poster of Michael Jordan, walk through departments centered on different sports, and witness audio and video effects that lend a special ambiance to the shopping experience. In the basketball department, there is even a basketball court! This store became the most visited retail attraction in Chicago, drawing more out-of-town visitors than the famous Art Institute of Chicago.

Distribution, clearly, poses a number of challenges. Companies recognize that their distribution choices establish a fairly long commitment that they may have to live with even when new and more attractive channels appear. For example, automobile manufacturers have traditionally sold their cars through franchised dealers. Yet people report many unpleasant experiences when buying a new or used car, including hard-sell pushiness, lies, and other ordeals. A growing number of buyers may want to buy cars in a different way, maybe from manufacturer owned and operated dealerships, at multibrand dealerships, or over the Internet. But auto manufacturers are constrained, given their tieup with franchised dealers, in how far they can go in revising their current distribution channels. Meanwhile, such new companies as Auto Nation and CarMax have a free hand in choosing or developing more effective new distribution channels.[10]

Promotion

The fourth P, promotion, covers all those communication tools that can deliver a message to a target audience. The tools fall into five broad classes:

- Advertising
- Sales promotion
- Public relations
- Sales force
- Direct marketing

Specific examples of these tools are shown in Exhibit 6–4. Here we shall review the five communication tools.

Advertising

Advertising is the most potent tool for building *awareness* of a company, product, service, or idea. On cost-per-thousand people reached, advertising is hard to beat. If the ads are also creative, the advertising campaign can build *image* and even some degree of *preference* or at least *brand acceptability*. But most ads are not creative. One need only examine car ads to see how similar and inconsequential they are. In fact, if one's ads are not different from and better than competitors' ads, the company may be better advised to spend money on other marketing communication tools, such as public relations, sales promotion, or direct marketing.

Add to this that fewer people may be viewing ads, especially TV ads. Furthermore TV ads have grown shorter, often down to fifteen seconds, leaving hardly enough time to absorb the message. And there are more ads, causing clutter. The ads tend to broadcast a message to everyone rather than to narrowcast the message to a target group for whom the message is important. How effective is a TV commercial for cat food if only 5 percent of the audience owns a cat! Finally, people seem quite prepared to use their remote to switch channels when ads appear.

EXHIBIT 6-4

Examples of Different Promotion Tools

Advertising	Sales Promotion	Public Relations	Sales Force	Direct Marketing
Print and broadcast ads	Contests, games, sweep-stakes, lotteries	Press kits	Sales presentations	Catalogs
Packaging — outer	Premiums and gifts	Speeches	Sales meetings	Mailings
Packaging inserts	Sampling	Seminars	Incentive programs	Telemarketing
Motion pictures	Fairs and trade shows	Annual reports	Samples	Electronic shopping
Brochures and booklets	Exhibits	Charitable donations	Fairs and trade shows	TV shopping
Posters and leaflets	Demonstrations	Sponsorships		Fax mail
Directories	Coupons	Publications		E-mail
Reprints of ads	Rebates	Community relations		Voice mail
Billboards	Low-interest financing	Lobbying		
Display signs	Entertainment	Identity media		
Point-of-purchase displays	Trade-in allowances	Company magazine		
Audio-visual material	Continuity programs	Events		
Symbols and logos	Tie-ins			
Videotapes				

Advertising is most effective when it is narrowly targeted. Ads placed in specific magazines targeted to fishermen, motorcycle afficionados, packaging purchasing agents, chief hospital administrators, or other specific groups will have a greater impact. In such cases, advertising serves more as an investment than an expense. Although it may be difficult to measure the rate of return on advertising investment (ROAI), it is probably higher for highly targeted ads.

Advertising ROAI is easiest to measure when doing direct marketing. The company sends offers to specific individuals and can tally the number of persons requesting information or placing an order. The number and value of orders divided by the total direct marketing cost gives the ROAI. Outside of direct marketing ads, however, it is more difficult to measure ROAI. Not much has changed since John Wanamaker observed: "I know that half of my advertising budget is wasted; however, I don't know which half."

The difficulty in measuring ROAI lies in trying to separate it from other concurrent communication and marketing mix actions. If a new advertising campaign is accompanied with a price increase, a new sales promotion, and a heightened public relations campaign, how can we segregate advertising's effect? Unless experimental controls are used, it is next to impossible to assess advertising's pure effect.[11]

Advertising involves making decisions on the five Ms—*mission, message, media, money,* and *measurement.* The first step is mission: Is the ad campaign's aim to *inform, persuade,* or *remind* target customers? Are the ads designed to create Awareness, Interest, Desire, or Action (AIDA)?

As for message, it is shaped by earlier decisions on the brand's intended target market and value proposition. The challenge is to present the value proposition creatively, and this is where the advertising agency's skills are tested. Advertising is largely a waste if the company finds nothing arresting to say or says it badly.

The message design decision interacts with the media decision. Although the same coherent message must be delivered through all media, execution will vary with the medium, whether newspapers, magazines, radio, TV, billboards, direct mail, or telephone. And such new media as e-mail, faxes, and the Internet will each require different creative approaches.

Companies must carefully make the money expenditure decision. If they spend too little on advertising, they may be spending too much, since the ads won't draw much attention. Companies resort to advertising spending rules such as setting the advertising budget on what they can afford, or as a percentage of past or expected sales, or as a percentage based on what competitors are spending on their advertising. But the more effective approach is to set the advertising budget on an *objectives and task* basis. Here the company decides how many people it wants to *reach* in the target market, with what *frequency*, and with what media qualitative *impact*. Then it becomes easier to calculate the budget that would deliver the desired reach, frequency, and impact.

With regard to measurement, too many companies settle for measuring recall or recognition scores when they should be measuring persuasion scores, namely the amount of increase in brand preference resulting from exposure to the ad campaign. The best measure, of course, would be the sales impact of the advertising.

Given the expense and complexities of advertising decision-making, I would counsel companies to review and evaluate their advertising programs periodically. Companies too often continue the same advertising programs and policies because it is the safe thing to do; any departure represents a risk that advertising managers prefer to avoid. It makes sense to invite an independent assessment of the advertising program in the hope that it might outline a more promising five-M approach for the company's advertising.

Sales Promotion

Most advertising does not deliver sales quickly. Advertising works mostly on the mind, not on behavior. It is sales promotion that works on behavior. The customer hears of a sale, an offer of two for the price of one, a gift, or a chance to win something. Now the customer acts.

Sales promotion, which comprises a wide-ranging set of incentives, has been spinning out of control. Consumer packaged goods companies, which used to spend about 30 percent of their total promotional budget on sales promotion, now often spend 70 percent. A good percentage is spent on *trade promotion*, giving supermarkets and other retailers special allowances, discounts, and gifts. In fact, many supermarkets depend on trade money to feed into their profits. The retailers buy more during the trade promotion period than they can sell to take advantage of the discounts, and they will buy less during nonpromotion periods, causing wide swings in the manufacturers' production schedules or inventory levels.

Consumer promotion, the other part of sales promotion, has the effect of weakening customer brand preference and therefore brand equity. Any product that is highly sales-promoted gives the lie to the product's list price. Consumers increasingly expect to find or negotiate prices lower than the list prices. This, coupled with the growing perception that most brands are similar, leads consumers to define an acceptable set of brands, rather than an insistently preferred brand. The consumer examines what brands are on sale each week and buys the brand that falls in the acceptable set.

Companies worry that they will lose market share if they don't match their competitors' sales promotions. It takes special courage to reduce sales promotion spending and to use the funds to build better advertising, or to invest in innovation or better customer service. Procter & Gamble took the initiative to reduce its sales promotion expenditure and compensated by introducing "everyday low prices." P&G saw sales promotion not only as diluting brand equity but also as causing wide and costly swings in production.

This is not to say that all sales promotion is bad.[12] For example, sales promotion is warranted when the company has a superior brand but low awareness. Then sales promotion, by stimulating trial, will cause the customer base to grow. Sales promotion is also effective when it attracts new customers who have a loyalty bent. But most sales promotion brings in switchers and deal-prone customers who are "here today, gone tomorrow." According to many observers, most sales promotions lose money for the company.

Public Relations

Public relations, like sales promotion, comprises a diverse set of tools. Public relations can be quite effective, although it tends to be underutilized in the promotion of products and services. One reason is that a company's public relations is normally located in a separate department handling not only marketing public relations (MPR) but also financial PR, employee PR, government PR, and so on. So marketers have to beg for resources from the PR department or must engage a separate PR agency.

As advertising loses some of its brand-building power, and as sales promotion has grown far beyond its optimum size, companies may recognize more potential in MPR. MPR consists of a set of tools that can be classified under the acronym of PENCILS, namely:

P = *publications* (company magazines, annual reports, helpful customer brochures, etc.)

E = *events* (sponsoring athletic or art events or trade shows)

N = *news* (favorable stories about the company, its people, and products)

C = *community involvement activities* (contributions of time and money to local community needs)

I = *identity media* (stationery, business cards, corporate dress codes)

L = *lobbying activity* (efforts to influence favorable or dissuade unfavorable legislation and rulings)

S = *social responsibility activities* (building a good reputation for corporate social responsibility)

Each tool has further breakdowns. Consider identity media. The company's stationery, business cards, and brochures all create an impression. So do the company's factories, offices, and trucks. An important communication tool is the corporate dress code, which may include wearing uniforms such as in fast food stores, airlines, and hotels. Or it may be a "soft" dress code such as the rule laid down by Thomas Watson of IBM that IBM salesmen must wear a dark suit, a white shirt, and a good-looking tie. They must look "professional." The source of the rule was an experience that Watson had when visiting Chase Manhattan Bank's president and noticing out of the corner of his eye that one of the bank's employees looked disheveled. When Watson commented on this, the Chase president said, "Oh, he is not my employee. He is yours. He is visiting us today to do some work." Watson was aghast and that night drew up the IBM dress code.

Most PR expenditures represent solid investments designed to create and deliver a positive image to the target market. They are less blatantly perceived as self-serving than advertising campaigns. "While advertising is what you pay for, public relations is what you pray for." A favorable magazine story about a new software product is worth much more than tens of thousands of dollars spent in advertising. Regis McKenna advises his hi-tech clients to do a lot of public relations work in advance of launching their new products.[13] He identifies a whole set of influential personages and opinion leaders—computer magazine editors and columnists, lead users, and so on—who will have much more influence on the success of a new hi-tech product than strong advertising. He helps his clients garner the good opinion of these influentials prior to launching their advertising campaign.

Perhaps the main problem management faces in using more PR is to find those PR agencies that can develop creative ideas. Routine PR work can be obtained from most PR agencies, but it takes some talented PR people to come up with big ideas that will bring positive attention and repute to the company.

Sales Force

One of the most expensive marketing communication tools is the company's sales force, especially when out in the field, traveling a lot, and spending considerable time hunting for prospects and keeping existing customers satisfied. When one considers that the average salesperson is with customers only 30 percent of the time and spends the remainder learning about products and selling techniques, filling out reports, attending sales meetings, traveling, and so on, clearly this resource requires the utmost skill in managing it carefully.

Salespeople have the advantage of being much more effective than a series of ads or direct mail pieces. The salesperson sees the customer and can take him to lunch, gauge his interest, answer questions and objections, and close the sale. The more complex the product or service, the more necessary it is to use salespeople. Where products and prices are fairly similar, the salesperson may be the only factor that inclines the customer to purchase from one vendor and not another.

Some salespeople have a true gift for selling. Some even boast that they could sell sand to oil sheiks and ice to Eskimos. The top people in a sales force can often sell five to ten times as much as the average salesperson. Companies would therefore be smart to hire the best salespeople and pay them more. What is important is not the salesperson's cost but his cost in relation to the generated sales. Top salespeople produce sales at a lower cost to sales revenue than poor salespeople. Companies that try to save money by offering low pay to salespeople often have the highest cost to sales. Poor salespeople sell less, become frustrated, and either quit or are fired, thus necessitating new recruitment, selection, and training costs that would not be necessary in a strong and well-paid sales force.

At the same time, salespeople can no longer win business simply with "a smile and a shoeshine." A good smile and a shoeshine cannot compensate for an inferior product offering. Purchasing agents, no matter how much they might favor a certain salesperson, are under great pressure to justify their vendor choices. Salespeople know this, and increasingly they are "back-selling" to their companies, urging them to make better products and value propositions, which would be easier to sell.

As important as salespeople may be, companies nevertheless keep searching for ways to reduce sales force size and cost. One common approach is to increase the *inside sales force* relative to the *outside sales force*. Early on, companies recognized that telemarketers could be effective in selling to smaller customers, especially where the revenue from smaller customers would not cover the field sales call expense. Companies then expanded the telemarketing operation to cover even larger customers, many of whom prefer to deal with salespeople over the phone rather than in person. Many customers today feel that they can get the needed information and service through a phone call instead of tying up the time seeing salespeople in their office. Today it is possible to see the telemarketer face to face on the computer screen, thanks to video transmission. There are an increasing number of salespeople who have made five- and six-figure sales without ever meeting the customer face to face. As salespeople and buyers become more comfortable with electronic commerce, sales travel costs will go down. The customer saves time, and the selling company saves considerable time and money turning its sales force into competent telemarketers.

But the company's field sales force is not happy to see more of its clients handled by telemarketers. Salespeople see their commissions going down. They argue that they could turn even the smaller customers in their territory into larger customers. They insist that if the small customer becomes a larger customer, this customer should be returned to the field salesperson. One company told a customer who had grown larger in size that the customer now would get a visiting salesperson. When the customer said he was perfectly happy using the phone, the company said, no, he would have to accept the visiting salesperson. The customer promptly took his business elsewhere.

Most companies, in trying to gain their sales forces' acceptance of a telemarketing operation, have finally agreed to pay a small commission to the field salespeople for any telemarketing sales within their territory. The company's cost is higher, but that is the price of gaining the sales force's cooperation.

Another approach to reducing the size of the company's direct sales force is to sell through distributors. The distributors have their own sales forces and normally represent several noncompeting suppliers. Distributors offer economies of scale and scope that are highly appealing to manufacturers. Normally, a new company seeking fast national market coverage will hire distributors to carry its products. But as the company's business grows, the company may eventually find it more economical to hire its own sales force and replace its distributors. Further incentive is added when the company is dissatisfied with the distributor's sales coverage, effort, or cost.

As long as the company employs a direct sales force, it needs to invest in its productivity. One step is to carry out *time-and-duty analysis*, which will reveal how salespeople allocate their time to sales meetings, report writing, product and selling technique studies, travel, and customer contact time. Usually the company can find ways to reduce the salespersons' report writing time, travel time, and so on. Sometimes the company will redesign sales territories so that they can be covered more efficiently.

The other chief tool for increasing sales force productivity is *sales automation*.[14] Today's salesperson needs a laptop computer, printer, copy machine, fax machine, cellular phone, electronic mail, software, and so on. While all that is expensive, companies have found that salespeople who know how to use such equipment are more productive. Hewlett-Packard, which coined the term "sales automation," arrived at this conclusion when it trained some of its sales force to use laptops and saw their productivity increase by 30 percent over the salespeople who did not use this equipment.

Today's salespeople, when asked where their office is, often point to their laptop. With their laptop, they can access industry, product, and customer data, download brochures, and print contracts. In fact, some companies no longer see the need of providing offices for their salespeople. Compaq and Hewlett-Packard have asked their salespeople to work out of their homes rather than drive to an office each day and lose time. By closing down sales offices, those companies have reduced their rent, heat, and lighting expenses, while their salespeople have gained time and become more productive.

Managing the sales force involves complex questions in recruiting, selecting, hiring, training, motivating, compensating, and evaluating salespeople. Years ago, companies would hire one sales manager to supervise every six to eight salespeople. Today the span of control is more like twenty to forty salespeople for each sales manager. The fact is that salespeople are getting better at managing themselves without Big Brother constantly peering over their shoulders.

Companies are increasingly organizing their sales force by *vertical markets*. Instead of an IBM salesperson calling on a bank in the morning and a hotel chain in the afternoon, there will be IBM salespeople who concentrate on banks and another group who concentrate on hotels. In this way the salespeople learn more about customer needs within an industry and are in a better position to make useful suggestions.

An increasing number of companies are setting up *key account management systems*. Companies know that a few customers account for a large share of their sales and profits. The company appoints key account managers to manage their more important accounts, thus increasing the likelihood that important customers will be better served and will remain loyal. Key account managers manage anywhere from four to ten accounts, although their effectiveness diminishes with higher numbers of accounts to manage. Key account managers typically are judged by whether they reach their sales and profit goals and by the accounts' level of satisfaction. One problem is that key account managers may be overmotivated to increase sales and profits and provided with weak incentives to build long-run customer satisfaction.[15]

Direct Marketing

Today's markets are fracturing into smaller collections of minimarkets. As a result, more specialized media are appearing. There is an exploding number of magazines, each designed to deliver ads and editorial material to a specific customer group. Advances in television, cable networks, and satellite transmission are leading to an explosion in the number of available TV channels, expected to reach several hundred in the not-so-distant future. Not only can segments and niches be more efficiently reached, but also individuals, "segments-of-one," as a result of *database marketing*. Many companies possess proprietary databases comprising profiles on thousands or millions of customers and prospects. Consider the following:

- General Motors has a database of 12,000,000 names showing everything that these customers charged to their GM credit cards.
- Land's End has a database of more than 2,000,000 names of people who bought one or more clothing items from Land's End.
- WaldenBooks has the names of 4,000,000 members of its Preferred Reader Program.

Those companies can sort the names in their databases to collect any subset of names that might represent a marketing opportunity. They may be recent PC buyers who might respond to an offer of a low-priced scanner. They may be women who spend a lot at Saks Fifth Avenue to whom the company wants to send a gift. Or they may be lapsed subscribers to *Time* whom the company wants to attract back.

Since company databases contain so much data, various customer groupings would not be detectable without advanced technical analysis.

The customer database represents a *data warehouse* calling for *data mining* through advanced statistical and mathematical tools. Using those tools, companies are able to define their market targets better and to improve their response rates.[16]

Moving Toward Integrated Marketing Communications (IMC)

There is a growing awareness that companies generally do a poor job of integrating their marketing communications. They choose an advertising agency for their advertising; a public relations firm for their PR; a sales promotion firm for their sales promotion; and so on. Not only may they end up using these promotional tools in the wrong proportions, but they may also fail to create and deliver a consistent message with the different tools.

For example, Exhibit 6–5 lists nineteen tools available to pharmaceutical companies for communicating with and promoting to physicians. In principle, a pharmaceutical company should estimate the cost-effectiveness of each tool and choose the combination of tools that maximizes the total impact on the brand-prescribing behavior of their target doctors. In practice, these estimates are fairly hard to make.

Selecting the appropriate mix of promotion tools would be facilitated if the company had some theory of customer purchase drivers. Exhibit 6–6 provides an example. Three drivers are identified: the physician's adoption probability is higher, the more favorable his or her evaluation of the product is, the more favorably he or she regards the salesperson, and the greater the physician's regard for the company. Under each are listed, on the left, the evaluation criteria used by the physician, and on the right, the appropriate communication tools that can deliver messages in support of the evaluation criteria. For example, sampling is a way to let the physician learn about the effectiveness and side effects of the drug. In general, a company must distinguish the roles played by different promotional tools, so that they can be chosen and combined efficiently.

The solution to the IMC problem is fairly straightforward. The company should appoint a Vice-President of Communications (VPC). The VPC would be responsible for managing and integrating all the company's communications. That would include advising on everything that communicates something to the customers, not only the standard media vehicles but company dress code, the look of company trucks and company factories, and so on. A prospect or customer will form judgments about the company and its products based on a wide range of exposures:

EXHIBIT 6–5

Promotion Tools Used by the Pharmaceutical Industry

1. Detailing
2. Doctors' meetings (symposia, panel discussions)
3. Congress exhibitions (sponsored by pharma cos.)
4. Lunch or dinner meetings
5. Teleconferences
6. Seeding trials
7. Samples
8. Entertainment and gifts
9. Scientific publications and reprints
10. Journal advertising
11. Direct mail
12. Medical-subject audiotapes and videotapes
13. Company magazine
14. Company hotline and/or computer link
15. Name reminders (pens, calendars, clocks)
16. Couponing
17. Distributor/Wholesaler Programs
18. Public relations (aimed at patients, doctors, opinion leaders, government, health groups, etc.)
19. Social investments

- A prospect visits the company's factory and is appalled by the disorder and litter on the floor.
- A prospect receives a visit from a company salesman who is dressed poorly and has bad breath and a bored manner.
- A customer sees a company ad and thinks it is in poor taste.
- A customer notices that trucks of a certain highly advertised moving company are old and in poor condition.

The IMC solution calls for recognizing all contact points where the customer may encounter the company, its products, and its brands. Each

EXHIBIT 6–6

Classification of Major Promotional Tools Used by the Pharmaceutical Industry

---

1. Product Evaluation

   Product Management

   A. Effectiveness — Samples
   B. Dosage features — Journal ads & articles
   C. Side effects — Direct mail
   D. How long in market — Symposia

2. Salesperson

   Relationship Management

   A. Knowledge — Selection
   B. Character — Training
   C. Responsiveness — Entertainment
   D. Likability
   E. Special talents

3. Company

   Image Management

   A. Scientific standing — Feature articles
   B. Trustworthiness — Sponsorships
   C. Helpfulness — Civil actions
   D. Image
   E. Samples
   F. Well-known experts

---

brand contact will deliver a message, either good, bad, or indifferent. The company must strive to deliver a consistent and positive message at all contact points.

There is a further meaning of Integrated Marketing Communications. Too often a campaign is based on a single instrument, such as advertising, when in fact it should be designed as a *multimedia campaign*. Suppose a company wants to launch a product that embodies an exciting new feature. Instead of running ads as the first step in the campaign, it might call a press conference and get "free" press coverage. In that way, target market awareness will be created at a much lower cost than using expensive advertising. At the next step, the company can run a print advertising campaign offering to send a free booklet describing the product. Those who request the free booklet will receive the booklet along with an offer to sell the product at a reduced price before it is available in normal retail channels. Suppose 5 percent of those receiving the free brochure place an order. Not stopping there, the company next phones the 95 percent of the customers who received the brochure but did not place an order to see if they are still interested. That may produce another 5 percent sales response. Those who choose not to buy may be invited to a free product demonstration or, if they prefer, can receive a visit from a company salesperson. Thus, the company's product launch might consist of a carefully crafted sequence looking like this:

Press release → Ad with brochure offer → Direct mail
→ Telemarketing → Sales demonstration

Admittedly, this involves more communication work in contrast to simply spending the whole communication budget on advertising. On the other hand, those steps will probably deliver much more sales per dollar.

Here is another example of blending the various communication tools:

Warner-Welcome, maker of Benadryl, wanted to promote its antihistamine to allergy sufferers. The company used advertising and public relations to increase brand awareness and to promote a toll-free number that provided people with the pollen count in their area. People who called the number more than once received free product samples, coupons, and in-depth materials describing the product's benefits. These people also received an ongoing newsletter that included advice on how to cope with allergy problems.

Not only must the promotion tools be integrated; all four Ps must be integrated. The company cannot charge a high price for a poor-quality product or charge a high price for a good-quality product but provide poor service.

Each of the four Ps are in a competing as well as a complementary relationship. An automobile dealer decided one day to fire his ten salesmen and to use the saved cost to lower his car prices substantially. That resulted in a "land office" business. Apparently customers cared more for a low price than a car salesperson's dubious service.

The great number of interdependencies among marketing elements require the most careful planning. The choice of one element often dictates other elements. Selling through retailers may require offering to pay for "co-op ads." Catalog selling might require providing telephone ordering service seven days a week, twenty-four hours a day. Choosing to be the lowest-price firm may require a "hard-bargaining" stance toward suppliers and dealers. For those reasons, it is important once again to emphasize the need for developing a clear total value proposition around which all the marketing elements can be integrated in a seamless fashion.

Questions to Consider

A company needs to flesh out its basic strategy by preparing the most potent marketing mix. The word "mix" is well-chosen because of the large number of elements that must be considered, chosen, and coordinated. Not only must the elements be coordinated within each of the four Ps but also among the four Ps themselves. The customer needs to believe that the company's offer will be superior in delivering the four Cs: customer value, lower costs, better convenience, and better communication.

Here are some questions to answer about your business.

1. List all the marketing mix tools that your business unit currently uses. Which are the most important? Are any tools missing from the list that should be added? Are any tools in the list "a waste of money"? Can you sort the tools into their roles within the main customer driving forces?
2. Does your business unit deliver a consistent brand message through all customer brand contacts? Do your separate marketing service agencies (advertising, sales promotion, public relations, etc.) work well together?
3. Are you satisfied with the proportion of funds that your business unit spends on each promotional tool? If you were to shift funds, which tools would you reduce and which would you increase?
4. How do you currently assess whether your advertising is effective?
5. What steps are you taking to bring down sales force costs? Have you invested in time-and-duty studies, sales automation, moving into more telemarketing?
6. Have you identified your most important customers? Do you have enough information about each important customer to anticipate his needs and level of satisfaction? Are you now doing one-to-one marketing or planning to do so?

7

Acquiring, Retaining,
and Growing Customers

The only profit center is the customer.—*Peter Drucker*

If you're not serving the customer, your job is to serve somebody who is.—*Anonymous*

The paradigm has shifted. Products come and go. The unit of value today is the customer relationship.—*Bob Wayland*

If we're not customer driven, our cars won't be either.—*Statement by a Ford executive*

MARKETING HAS BEEN defined by several observers as "the art of finding and keeping customers." We should extend the definition to read: "Marketing is the science and art of finding, keeping, and growing profitable customers." How can a company find, keep, and grow profitable customers?

Yesterday's marketers thought the most important skill was the ability to find new customers. Salespeople spent most of their time hunting for rather than cultivating customers. They celebrated every new customer, like winning a trophy. They serviced their current customers with less gusto.

Today's consensus by marketers is the reverse. Keeping and growing customers are primary. The company has spent a lot of money getting each of its current customers, and competitors are always trying to snatch them away. A lost customer represents more than the loss of the next sale; the company loses the future profit on that customer's lifetime purchases. Then there is the cost of attracting a replacement customer. The cost of attracting a new customer, according to the TARP studies, is five times the cost of keeping a current customer happy.[1] Still worse, it will take some years before the new customer buys at the rate of the lost customer.

So the mantra goes: Monitor your current customers' level of satisfaction with your products and services; don't take them for granted; do something special for them from time to time; encourage their feedback.

In truth, great companies are skillful in both finding and keeping new customers. Here we shall examine the main processes involved in (1) locating prospects, (2) selling first time to the prospects, and (3) keeping and growing the new customers, if possible forever.

Locating Prospects

Locating customers is a problem only if customers are scarce. They are not scarce during a shortage; they stand in line for rations of bread or gasoline. When a company launches an extremely attractive product, customers queue up. When Ford launched its Mustang in the 1960s and Mazda launched its RX-7 in the 1970s, young people rushed into the dealerships to see and buy those cars.

But such situations are rare. Today most markets are characterized by an abundance of suppliers and brands. There is a shortage of customers, not products. It has been estimated that Europe's car makers have the capacity to produce 75 million cars a year, but the demand will be for only 45 million. Clearly, auto companies, as well as most other companies, must fight hard for each customer.

Industrial companies used to give their new salespeople a territory, a catalog, and an order book, then would tell them to spot factories that were spewing smoke. Each busy factory needed inputs. So knock on its door and show it that you have something worth buying.

Today many companies still leave it to their salespeople to find customers. But with the high cost of sales force time (for some companies, $500 a call when all costs are added together), finding new customers is too costly a use of sales force time. Salespeople should be selling, not looking for customers. Companies today are increasingly taking responsibility for *lead generation*. Companies are able to find leads at less cost. By turning good leads over to their salespeople, they give their salespeople more time to sell.

How can companies generate high-quality leads for their salesforce? *Lead generation* is a three-step process: defining the target market; using communication tools to gather leads; and qualifying the leads.

Defining the Target Market

No company in its right mind tries to sell to everyone. Gillette does not try to sell razor blades to preteens, and Kimberly-Clark doesn't try to sell its Huggies to childless families. A savvy steel company doesn't try to sell steel to every steel-using company. Presumably the steel company has gone through the STP process (segmentation, targeting, and positioning), and has chosen target markets. The steel company may decide to concentrate on fabricating steel for the auto industry, the office construction industry, or the kitchen appliance industry. Once the target market is chosen, it is relatively easy to identify the names of potential buyers. As the company deepens its knowledge of the target market—what it wants; what it buys; where and when it buys; how it buys; and so on—the company improves its ability to find good leads.

Soliciting Leads Through Communication Tools

A company can use several tools to gather prospect names. It can use *advertising*, *direct mail*, *telemarketing*, and *trade show exhibits*. Ultimately it can buy names from list brokers and others who happen to possess the names that the company wants.

For example, suppose a cat food manufacturer such as Mars wants to obtain the names of cat owners in Germany. One approach is to place an ad in a leading newspaper offering a free booklet titled "How to Take Care of Your Cat." Any cat owner needs only to fill in a coupon and supply the family's name, the cat's name, the cat's age and birthday, and any other information that Mars would find useful. Most cat owners who see the ad would probably request a free booklet.

Or Mars can approach German veterinarians and offer to buy names of cat-owning families. That is similar to the way baby food companies such as Nestlé and Gerber obtain the names of new mothers, that is, by soliciting obstetricians or examining birth records.

Mars uses the information it gets in several ways: to send a cat lover's magazine or catfood announcements to the cat-owning families; to send coupons for discounts on its brand; and even to send a birthday card to each cat on its birthday!

Let's look at how Toyota obtained the names of prospects for its new Lexus automobile, which it introduced in the United States in the early 1980s. One source of names comes from defining your competitors. In this case Lexus wanted to take sales away from Mercedes. So it proceeded to gather the names of Mercedes owners from car registration records and to use direct mail and telemarketing to get Mercedes owners to consider a Lexus on their next purchase.

Another approach was to sponsor an antique car show. Lexus marketers assumed that people who attend an antique car show are interested in interesting cars. The show was advertised, and ticket admission was $15, which was a way of limiting the audience to more affluent persons. Each attendee signed his name and address in a visitor book and this became a database for sending mailings to prospects about the Lexus.

In industrial marketing, finding the names of prospects is made easy by the Census Bureau's Standard Industrial Classification (SIC), which lists information on companies and businesses selling different products and services. Those data have been further enhanced and enriched by such information organizations as Dun & Bradstreet and made available on CD-ROMs for a price. Thus a company making a special glue for joining wood furniture would have no trouble finding the names of every furniture manufacturer in the United States, along with addresses, officers' names, sales, and number of employees.

Qualifying the Leads

Not all leads are worthwhile. Companies rightly draw a distinction between *suspects* and *prospects*. Suspects are people or organizations who might conceivably have an interest in buying the company's product or service, but they may not have the means or the real intentions to buy. A lot of people would like to own a Mercedes, but most are not qualified prospects.

One of the problems with the business cards left by visitors in a trade show booth is that many visitors are just curious or want some taste treat or complimentary pen, and they leave their business cards. Savvy salespeople usually throw away most of the business cards that come from people dropping by a booth.

What matters is discerning who are the best prospects. Companies distinguish between *cool, warm,* and *hot prospects,* the last being the most able, willing, and ready to buy. Every salesperson wants the list to start with the hottest prospects.

Companies can help discern the best prospects by using the mail or the phone. They can call the prospect and ask if he wants product literature or a sales call. Even when the prospect says he would welcome a sales call, the company might call the prospect's bank to make sure that the prospect can afford the product.

The company's aim is to supply high-quality leads to the sales force so that the sales force can use its expensive time to do what it can do best, namely sell. Lead generation needs to be set up as a specialty within the marketing department manned by marketing researchers and marketing communicators working together to locate good leads in the most efficient manner.

Selling to the Prospects

The salesperson, armed with good leads, can now call on the best prospects. Before the age of electronic media, that meant making an appointment to visit the prospect. Salespeople would prepare their weekly calendar of planned visits, including the modes of transportation and the motels they would stay in. They would also use a fairly standard approach when arriving in the prospect's office, such as AIDA: get the prospect's Attention, create Interest, develop his Desire, and move him to Action.

Each stage contains a set of techniques. The prospect's attention could be captured by claiming that the product will make money, save a large amount of cost, give the buyer peace of mind, or help him beat competitors. The salesperson would try to arouse interest by telling stories of other satisfied customers. To stimulate desire, the salesperson would say that the product is priced at a deep discount for the first purchase and that the offer could be made only today. Finally, to produce action, the salesperson would carefully answer each objection, and offer a money-back guarantee if the customer signs and is not completely satisfied.

The AIDA approach has the salesperson take the initiative and "lead the dance." In more recent times salespeople have been taught to talk less and listen more. Gone is the script of the slick salesperson, and in its place is the salesperson who knows how to raise good questions, how to listen and learn. Neil Rackham, in his SPIN Selling Method,[2] trains salespeople to raise four types of questions with the prospect:

Situation questions:	These ask about facts or explore the buyer's present situation. For example, "How many people are there in this location?"
Problem questions:	These deal with problems, difficulties, and dissatisfactions that the buyer is experiencing with the present situation and that the supplier can solve with its products and services. For example, "What parts of the system create errors?"
Implication questions:	These ask about the consequences or effects of a buyer's problems, difficulties, or dissatisfactions. For example, "How does this problem affect your people's productivity?"
Need-payoff questions:	These ask about the value or usefulness of a proposed solution. For example, "How much would you save if we could reduce the errors by 80 percent?"

Rackham suggests that companies, especially those selling complex products or services, should initially be selling not products or services but *capabilities*. The salesperson should move from preliminaries to demonstrating the supplier's capabilities, and then should work toward obtaining a long-term commitment to work together. That approach reflects the growing interest of many companies to move from pursuing an immediate sale to developing a long-term satisfying customer relationship.

We have assumed that the salesperson starts the process by visiting the prospect in his office. It may turn out that the prospect doesn't want a personal visit, that he prefers that the salesperson send information or talk over the phone before any visit occurs. As a result salespeople have had to develop good telephone skills. Some are so good on the phone that they can complete many sales without ever visiting the customer. In fact, companies now prefer to set up a telemarketing group to reach prospects, especially smaller prospects, as a way to contain selling costs.

In the electronic age, selling to prospects will increasingly involve less personal travel to the prospect's office. Computers will also have cameras. The salesperson will set up an appointment for a video conference with the buyer and his colleagues. They will see each other on the screen. The salesperson can show his product on the screen and/or fax exhibits to the buyer. The computer-trained salesperson will replace the costly traveling salesperson.

The computer will also reduce other costs of supporting the salesperson. Most salespeople will work out of the home in the future. They will be adept on the computer, on the phone, in using e-mail and the fax machine, in getting information and communicating on the Internet and the company's Intranet. Companies need people who are skilled in using lower-cost information and communication channels to carry on their selling and customer relationships.

One of the key uses of the computer is to manage the *prospect and customer database*. Let's return to the example of the Lexus, where the company has gathered the names of affluent car owners. Lexus developed an elaborate selling process for reaching those prospects. First it sent what looked like a gift by express mail to the prospects who had attended the antique show. The parcel contained a letter and a videotape from a nearby Lexus dealer. The letter invited the prospect to attend a party at the dealership the following Saturday. The videotape itself ran for twelve minutes and illustrated many ways in which the Lexus was as good as or even superior to the Mercedes. One example showed a mechanic putting glasses of water on the engines of a Lexus and a Mercedes, and starting both engines, with the result that the water on the Lexus engine block hardly moved while the one on the Mercedes engine shook badly. That was Lexus's way of suggesting that the Lexus offered a smoother ride.

The Lexus dealer would phone the prospect a few days before the Saturday party to confirm whether he would attend. If the prospect said that he couldn't make it, the dealer would ask if he would be interested in coming another time. If yes, the dealer would put into the "tickler" file a reminder to send another invitation later.

If the prospect didn't visit the dealer, the dealer would call a few weeks later and offer to bring the car to the prospect's home and provide a test drive for his family. Or the dealer might offer to lend a Lexus to the prospect for a weekend.

All those steps were recorded in the dealer's database, so that he would know where each prospect stood. He would know which ones to continue to pursue and which ones to drop.

The computer has given marketing people and salespeople an enormous advantage by enabling them to retain all kinds of details about prospects and customers. It is revolutionizing the sales process. Today's salespeople, after working out a basic agreement with a customer, can even print out a customized contract in the prospect's office, ready for his signature, thus turning the prospect into a first-time customer.

Was the Customer Worth Getting?

Given all the effort that goes into converting a prospect into a customer, companies need to analyze whether the *customer acquisition cost* (CAC) will be covered by the *customer lifetime profits* (CLP). Here is an example where the average customer acquisition cost exceeds the average customer lifetime profit.

1. Annual cost of a salesperson	$100,000
2. Number of annual calls by a salesperson	200
3. Cost of an average sales call (1 ÷ 2)	$500
4. Average number of sales calls to convert a prospect into a customer	× 4
5. Cost of attracting a new customer (CAC) (3 × 4)	$2,000

The $2,000 cost is an underestimate, because we are omitting the cost of advertising and promotion and operations, as well as the fact that not all prospects end up being converted into customers.

Now suppose this company estimates average customer lifetime profit:

1. Annual customer revenue	$10,000
2. Average number of loyal years	× 2
3. Company profit margin	× .10
4. Customer lifetime profit (CLP) (1 × 2 × 3)	$2,000

Even this estimate of CLP is overstated, since it omits the cost of maintaining the account through salesperson visits, ads, and so on. The conclusion, then, is that this company is paying more to get a new customer than the average new customer is worth!

To avoid heading toward bankruptcy, this company must find a way to reduce its CAC and to increase its CLP. To reduce its CAC, the company must reduce the cost of supporting its salespeople (e.g., reduced sales expenses, increased use of the telephone instead of personal visits), and increase the prospect conversion efficiency. To increase its CLP, the company must sell more to each new customer, keep them for more years, and sell them more high-profit items. With those steps, the company can hope to create a better balance between its CAC and its CLP.

Keeping Customers for Life

Now we can appreciate the importance of keeping and growing customers. Today's smart companies do not see themselves as selling products; they see themselves as creating profitable customers. They not only want to create customers, they want to "own" them for life. Recent books bear testimony to this interest: *Market Ownership: The Art and Science of Becoming #1* and *Customers for Life,*[3] among others. That does not mean the customer wants to be owned. In fact, he wants to keep his options open. Nevertheless, the marketer wants to own the customer, to "loyalize" him.

It goes further. The marketer wants to increase his share of the customer's business constantly. He wants not only to be the sole supplier of a particular product but to supply more of whatever the buyer buys. That is known as pursuing *share of customer.* Banks, for example, want to increase their share of the customer's "wallet." Supermarkets want to increase their share of the customer's "stomach." Today Harley-Davidson sells not only motorcycles but leather jackets, sunglasses, shaving cream, Harley beer, and Harley cigarettes, and even runs a Harley restaurant in New York City. We might say that Harley wants to create and own a "customer lifestyle."

That is also the aim of *affinity marketing.* A company will target a group such as dentists or beauticians and try to sell them an array of goods and services that will meet their needs. The members of such a group have common problems, needs, and lifestyles. The company can sell them insurance, travel plans, and banking services.

Developing a new customer into a stronger and more loyal customer involves moving that customer through several stages. The main *customer development stages* are as follows:[4]

First-time customer
Repeat customer
Client
Advocate
Member
Partner
Part-owner

Here we shall examine each stage and consider what can be done to move the customer into each subsequent stage.

First-time Customer

The first-time customer—whether he is buying a tennis racket, an automobile, legal services, or a hotel stay—will end up with a feeling about the purchase and the supplier. Before buying, he had developed a certain expectation, based on what others had said, what the seller had promised, and his general past experience with similar purchases. After buying, he will experience one of five levels of satisfaction:

Highly satisfied	Satisfied	Indifferent	Dissatisfied	Very dissatisfied

The probability that the new customer will buy again is strongly related to his level of satisfaction with the first purchase. He will be a "lost customer" if he is very dissatisfied, dissatisfied, or even indifferent. He will probably buy again if he is satisfied, and there is a high probability that he will buy again if he is very satisfied. Companies often fail to distinguish between the satisfied customer and the very satisfied customer. Satisfied customers can easily switch when another supplier can offer equal or greater satisfaction. But very satisfied customers will be less likely to find another supplier who they believe can satisfy them at the same high level. Xerox reports that totally satisfied customers are six times more likely to repurchase Xerox products over the next eighteen months than are satisfied customers.

Companies that want to attract repeat customers must periodically survey their customers' level of satisfaction. In the best case, their Customer Satisfaction Index (CSI) would show that most customers are satisfied or highly satisfied. Unfortunately, that is often not the case. Studies of customer satisfaction show that customers tend to be dissatisfied with their purchases about 25 percent of the time! What's worse, about 95 percent of them do not complain, either because they do not know how or to whom to complain or they believe that it is not worth the effort.[5]

If the company's CSI shows a lot of dissatisfied customers, the company must figure out why. One possibility is that the company's salespeople are overly aggressive; they persuade customers to buy products or services that really don't fit their needs. Another possibility is that the company has exaggerated the performance of its products or services, leaving customers disappointed. In either case, the company will probably not see those customers again.

A company should estimate the cost of its lost customers. For example, a transportation company estimated that it loses approximately 5 percent of its customers each year because of poor customer service. Here is their calculation of the cost of losing those customers:

The company had 64,000 accounts.
The 5 percent loss of customers a year due to poor service amounted to 3,200 accounts (.05 x 64,000).
The average lost account had grossed an average of $40,000.
Therefore the company lost $128,000,000 (3,200 x $40,000) in sales a year because of poor service.
The company's profit margin was 10 percent. Therefore, the company's net loss was $12,800,000 (.10 x $128,000,000).

This company would benefit greatly by spending money to improve its customer service. It would be worth spending at least $12,800,000 for advice or programs to ensure never having any losses of customers due to poor service. In fact, it would be worth spending some multiple of that figure, because each saved customer will yield a several-year stream of customer profits.

The damage done by disappointed customers goes beyond the loss of these customers' lifetime spending. A company should never underestimate the power of an irate customer. The TARP studies found that a very dissatisfied customer might tell as many as eleven other people about his disappointment, and each of them will tell others, leading to a possible exponential growth in the number of prospects who hear bad things about the company. So the company loses not only the lifetime earnings from the dissatisfied customer but also many potential customers who have decided not to buy from the company.

Disappointed customers, of course, need not necessarily be lost. Alert companies set up systems making it easy for dissatisfied customers to reach them. No longer do small hotels post a sign saying "Complaints only accepted between 9 A.M. and 10 A.M. daily." Procter & Gamble, Whirlpool, and General Electric provide a toll-free phone number with their products that customers can use to complain, inquire, or deliver suggestions to the company. Pizza Hut prints its toll-free number on all delivered pizza boxes; when a customer complains, Pizza Hut sends voice mail to the store manager, who must call the customer within forty-eight hours and resolve the complaint. Those companies use the following procedure to recover customer goodwill:

1. Set up a seven-day, twenty-four-hour toll-free "hotline" (by phone, fax, or e-mail) to receive and act on customer complaints.
2. Contact the complaining customer as quickly as possible. The slower the company responds, the more the dissatisfaction may grow and lead to negative word-of-mouth.
3. Accept responsibility for the customer's disappointment; don't put the fault on the customer.
4. Use customer service people who are empathic.
5. Resolve the complaint swiftly and to the customer's satisfaction. Some complaining customers are not looking for compensation so much as a sign that the company cares.

Ironically, customers whose complaints are satisfactorily resolved often become more loyal than customers who were never dissatisfied. About 34 percent of customers who register major complaints will buy again from the company if their complaints are resolved, and the number rises to 52 percent for minor complaints. If the complaint is resolved quickly, between 52 percent (major complaints) and 95 percent (minor complaints) will buy again from the company.[6]

There are many ways of winning back the goodwill of a disappointed customer. The company can offer a discount on the next purchase or a small gift to make up for the error. Timothy Firnstahl, who runs a Seattle restaurant chain called Satisfaction Guaranteed Eateries, Inc., sets down these recovery guidelines: "When guests have to wait more than ten minutes beyond their reservation time, but less than twenty, we suggest free drinks. If they wait for more than twenty minutes, the entire meal may be free. If the bread arrives more than five minutes after the guests sit down, we suggest free chowder."[7]

Repeat Customers

First-time customers are of varying profitability. Some make an expensive purchase and have the means and interest to buy much more. Others buy a small amount and may never buy again. The marketers then will focus on the best first-time customers in the effort to convert them into repeat customers.

Companies find it useful to classify customers by their "depth-of-repeat." An auto company might distinguish between customers who bought its car only once, customers who bought two cars, three cars, or more from the same dealer. A catalog company like Land's End classifies its customers by their *recency*, *frequency*, and *monetary value* (known as the RFM formula). Its best customers are those who bought recently, who buy frequently, and who spend a lot.

Companies have discovered that the longer that customers stay with a company, the more profitable they are. Longer-tenured customers are more profitable because of four factors:

1. *Retained customers buy more over time if they are highly satisfied.* Once customers have established a purchasing relationship with a seller, they continue to buy from him, partly because of inertia. If their needs grow, they buy more. And the seller engages in two processes:
    - *Cross-selling:* The seller adds other items to his product line that will appeal to the same customers and brings the new items to the customers' attention. A computer salesman will show the customer a printer, modem, software, and other items that support the computer. A bank may try to interest a customer who opened a new savings account to think also about loans and trust services.
    - *Upselling:* Where there is equipment wearout or resupply needs, the seller helps customers see the advantage of early or upgraded replacement. By keeping a record of when a customer bought his car or computer, the company can know when to promote the availability of a newer, better-performing version. Upselling should not occur too early: the buyer of a new car is not going to consider replacing it for a few years. On the other hand, if the seller waits too long, he might find that the buyer has already bought another car.
2. *The cost of serving a retained customer declines over time.* Transactions with a repeat customer become routinized. Much is understood without signing a lot of agreements. Trust is built, and it saves both parties a lot of time and cost.
3. *Highly satisfied customers often recommend the seller to other potential buyers.*
4. *Long-term customers are less price-sensitive in the face of reasonable price increases by the seller.*

As a result of these factors, companies that have a high customer retention rate are more profitable. Fred Reichheld has gathered data on companies with high customer retention levels and has documented

EXHIBIT 7–1

Relationship Between Customer Retention and Profitability in
the Insurance Brokerage Industry

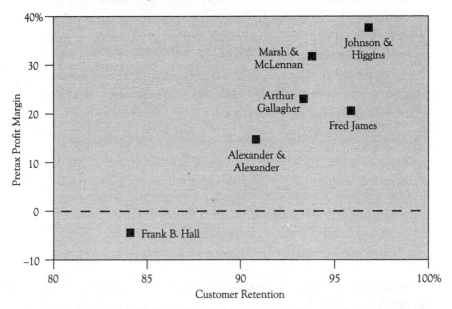

Source: Frederick Reichheld, *The Loyalty Effect* (Boston: Harvard Business School Press, 1996),
p. 13. Based on Bain estimates, U.S. Operations.

their higher profitability. As an example, Exhibit 7–1 shows the customer retention rates and profitability of several insurance companies. Clearly those companies with higher customer retention rates are more profitable. In fact, Reichheld concludes that a company that can increase its customer retention rate by five percentage points can increase its profitability anywhere from 35 to 95% percent depending on the economics of the particular industry.[8]

Because customers with a longer tenure are more profitable to the company, companies often treat them in a special way. After identifying their Most Valuable Customers (MVCs), companies might send them birthday greetings, small gifts, invitations to special sports or art events, and other thoughtful gestures.

Client

We have used the word "customers" to describe those who buy from the firm. However, professional firms—accounting firms, law firms, architectural firms—use the word "clients," not customers. What is the difference? First, members of professional firms know much more about their clients. Second, they devote more time to helping and satisfying clients. Third, their relation to the client is more continuous and leads to more familiarity and empathy.

With the power of database marketing, it is now possible for a firm with many customers to start seeing them and treating them as clients. Today when a customer phones a company like L. L. Bean (clothing catalog) or USAA (insurance for military families), its telemarketers immediately see data about the customer on their screens, thanks to caller-ID. The L.L. Bean telemarketer might say: "Mrs. Jones, how did you like that jacket you bought last month?" The USAA telemarketer might ask: "Lieutenant Smith, did the garage manage to fix the car door in a satisfactory manner?" Those companies are viewing their customers as clients and show an interest that goes beyond simply selling the next product.

Advocate

The more a client likes the company, the more likely he is to talk favorably about it, either when asked for an opinion or without being asked. "The best advertisement is a satisfied client." "Satisfied customers become apostles," according to Duane Collins, CEO of Parker-Hannafin. The aim of many companies is to create not customers but *fans*.[9] Fan is short for *fanatic*, which describes how Harley-Davidson motorcycle owners feel about the Harley-Davidson Company and its products. People trust much more the opinions of friends and acquaintances than the ads they read or the spokespeople who hype the product. The real question is whether companies can take additional steps to stimulate positive-word-of-mouth.

One clear option is to ask satisfied customers for the names of friends or whether they would act as references for the company. A dentist might post a sign in his office saying: "If I have satisfied you, I would be happy to also satisfy your friends." A company selling an installed swimming pool system called Endless Pools has arranged for its most satisfied customers to receive and show their pool to new prospects.

Companies also try to win over opinion leaders to recommend their product. Regis McKenna has carefully documented the steps in harnessing opinion makers to spread favorable information about new hi-tech products.[10]

Member

To further "loyalize" clients, the firm might launch a membership program that carries privileges. The idea is that if enough special benefits come with membership, members would be reluctant to switch away and lose the privileges.

There are many levels and kinds of membership programs. Some are open to everyone; some can be joined only by invitation. The benefits and costs vary greatly. We shall describe several of these programs in Chapter 8.

Partner

Some companies have gone further and view their customers as partners. That becomes manifest when a company solicits customers' help in designing its new products, asks for customer suggestions for improving the company's service, or invites customers to serve on a *customer panel*.

Partnering is more readily seen in business-to-business relations than in mass consumer markets. Caterpillar, the world market leader in construction equipment, views its dealers not just as customers and resellers but as partners in the enterprise. Caterpillar actively solicits the opinions of its dealers with respect to new equipment models, marketing strategies, and pricing policies. In a similar manner, a sole supplier to an automobile company, such as Johnson Controls, which designs the whole seating system for Chrysler, sees Chrysler, its customer, as its partner. In fact, Chrysler reciprocates by encouraging all of its important system suppliers to see Chrysler as its partner.

Milliken & Company, a leading textile manufacturer of carpeting, seat upholstery, and towels, sees its customers as partners; it encourages them to be "Partners for Profit" (PFP). Industrial laundries that agree to sign a five-year contract with Milliken to buy its towels receive several benefits: proprietary software for transportation routing, software for keeping laundry books, a newsletter on developments in the industrial laundry industry, and free sales training for the laundry's sales force. Milliken is really not selling towels; it is selling "laundry profitability." Its aim is to make its customer-laundries rich and, in the process, to make itself rich. To Milliken, "the success of our company depends on the success of our customers."

Part-owner

Perhaps the highest view of the customer is that he is a stakeholder, virtually a part-owner of the firm. There are, in fact, businesses where the customers are the legal owners. For example, a mutual insurance company is owned by its customers. (It doesn't follow that the mutual insurance company acts especially solicitously toward its insured customers, but in principle it should.) Cooperatives, too, have customers who are owners of the firm. In a wholesaler-sponsored coop, the retailers own shares in the coop. They make their purchases through the coop and receive dividends based on how much they have purchased. And in a consumer cooperative, the consumers have a say in the policies of the coop and receive dividends based on spending level.

This is not to suggest that every company should strive to turn its customers into partners, owners, or co-owners. Often those terms express more an attitude smart companies manifest toward those who buy from them than a legal status of the customers.

Are All Customers Worth Keeping?

Today the rage is to say "Customers are number 1." Stu Leonard, who operates one of the most profitable supermarkets in the world, advertises two rules to his employees:

Rule 1: The customer is always right.
Rule 2: If the customer is wrong, go back to rule 1.

If a manager spots an unhappy customer, the manager will do anything to resolve the grievance. A lost customer will cost the store $50,000 in lost sales. The average customer normally spends $100 a week on groceries, shops fifty weeks a year, and stays in the area about ten years ($100 × 50 × 10 = $50,000).

Yet most companies recognize that while all customers are important, some are more important than others. We saw earlier that customers can be classified by their recency, frequency, and monetary value. Often companies think their largest customers are the most profitable and their smallest the least profitable. But consider that the company's largest customers tend to get the deepest discounts and demand the most services. There is some evidence that medium-size customers often yield a higher return on investment than the company's largest customers.

In short, companies must find a way to measure individual customer profitability. One must allow for the fact that customers receive special discounts, free services, and other attentions that cause their real profitability to vary. Companies are starting to apply activity-based costing (ABC) to determine the actual cost of services delivered to each customer, so that true customer profitability can be determined.

Once that is done customers can be ranked in deciles of profitability. One frequently quoted rule is the 20/80 rule, which says that the top 20 percent of profitable customers account for 80 percent of the company's profits. The formulation has been modified more recently into the 20/80/30 rule, which adds the observation that the poorest 30 percent of the company's customers cuts the company's potential profits in half.[11] Stated otherwise, most companies lose money on some percentage of their worst customers. Specifically, some banks report that they lose money on as many as 40 percent of their weakest retail customers.

What should companies do with their unprofitable customers? Some companies say: "Fire them." Release the unprofitable customers so that they can bleed the competitors. More thoughtful companies ask the question: "How can we turn our unprofitable customers into profitable ones?" There are several possibilities. The company can require unprofitable customers to buy more, order in larger quantities, forgo certain services, or pay more. Recently banks have raised their fees for deposit withdrawals and low deposit accounts, in the interest of raising customer profitability.

Are all customers worth keeping? No, certainly not those who cannot be turned sooner or later into profitable accounts.

Questions to Consider

Marketing is defined as the science and art of finding, keeping, and growing profitable customers. Today's companies are shifting their emphasis from finding customers to learning how to keep and grow them. As more companies master the art of satisfying and retaining customers, it will become increasingly hard for companies to attract new customers through getting them to switch. That forces still more companies to master the art of creating loyal customers.

Here are some things for your company to think about.

1. How does your company generate leads? Are they largely the sales force's responsibility, or has the company taken the initiative to collect and qualify "hot leads" in an efficient manner?

2. Are the salespeople trained according to the AIDA formula (Attention, Interest, Desire, Action), the SPIN formula (Situation, Problem, Implication, Need-payoff), or some other method? Do you see a reason for switching to a new sales approach that would be more effective with today's customers?

3. Has your company analyzed the average customer acquisition cost (CAC) and compared it with the average customer lifetime profits (CLP)? How does it look? What steps can be taken to improve the ratio of CLP to CAC?

4. Do you treat customers as transaction customers only, or as clients, advocates, members, or even partners? Can you develop all customers or at least move the more valuable customers to a higher level of "partnering?" Do you encourage your customers to be referral sources or word-of-mouth initiators?

5. What programs do you operate for encouraging cross-selling and upgrading of customer purchases? How can these programs be improved further?

6. Do you measure the profitability of individual customers? What percentage of your customers are unprofitable? How do you handle them? How should you handle them?

8

Designing and Delivering More Customer Value

We're in the value business.—*Ed Rensi, President and CEO, McDonald's*

Get fewer, smarter people to deliver more value to customers faster.—*John Thomson*

IF CUSTOMERS ONLY bought products and didn't care about services and surrounding benefits, and all products in the category were the same, all markets would be price markets. Then all companies would have to accept the market-made price. The only winner would be the lowest-cost firm.

Clearly there are markets like that. An investor who wants to buy IBM shares won't pay a cent more to one seller over another. We call such markets "commodity markets." We hear laments from gasoline companies, produce companies, bulk chemical companies, and steel companies that "price is everything."

But if that's the case, we would have to explain some anomalies:

- Why does Frank Perdue get 10 percent more for his brand of chicken?
- Why does Evian get 10 percent more for its bottled water?
- Why does Starbuck's get 20 percent more for its cup of coffee?
- Why does Morton's get 10 percent more for its brand of salt?

140

People form brand preferences. Brands are familiar, and they create an expectation. Frank Perdue's brand means that his chicken will be tender, not tough. Evian's brand means that the water will be pure. Starbuck's brand means that its coffee will be tastier and fresher. Brands represent more than the product. Brands represent a configuration of services, values, and promises made by the seller.

In today's hypercompetitive marketplace, companies are struggling to differentiate their offerings. Carl Sewell, in his Dallas Cadillac dealership, is not simply selling Cadillacs; he is selling fine service and a promise to help his customer get the maximum use out of his Cadillacs. His dealership can be reached day or night in an emergency and gives a free car wash with every service. He has transformed the *core product* into an *augmented product*. Today's smart marketers don't sell products; they sell *benefit packages*. They don't sell *purchase value* only; they sell *use value*.

There are three ways a company can deliver more value than its competitors:

- It can charge a lower price.
- It can help the customer reduce his other costs.
- It can add benefits that make the offer more attractive.

Let us now examine the various ways under each strategy by which companies can gain a competitive advantage.

Winning Through a Lower Price

Michael Porter, in his *Competitive Strategy*, cited "price leadership" as one of three winning competitive strategies. The Japanese won several markets by practicing price leadership. The American company Texas Instruments also employed this strategy, using "experience curve pricing." It would price its chips and other components lower than its competitors and would achieve volume leadership. That in turn would lower its scale cost and experience curve cost, permitting it to lower its price still further. In the meantime, its competitors, having lower volume and less accumulated production, would operate from a higher cost position and would be forced to charge higher prices for what was often seen as "commodity products." That theory worked well, although it was not without its risks.[1]

Companies Winning Through Aggressive Pricing

Aggressive pricing is best practiced by firms that enjoy the low cost position in the industry. A firm may be low-cost as a result of many factors, including scale, experience, inexpensive locations, superior cost control, or stronger bargaining power with suppliers and distributors. Here we shall examine four firms that have won substantial market shares by offering the lowest prices to their customers.

SOUTHWEST AIRLINES. Sensing that the high cost of flying keeps many people from taking occasional short trips, the founders of Southwest Airlines started inexpensive flights between regional city pairs. The low fares resulted from several cost savings. Southwest did not use travel agents and therefore saved 10 percent commission costs. Southwest did not serve food and therefore could land and take off in less time than other carriers, which had to load food on the plane; without food service, the crew size could be smaller. Southwest did not preassign seats, which tends to slow down boarding. The strategy amounted to offering passengers "less for much less." Passengers preferred the savings over the dubious quality of airline food. Southwest hired and trained enthusiastic crew members known for their friendly attitude toward the passengers. Some devoted Southwest passengers say that Southwest really offers "more for less," rather than "less for much less."

COMPAQ. Compaq has been the most aggressive price-cutter in the personal computer market, earning it the number one market share. It didn't do so at the sacrifice of quality; in fact, Compaq also led in introducing new features. It accepted smaller margins in exchange for more volume, and seems to be using *experience curve pricing*. Recently, however, it has confronted lower-cost direct marketing firms, such as Dell and Gateway, which don't pay resellers for their services. Dell enjoys 12 percent lower costs because it produces the computers to order with the right software, one at a time, whereas Compaq has to forecast demand and ship computers to its retailers, risking larger inventories and even outdated computers. Compaq is now experimenting with new ways to compete with direct computer marketers, including doing some direct marketing itself. Compaq may have to decide whether it can live with the higher costs of its reseller network or if it should move totally into direct marketing.[2]

WAL-MART. Wal-Mart today is the world's largest retailer. Sam Walton built his retail empire on a number of principles, including "Satisfaction

Guaranteed" and "Everyday Low Prices." Wal-Mart has the lowest costs in the industry, less than its rival Kmart and substantially less than Sears and other mega-retailers. Its low costs are the result of several factors: very hard bargaining with its suppliers; locating in low-cost real estate areas; playing off competing municipalities trying to attract a Wal-Mart store and going with the one offering the largest subsidy; and a superb information system allowing Wal-Mart to carry more efficient levels of inventory. Wal-Mart uses its lower cost position to signify that its prices cannot be beaten, and many shoppers first go to Wal-Mart when they must make some purchases. Unlike the early discount stores, with their stark buildings and furnishings, Wal-Mart provides excellent shopping aisles displaying national brand goods, a friendly door greeter, and a "no-questions-asked" return policy.

TOYS 'R' US AND OTHER CATEGORY KILLERS. Category killers are stores that feature the largest product assortment within a category at the lowest prices. Toys 'R' Us was one of the first category killers and today accounts for about 40 percent of all toys sold in the United States. Parents know that they will find the largest toy assortment at the lowest prices. So powerful is Toys 'R' Us that no toy manufacturer will design and market a new toy before checking it out with Toys 'R' Us. Toys 'R' Us often insists on some design changes, a heavy promotion program, and other conditions for carrying the new toy on its shelves. The same practices characterize such other category killers as OfficeMax, Home Depot, and Sportmart.

Offering a Low Price to Customers Willing to Give Up Some Services

When customers insist on a lower price, one strategy is to ask them to relinquish some service normally included in the price, such as free delivery, free installation, or free training. The company can quantify the potential savings with each eliminated service. The key is for the company to reduce its price by less than the company's actual cost savings. Thus if the company normally spends $100 to provide delivery, the company can offer to cut, say $80 off the price. The company adds $20 to its profit through unbundling.

Limitations of the Low Price Strategy

Low-cost companies are in the best position to set low prices—although they also have the option of charging higher prices and plowing the money into product and service improvements. But the real question is, How long can a low-cost firm maintain its low cost position in a global competitive era? Such a firm originally might have been producing in the United States, then, in search of lower costs, may have moved its production to Taiwan. As Taiwan grows more expensive, the firm may move its production to Malaysia. Then China and India become cheaper, or a new low-cost competitor emerges in Central Europe. Another country, intent upon building up this industry, subsidizes an infant industry at prices lower than our firm's prices. Clearly, maintaining the lowest cost position over a long period is not easy and makes a low-price winning strategy less reliable in the long run.

Helping Customers Reduce Their Other Costs

Companies have two other ways to help customers realize lower costs. One is to argue that while the company's price is higher, the customer's long-run total cost will be lower. The other is to advise how the customer can reduce some of his other costs. Let's examine each of these.

Showing the Customer His Total Cost Is Less Despite Its Higher Price

Caterpillar is a master at charging higher prices but showing that the customer's costs will actually be lower. A construction company may want to buy a large tractor and is trying to decide between Caterpillar and Komatsu. Komatsu quotes a price of $45,000, and Caterpillar says it must charge $50,000. The Caterpillar salesperson will provide evidence to show that the construction company is better off buying the Caterpillar tractor. The Caterpillar salesperson itemizes Caterpillar's superior cost savings and what they are worth to the customer:

Caterpillar equipment has fewer breakdowns	$3,000
Caterpillar can fix its equipment faster	2,000
Caterpillar equipment lasts two years longer than competitor's equipment	4,000
Caterpillar equipment fetches a higher price on the second hand market when sold	2,000
Amount saved by the customer in buying a Caterpillar	$11,000

The Caterpillar salesman, having demonstrated that his tractor is worth $11,000 more than the Komatsu tractor, then says Caterpillar will charge only $5,000 more.

Otis Elevator has an 80 percent market share of the elevator business in India and yet charges higher prices than its competitors. The reason: Otis can show up within an hour after receiving a service call. Elevator owners will pay substantially more to avoid breakdowns, slow repairs, and irate users.

Some higher-price companies make an offer to their customers to "share-the-gain, share-the-risk." One consulting firm was so sure it could help its client save a million dollars a year that it offered to drop its consulting fees if it failed. In another case, a medical equipment firm promised to hold its prices steady for three years. In that case, the medical equipment firm would gain if its costs went down and lose if its costs went up.

Yet even when customers are convinced of lower long-run costs, some purchasing agents will buy from the lower-price firm because they are under pressure to keep their purchase costs down. Furthermore, their department typically doesn't bear the costs of the subsequent breakdowns and troubles.

Actively Helping the Customer to Reduce His Other Costs

Some companies charge a higher price but show the customer how he can reduce his other costs. Lincoln Electric, a manufacturer of welding equipment and supplies, provides a vivid example. Suppose General Motors (GM) needs to buy new welding equipment and supplies. Lincoln quotes the price at $400,000 to GM. GM checks with a competitor who offers the same equipment and supplies for $350,000. Suppose GM prefers to deal with Lincoln and asks Lincoln to meet the competitor's price. Lincoln will probably say no, on the grounds that its equipment, supplies, and service are superior to that of the competitor. If they can't agree, Lincoln then proposes the following: Lincoln will guarantee that it can help GM save the $50,000 difference. It will offer to GM a *conditional rebate* of $50,000 if it can't find a way to help GM save $50,000 in costs. Since GM has nothing to lose, it signs the contract with Lincoln for $400,000.

Now Lincoln sends its crackerjack team of factory specialists into GM's plant to see how welding is done and how the flow of work is organized. Typically, those experts can spot ways for GM to save not $50,000 but a lot more. When at least $50,000 of potential savings is pointed out, GM is satisfied and Lincoln is satisfied. Lincoln might even show GM a larger saving to impress GM with how good a partner Lincoln is. Yet Lincoln will be tempted to hold back some cost-saving suggestions if it expects future tough negotiations with GM.

How can a company help its customers save money? The Corning company provides its sales engineers with many cost-saving ideas. In fact, Corning now sells training seminars to other companies on ways to save customers money. The approach is to think through the customer's product purchase and use cycle and search for savings out of the customer's *ordering, inventory, processing,* and *administrative* routines. We review these cost-saving areas below.

HELPING CUSTOMERS REDUCE THEIR ORDERING COSTS. Customers who place frequent orders typically face a lot of paper work. The supplier can make the customer's life easier by supplying a computer software program for ordering with electronic links to the supplier. The McKesson Corporation, a multibillion-dollar pharmaceutical wholesaler, provides its many pharmacy customers with hardware and software to facilitate their ordering and reduce their costs. Its Omnilink Program automatically performs pre- and post-edits that check for errors in dosage information, pricing, refill limits, and brand recommendations to ensure that proper claims are submitted to insurance companies and government agencies.

In a similar fashion, travel agents have benefited greatly from American Airlines' SABRE reservation system. Without SABRE, travel agents would have to phone various airlines for ticket information. SABRE saves them time and cost. Robert L. Crandell, head of American Airlines, once remarked that he would rather sell American Airlines than SABRE if he had to make the choice, since SABRE has been more profitable.

HELPING CUSTOMERS REDUCE THEIR INVENTORY COSTS. In earlier times, suppliers would try to load their customers with high inventories for two reasons. One was to make sure there were no stockouts. The other was to put the customer under great pressure to favor the supplier's brand. Today's customers, however, are under great pressure to reduce all their costs, including their high inventory costs. At least three different solutions are available:

Just-in-time supply: Suppliers can offer to ship fewer units more frequently to their customers. As an example, 7-Eleven convenience stores in Japan carry small inventories because of a lack of storage space. Each convenience store transmits to headquarters the exact items sold in real time. 7-Eleven warehouses send supplies three times a day to each store based on what it needs for the coming few hours, which is known from historical records of what people buy at each store at each hour.

Levi Strauss uses a just-in-time stock replenishment system for its blue jeans. Each night, Levi Strauss receives information from Sears and other major retailers on how many Levi jeans sold of each size and style. Levi that night sends an electronic order to its main denim supplier, Milliken, specifying how much denim material it needs at its various factories the next day. Milliken loads its trucks with the needed amount, and they arrive a few hours later at Levi's factories. The denim is unloaded and delivered right to the machines to be cut and sewn into jeans. Meanwhile, DuPont has been notified as to how much fiber Milliken needs to make the denim. The whole supply chain keeps product flowing. The goal is "flow," not "stock," to keep down inventory carrying costs.

General Electric uses just-in-time arrangements in selling its large appliances. Its resellers carry sample appliances, take orders for them, and send the orders electronically to GE's factory, which makes the ordered units and sends them to the dealers or customers. The result is lower inventory carrying costs and satisfied dealers.

Consignment: Suppliers can reduce reseller inventory costs by selling the goods on consignment. The reseller pays for the goods only when they are sold.

Outsourcing inventory management: Another approach is for the supplier to offer to manage the customer's inventory system. Baxter Healthcare found that many hospitals have poor inventory control; they will be caught with too many items or too few. Baxter took over management of Massachusetts General Hospital's inventory and reduced inventory levels by 80 percent leading to a 20 percent cost saving. Hospitals gain by having the right supplies available at a lower cost. Baxter gains by becoming the channel gatekeeper through whom other hospital supply firms have to sell.

HELPING CUSTOMERS REDUCE THEIR PROCESSING COSTS. Companies can justify higher prices by showing their customers how they can save money on their processing costs. We saw how Lincoln Electric could help its buyers of welding equipment use the equipment more effectively. Here are ways in which a supplier can help customers save on their processing costs:

- Helping the customer improve yields
- Helping the customer reduce waste or rework costs
- Helping the customer reduce direct or indirect labor
- Helping the customer reduce accidents
- Helping the customer reduce energy costs

For example, the company can supply a machine that can replace some direct labor. Or the company can produce six sigma quality, in which case the customer would be saved inspection costs. The supplier should understand the customer's business so well that he can spot numerous opportunities for reducing the customer's processing costs.

HELPING CUSTOMERS REDUCE THEIR ADMINISTRATIVE COSTS. Customers often encounter a number of frustrating administrative experiences. For example, the customer may not understand the supplier's invoice. He should find it easy to phone the supplier's billing department for clarification. Or the customer may be upset about a late shipment. The supplier should make it easy for the customer to trace the shipment. Procter & Gamble and General Electric have set up large call centers that customers can call on a seven-day, twenty-four-hour basis to vent complaints, make suggestions, or ask questions. Suppliers who are accessible to their customers will have a better chance of building customer loyalty.

Winning Through Offering More Benefits to the Customer

Companies may have to "sweeten" their offerings to customers in other ways than through a lower price or helping customers reduce their other costs. *Value-adding companies* have figured out a stronger value offering or benefit bundle to win the buyer's preference. They can offer one or more of the following benefits to win the customer's business:

- Customization
- More convenience
- Faster service
- More and/or better service
- Coaching, training, or consulting
- An extraordinary guarantee
- Useful hardware and software tools
- A membership benefits program

Customize the Company's Products and Services

A company practices "customer intimacy" when it can customize its offering to a particular customer's requirements. In Burger King's battle with McDonald's, Burger King used the positioning "Have It Your Way," indicating that it would modify its standard offering to the customer's taste. McDonald's, on the other hand, wanted its customer to "Have It McDonald's Way." Burger King invited customers to ask for a variation and see which company would do it faster and better.

Some companies customize their products routinely. A specialty chemical company will formulate its chemicals to the customer's specifications. A packaging machine company will design special equipment to serve each customer's packaging requirements. Boeing will design the 747 features and interiors that each purchasing airline wants.

More recently, some companies have exploited the opportunity called *mass customization*.[3] Mass customization is the ability to prepare on a mass basis individually designed products, services, and communications. Thanks to flexible manufacturing and computer databases, companies can offer one-of-a-kind products to hundreds, thousands, or millions of their customers. Here are some examples:

Women's swimsuits. A Maryland swimwear manufacturer, Suited for Sun, has installed in several retail stores a computer/camera system that facilitates designing a custom-tailored swimsuit for each woman client.

Jeans. Levi's sales clerks can measure a person's exact dimensions, customize a pair of jeans, and deliver it in two days, at the normal cost plus $15. The customer can order additional jeans without again visiting a store.

Bicycles. The National Bicycle Industrial Company of Japan manufactures custom-made bikes fitted to the preferences and anatomies of individual buyers. The factory can produce any of 11,231,862 variations of eighteen bicycle models in 199 color patterns.

Custom music tapes. Personics allows music buyers to customize a personal audiotape by choosing from more than 5,000 songs.

Seeding equipment. John Deere's Moline, Illinois, plant manufactures seeders that can be configured in more than 2 million versions to customer specifications. The seeders are produced one at a time, in any sequence, on a single production line.

Medical supplies. Becton-Dickinson, a major medical supplier, offers to its hospital customers a great number of options: custom-designed labeling, bulk or individual packaging, customized quality control, customized computer software, and customized billing.

Not only can companies offer customized products and services, but they can also customize their communications. We mentioned earlier that Mars sends a birthday card to individual cats! "Dear Felix. Congratulations on your second birthday. We are including special coupons for buying appropriate food for this age in your life." Felix's cat-owning family is surprised, amused, and delighted by the personal gesture and increases its preference for Mars cat food.

More Customer Convenience

Sellers have a better chance of attracting and satisfying customers when the customers find it easy to reach the sellers, to see their products, and to place orders. Accordingly, sellers establish extensive market coverage, set up showrooms, distribute catalogs, and set up a Web page. Recently, BMW put a feature on its Web Page that permits a prospect to design his own BMW, learn when it will be ready, and even pay for it.

One aspect of convenience is offering customers more hours for contact. Banks used to be open from nine to three and closed all weekend. Banks followed the 3-6-3 rule: borrow money at 3 percent, loan it out at 6 percent, and get to the golf course by 3 P.M. Today one of the fastest growing banks in England is First Direct, whose customers can transact banking business over the phone seven days a week, twenty-four hours a day. That is also true of such direct PC marketers as Dell and Gateway.

Even when a company doesn't go to 7/24, it may gain by offering longer hours than competitors. Barnes & Noble, the giant bookseller, keeps its stores open from 9 A.M. to 11 P.M. seven days a week. Many visitors come to browse, have coffee, hear authors, and meet friends. Their bookstores have become community centers.

The importance of providing convenience is no better illustrated than by the rise of *convenience food stores*. The 7-Eleven convenience stores were so named because they opened at 7 A.M. and closed at 11 P.M., thus offering shoppers convenient hours for buying milk, drinks, pastries, or other standard food items.

Faster Service

Some companies have positioned themselves as "speed leaders," serving those customers who want faster service. Wells Fargo Banks posted a sign in its branches; "Five dollars or five minutes," which offered to credit a customer's account with five dollars if he or she spent more than five minutes waiting in line. The whole fast food industry grew on the promise that it could provide a reasonably tasty and inexpensive meal in the shortest amount of time. The Minute Man stores in Europe will fix shoes, make keys, and offer a number of other conveniences quickly. Today one can have film developed in an hour, and some outlets are now promising film development in thirty minutes. Pearle Vision offers to make a new pair of glasses in one hour. One can order and receive a new mattress from Dial-a-Mattress or a new bed from Beds-to-Go within a few hours.

Service marketers can distinguish themselves by offering faster service. Citibank uses a software program and can tell mortgage applicants fifteen minutes after receiving their information whether the bank can extend a mortgage. The norm in the past was thirty days! Progressive Insurance dispatches a Ford Explorer equipped with a PC, modem, printer, and fax to an accident scene involving one of its insured clients to assess damages, issue a check, and arrange for a loaner car on the spot. The German company Krone, the world leader in bottle labeling machines, offers one of the fastest repair services in the world. According to Hermann Kronseder:

> At all times, we deploy 250 service and installation technicians around the world. Sometimes they cannot come home for weeks and months. . . . We store the data for each machine, totaling 20,000, in our central computer. These data can be made available at every one of our locations in the world within half a minute. The data are fed directly into the numerically controlled machines, and the spare parts are manufactured immediately. . . . Parts which are ordered before seven A.M. usually are sent in the afternoon, by truck, to Frankfurt Airport; from there they are airfreighted the same evening to their country of destination. At the same time, our subsidiary receives the flight and freight numbers so that the shipment can be cleared through customs without delay.[4]

More and/or Better Service(s)

The distinction between manufacturing businesses and service businesses is overdone. All businesses must be service businesses. In the first place, the customer who buys a product is actually buying an expected service from the product. A product delivers a service: a car delivers transportation; a bar of soap delivers cleanliness; a textbook delivers information and education.

In the second place, many manufacturers need to deliver service along with their product. Caterpillar promises to repair its equipment anywhere in the world within twenty-four hours. In fact, Caterpillar makes 60 percent of its profit by selling aftermarket parts and service.

In the third place, manufacturing companies include a lot of service workers: scientists, designers, engineers, market researchers, accountants, transportation specialists, senior and middle managers, and so on. The vast majority of employees in an auto company are service workers, not production workers.

Given that all companies are in the service business, how can a company differentiate its service mix and quality to achieve service leadership in its industry? Some companies have a reputation for legendary service. (A company can also become legendary for bad service.) Four Season Hotels and Nordstrom department stores have been mentioned elsewhere, but here are some others:

USAA Insurance. USAA is one of the most profitable American insurance companies. It sells insurance and banking services only to military people and their families, and it has no insurance agents who knock on doors. All insurance is sold through telemarketing. USAA keeps complete records on each customer. When a customer phones day or night, seven days a week, the customer's phone number is recognized immediately through caller ID and the customer's record is brought up on the telemarketer's screen. The telemarketer may even ask the caller how a family member is doing, did the son buy a car, and so on, much to the customer's surprise and delight. The telemarketer knowledgeably answers the caller's questions and gives insurance quotes typically much lower than competitors. Customers feel that USAA is one of the best service providers in their experience.

Saks Department Store. Saks, an upscale department store, runs a personal shopping service. A client can call for an appointment, arrive at the store, and enter a suite with sofas, desks, and telephones. She will be served a beverage and a personal shopper will bring clothes to her. Or Saks can send clothes to her home. If a storewide sale is scheduled, she will be notified. If a sale occurred after her purchase, she will receive a refund. Usually Saks sends a surprise gift each year to customers who spend over a certain amount of money. All these service steps build loyal Saks shoppers, customers who could easily buy their clothes elsewhere.

Amil Health Insurance Company. Amil, a Brazilian health insurance company, was started by four medical doctors. Today it is not only the leading health insurance company in Brazil but growing by 18 percent a month in Argentina and invading Austin, Texas, and Las Vegas, Nevada. Amil thinks of itself as a wellness company, not a sickness insurer. It is into "total care." Naturally, if an insurance company helps people stay well, they place fewer medical claims, and the health insurance company makes more money. Amil is outstanding at developing a high level of service and "customer delights":

- Amil can be phoned twenty-four hours a day, seven days a week and will give medical advice and assistance over the phone. It will do so even for nonmembers, causing many nonmembers to switch their insurance to Amil. The telephone number is the best-known phone number in Brazil and is part of every advertisement.
- Amil parks its ambulances at all big sporting events and will give emergency ambulance service to anyone who takes ill, whether or not he or she is a member. The presence of the ambulance further advertises the company. The ambulance itself is designed to be used as a small operating room if necessary.
- Amil owns helicopters and will fly them to pick up insured members who are stranded in remote locations and in need of emergency service.
- For an extra $25 a month, Amil will cover its members' costs who need an operation in another country.
- Amil operates a chain of pharmacies that sells drugs at 50 percent less to Amil members
- Amil classifies its members in the database by illness tendencies (smoking, heart disease, breast cancer, etc.) and encourages members to attend special educational programs to help them get better.
- Although Amil charges more for its health insurance, people gladly join because of Amil's superior service and caring.

HSM MANAGEMENT SEMINARS. Here is another world-class Brazilian service company. HSM invites leading management gurus (e.g., Peter Drucker, Tom Peters, Alvin Toffler) to come to Brazil and Argentina. As their sponsor, HSM delivers one of the highest-quality management seminar experiences in the world. HSM has the name of practically every middle and senior business person in the two countries and draws an average of 800 to 1,200 managers who pay $700 to attend the day-long seminar. During the seminar day, the following things take place:

- Good signage appears on the streets leading to the convention center welcoming cars; when the cars leave at the end of the day, the signage thanks the attendees for coming.
- The lobby of the convention center is filled with many exhibitors and sponsors, so there is a trade show atmosphere.
- The attendees can make free local phone calls and one free long-distance call.
- HSM has added additional cushions to all seats, making them more comfortable.
- Attendees are offered a choice of workbook for left- or right-handed people. Each notebook contains post-it notes and a pen.
- Attendees arriving late are given a special briefing during the first break summarizing what the speaker had said.
- During the seminar break, the latest currency results are flashed on a screen, because attendees are interested in the fluctuating value of their currency.
- Just before the resumption of the seminar following lunch, a famous comedian entertains the participants for twenty minutes.
- Everyone attending the seminar receives free medical insurance for the day, and HSM has arranged with Amil to keep an Amil ambulance stationed outside just in case someone becomes seriously ill.
- All the participants receive the choice of a man or woman's gift upon leaving the seminar.

In addition, HSM has developed a club for managers who have attended six or more programs. They receive red-carpet treatment when arriving at the seminar, a gold-lettered notebook, 10 percent discounts at certain stores, invitations to special events once a year, mailed articles of interest, personally autographed books from the speakers, and a free seminar for every ten seminars attended.

HSM leaves little doubt that it is the most customer-delighting seminar firm in the world. Its speakers all testify that they have never been better treated by any other sponsor. The speakers are set up in executive suites, are picked up and dropped off at the airport, are helped in designing a relevant seminar, can make free international phone calls, and, in general, enjoy superior hospitality from HSM.

Customer Training and/or Coaching

Smart companies will help their customers get maximum use value out of their offerings. They will seek to understand their customer's business. In some cases they know the customer's business better than the customer, partly as a result of working with similar customers. GE Plastics sends productivity teams to help customers use a "commodity" product and even shows them how to use less of it. Staples trains its customers on how to purchase office supplies better and even sets up electronic systems for ordering. Ceridian coaches its customers on how to use its special payroll software more effectively. Otis Elevator offers a remote elevator monitoring service so that it can anticipate imminent customer problems.[5]

One of IBM's chief competitive advantages in its mainframe business is the extensive training it offers customers who purchase its large computers. In the early days customers needed extensive help in learning and using computers. Later on, company data processing departments developed internal experts and needed IBM's services somewhat less. Today IBM is offering to run those departments at a cost saving to companies.

In general, the company offering the best training and coaching program can usually win. Citibank wants its commercial bankers to think of themselves as business consultants, not loan officers. Instead of just saying yes or no to a loan applicant, the Citibank officer will make suggestions on how the customer might improve his operation so that a loan might be more justified. Citibank hires bankers who have a broad business education, not just a training in finance.

Extraordinary Guarantee

Companies whose products perform much better than their competitors' should draw attention to the fact by offering an *extraordinary guarantee* that their competitors could not match.[6] Hampton Inn, one of the fastest-growing motel chains, attributes much of its success to its extraordinary guarantee, namely, if the guest is unhappy, the room is free. The guest simply has to say after the first night that he is dissatisfied— the mattress is too soft, the room was noisy—and he checks out without paying. Now if Hampton Inn was poorly run, a large number of guests would not pay and the motel chain would go bankrupt. But Hampton Inn is run with great service and care on the part of employees, who incidentally share in any money left over in a fund used to cover nonpaying guests. So the employees have a stake in serving the guests especially well. Hampton Inn reports that the percentage of guests who choose not to pay is minuscule when compared with the growth in the number of guests choosing Hampton Inn.

BBBK is a pest control firm that charges five times the price competitors charge, based on an extraordinary guarantee. When hired by a hotel, restaurant, or other establishment to eliminate a pest problem, BBBK gives the following guarantee:

- It will pay the cost of another pest control firm if BBBK fails to eliminate the pests.
- It will pay for any closing costs if the city insists on closing the establishment.
- It will pay for any guests who were injured in some way as a result of the pests.

Hotels and restaurants have too much to lose to complain about paying more for the services of hiring an expert pest control firm such as BBBK.

Saturn, the new car company started by General Motors, initiated an extraordinary guarantee never before offered by an automobile company. The new buyer could return the car within thirty days if not satisfied and get his money back! In a relatively mature market, Saturn was able to grow faster than most car companies, thanks partly to the confidence generated by the guarantee and other design elements in its service program. So loyal have its customers been that when Saturn celebrated its fifth anniversary as a company at its Spring Hill, Tennessee, factory and invited all Saturn owners to enjoy a weekend party, 44,000 owners and their families showed up, not the 2,000 that Saturn expected.

Useful Hardware and Software Tools for Customers

A company can build a stronger relationship with its customers by offering useful tools to run their businesses better. Federal Express gives its larger customers a tool called Powership, consisting of a computer, printer, and software. With Powership, the customers can print labels, dispatch and track packages, calculate costs, and bill their own customers. Similarly McKesson, the drug wholesaler, supplies its pharmacies with a computer and software for easy ordering.

A Membership Benefit Program

An effective way to win, keep, and grow customers is by rewarding them for being customers. Examples are airline frequent flyer programs and such membership groups as HOG (Harley Owners Group), which presents an attractive set of benefits to Harley motorcycle owners.

We can distinguish four types of membership programs that a company can create.

LEVEL 1: FREQUENT CUSTOMER AWARD PROGRAMS. In the 1960s a popular program involved supermarkets and other stores giving S&H stamps in proportion to customer purchases. Customers would paste the stamps in booklets and then turn the books in for gifts. When too many stores began to give away S&H stamps, store owners rebelled and the programs died.

In the 1980s American Airlines introduced its Advantage Program, which offered points that could be used to obtain free flights or upgrades. Because this program created a strong customer preference for American Airlines, the other airlines countered by introducing their own *frequency award programs*. Soon travelers would join several airline programs and accumulate points on whichever airline they chose, thus blunting the loyalty-building factor. Still, some airlines run their programs better than others and manage to attract more usage.

Other service companies began to offer frequency award programs, starting with car rental companies, later hotels, and more recently supermarkets. At a later stage, various program sponsors would invite other sponsors: American Airlines passengers would receive discount coupons if they would use Hertz Car Rental or stay at a Hilton hotel.

Each company would compete by expanding its set of benefits. For example, Sheraton Hotel sponsors ITT Sheraton Club International Gold, where membership provides a special set of benefits. By enrolling for $50 a year, the benefits include automatic room upgrades, guaranteed 4 P.M. late checkout, free travel awards, free night awards, free flight awards, and exclusive gold member events and discounts. The American Express Platinum card, for which the cardholder pays $300 a year, includes the following benefits: medical assistance when traveling, twenty-four-hour legal assistance, extra services at leading hotels, access to airline lounges, insurance for lost goods, and the ability to cash checks up to $10,000.

A few years ago Tesco, a leading British supermarket, launched a national "loyalty card" called Clubcard. Today more than 6 million British consumers are cardholders. Upon reaching the checkout counter, cardholders put their plastic cards into a machine and receive points every time they spend over a minimum amount. The points are added up each quarter, and money-off vouchers are sent to the shopper's home. Shopping at Tesco with the Clubcard saves an estimated 1 percent on the customer's shopping bills. Tesco feels that it has not only passed up its main competitor, Sainsbury, in market share but has also built a valuable customer database. Tesco can send announcements or money-saving coupons to individual customers who buy in certain categories. Sainsbury resisted introducing its own card but appears to be relenting.

Superquinn, the leading supermarket chain in Dublin, has a 70 percent market share. Run by an extremely creative marketer, Fergal Quinn, the stores offer membership cards to customers. Quinn's stores feature several "customer astonishment activities," including:

- Children receive balloons when they enter the store and can push a miniature shopping cart. There is also a child care center in each store.
- Customers can join the chain's Superclub (two-thirds of Dublin households have joined). The members receive one point for every 1 U.K. pound spent. The store awards bonus points for shopping on certain days or at certain times. A sixty-four-page redemption catalog offering a choice of gifts, toys, household items, etc., is mailed to members. There is a weekly lottery with prizes for cardholders. Every time there is a winner, a red light flashes in the store. Members are invited to special store events like cheese, wine, and food tastings.
- The Superclub card, when it is inserted in a machine at the cash register, reveals the person's name, making it possible for the clerk to greet the person by name. On the occasion of the customer's birthday (indicated on the card), the store's bakery immediately writes out the customer's name on a birthday cake and presents it to the customer upon exiting.

- Each time a customer reports a fault (such as a badly packed grocery bag or a dented can), the customer receives 200 points, thus turning customers into "quality control inspectors."
- Quinn has enlisted eighteen corporate sponsors (Texaco, National Irish Bank, UCI Cinemas, etc.), who also award points on the Super-Quinn card for sales at their establishments.

Other companies have created interesting frequency award programs. Ono-matic, an Australian company, provides detergents to households on a continuous replenishment program. The households collect points that the user can turn in for gifts, even a free washing machine if enough points are accumulated. General Motors issued its own credit card; customer charges on it earn points toward a deep discount on the purchase of a General Motors car.

Still not everyone feels that frequency award programs are the answer to building customer loyalty. Critics assert that when most competitors offer competing programs, customer loyalty is weakened. As loyalty programs add more benefits, it drains the margins for all players. Loyalty programs also tend to attract price-conscious buyers, whom a company is least likely to retain. Finally, a loyalty scheme will not compensate for offerings where the fundamentals are not right—such as poor products or service. The danger facing a company is that it will take its "loyal" customers for granted because of the scheme and fail to provide high and improving levels of performance.

LEVEL 2: MEMBERSHIP CLUB WITH A BENEFIT PACKAGE. Many frequency award programs call themselves membership programs but are really limited to offering points for purchases. Other companies offer a broader membership program with a rich set of benefits. Here are some leading examples:

Harley-Davidson: Buyers of a Harley-Davidson motorcycle receive a one-year free membership to the Harley Owners Group (HOG), renewable each year for $40, or for life for $350. Its 360,000 members—including blue-collar workers and millionaires—receive the following:

- An updated membership manual containing benefit information
- A forty-page bimonthly magazine, *Hog Tales*
- Free copies of *The Enthusiast* magazine about motorcycles
- A specially designed pin and patch

- The *HOG Touring Handbook*
- A mileage award program with twelve levels of attainment
- A contest involving the *ABCs of Touring*
- A *Fly & Ride* program to rent Harley-Davidson motorcycles throughout the world
- Local chapter invitations to monthly meetings, organized rides, and fundraising activities
- A monthly magazine with articles on taking care of a motorcycle and on the HOG lifestyle
- Lower rates on accident and life insurance

Not surprisingly, Harley-Davidson has succeeded in building a *brand community*, a group of customers who love Harley products and like to meet each other. To serve the community, Harley has extended its brand name to cover leather jackets, sunglasses, beer, and cigarettes.

Other companies have also built brand communities. Apple Computer has many loyal users who meet in user groups to exchange information and sociability. Saturn, the car company, has built a brand community. BMW and Porsche create opportunities for owner "get-togethers." Lexus has also pursued this strategy by arranging a number of "customer delights." Lexus owners in Sydney, Australia, when they drive up to the famous Sydney Opera, find a Lexus person who parks their car and who has arranged alcoholic refreshments waiting for them. Mercedes car owners have to park their own cars and buy their own drinks. And Lexus car owners in Germany receive each year a bottle of the best French wine and invitations to the famous Salzburg Festival.

Shiseido Club: The Japanese company Shiseido, one of the world's leading cosmetics companies, sponsors the Shiseido club, which now enrolls 10 million Japanese women members. For their $30 annual fee, members receive:

- A monthly magazine with articles appealing to women
- Discounts at selected theaters, hotels, and retailers
- Invitations to special programs such as speakers' presentations and concerts
- An affinity Visa card

Nintendo: This Japanese video game company has enrolled more than 2 million members in its Nintendo Club. For $16 a year, members receive a monthly magazine, *Nintendo Power*, and access to a "game counselor" whom kids and adults can phone with questions or problems.

Lladro: This Spanish maker of fine porcelain figurines sponsors a "Collectors' Society." For an annual membership fee of $35, members receive a free subscription to a quarterly magazine, a bisque plaque, free enrollment in the Lladro Museum of New York, and member-only tours to visit the company and the Lladro family in Valencia, Spain.

Companies interested in launching a membership program must think carefully about the benefits to offer, the cost of offering these benefits, the annual membership fee, the minimum number of members needed, and the cost of possibly having to terminate the program. Done well, a club can be a powerful loyalizing tool; done poorly, it could result in a heavy cost and embarrassment.

LEVEL 3: OFFERING A VIP PROGRAM TO THE COMPANY'S MOST VALUABLE CUSTOMERS. Although all customers are important, some are more important than others. Therefore companies need to identify their most valuable customers (MVCs). And the MVCs deserve very important person (VIP) treatment.

Elite department stores like Saks and Neiman Marcus welcome women as members who have spent more than, say, $3,000 a year. These women receive special invitations to programs and receive a gift each year.

There is a bank in Miami serving the Cuban community whose wealthiest customers don't stand in line for service but enter a separate suite where there is coffee, fruit, and personal service. They receive invitations to special seminars and sports events. The bank doesn't even require such a customer to visit the bank. It will send someone to his or her home to pick up a deposit or deliver cash.

LEVEL 4: ESTABLISHING A SPECIAL CUSTOMER RECOGNITION PROGRAM. Some companies will single out certain customers for special recognition, even honoring them in a formal ceremony. Arthur Andersen established a program in several cities to select and honor the local Entrepreneur of the Year. Andersen invites its clients in each city to the annual event. Until the client's name is announced, no one knows who will be selected.

Questions to Consider

Companies normally complain that they and their competitors are getting more alike and that it is difficult to maintain differentiation. That kind of convergence is part of a hypercompetitive world economy where any competitive advantage is soon copied. But as we have tried to show, a company that has failed to differentiate has failed to exercise its imagination fully, for there are many ways to add distinctive value and benefits to the company's customers. The company can lower its price, help the customer reduce his other costs, or add a whole array of positive benefits. While no value-added package lasts forever, alert companies will continuously review the possibilities and invest in new benefits that their customers will value.

Here are some questions for your business to consider.

1. Does your business enjoy lower costs than your competitors? If yes, have you turned this advantage into aggressive price cutting? If not, why not?
2. In what ways have you been able to help your customers reduce their ordering, inventory, processing, and administrative costs? Do you see further opportunities? How do you train your engineers and salespeople to recognize these cost-saving opportunities for customers?
3. How does your company rate with regard to offering each of the following value-adds: Customization? More convenience? Faster service? More and/or better service? Coaching, training, or consulting? An extraordinary guarantee? Useful hardware and software tools? A membership benefits program? Can one or more of these benefits be added to gain a competitive advantage?

PART THREE

ADMINISTRATIVE MARKETING

9

Planning and Organizing
for More Effective Marketing

Visions demand a strategy, strategy requires a plan.—*Anonymous*

You need battle plans, not business plans.—*Anonymous*

The sales department isn't the whole company, but the whole company better be the sales department.—*Anonymous*

We don't have a Marketing Department; we have a Customer Department. And we don't have a Personnel Department; we have a People Department.—*Herb Kelleher, CEO of Southwest Airlines*

A BUSINESS CAN BE very good at *strategic* and *tactical marketing* (the first two parts of the book) and yet fail if it is not also good at *administrative marketing*. Administrative marketing means having the capacity to prepare and carry out sound marketing plans. All the strategies and tactics must be integrated in a marketing plan that can be effectively executed by the marketing organization. Here we need to look at marketing planning and marketing organization.

Marketing Plans and the Marketing Planning Process

Someone said, "If you fail to plan, you are planning to fail." Granted, marketing planning is not much fun. It takes time away from doing.

One brand manager complained: "I am spending more time preparing plans than achieving them." James Brian Quinn complained that "a good deal of corporate planning . . . is like a ritual rain dance. It has no effect on the weather that follows." Are conditions changing so fast today that planning is presumptuous and futile?

Yet plan we must. The process of planning may be more important than the plans that emerge. The planning occasion requires managers to schedule "thinking time." Managers must think about what has happened, what is happening, and what might happen. Managers must set goals and get agreement. The goals must be communicated to everyone. Progress toward the goals must be measured. Corrective actions must be taken when the goals are not being achieved. Thus planning turns out to be an intrinsic part of good management.

Here we shall consider three planning issues:

- What types of marketing plans should a company develop?
- What should a marketing plan contain?
- How can we tell if the marketing plan is a good one and deserves the requested funds, or whether it should be modified?

What Types of Marketing Plans Should a Company Develop?

A company needs to prepare marketing plans for each major arena of marketing action. Specifically, there are six species of marketing plans:

- **Brand marketing plans.** Companies need to prepare brand marketing plans. Each Procter & Gamble detergent brand manager prepares a strategic and annual marketing plan each year.
- **Product category marketing plans.** Before the detergent brand managers prepare their separate brand marketing plans, the detergent category managers will set some assumptions, forecasts, and goals to drive the separate brand planning. After the brand plans are prepared and accepted, they are aggregated into the overall product category plan.
- **New product plans.** Each new product or brand requires a detailed development and launch plan. The product concept will have to be defined, refined, and tested, along with later prototypes. The launch phase will require a very detailed set of activities.
- **Market segment plans.** If the product or brand is sold to separate

market segments, then a plan would be prepared for each segment. IBM sells in several market segments—banking, insurance, hotels, air travel—and each IBM segment manager plans the products and services to offer to his or her segment.

- **Geographical market plans.** Marketing plans will be prepared for each country, region, city, and even neighborhood.
- **Customer plans.** National account managers will prepare separate plans for each valued customer.

In each case, really two plans are needed, a long-term strategic plan and an annual plan. The long-term strategic plan will cover a specific time horizon. It could be twenty years for public utilities or three years for high-tech industries. The strategic plan considers the forces driving the market, different scenarios that might take place, the company's hoped-for position in that future market, and the steps for getting there. The strategic plan provides the context for fleshing out the annual plan. But each year management must review and possibly revise the strategic plan.

All these plans must be synchronized. They cannot be written independently of each other. Thus market segment managers need information about product plans and area plans before they can recommend offerings and strategies for their specific segments.

Clearly management must invest a great deal of time in preparing plans. Therefore a reasonable and well-understood planning format should be designed that facilitates planning.

What Should a Marketing Plan Contain?

Marketing plans should be simple and to the point. Some CEOs want only a one-page plan! The CEO wants to know the goals, strategy, and cost to carry out the plan. That does not require a 200-page document loaded with numbers, text, diagrams, and ads that no one reads and that becomes obsolete before it is printed.

At a minimum, every marketing plan should contain the following sections:

- Situation analysis
- Marketing objectives and goals
- Marketing strategy
- Marketing action plan
- Marketing controls

We shall illustrate these sections with respect to designing the brand or product plan, although practically everything will apply to market segment and geographical plans as well.

Situation Analysis

The situation analysis includes four components:

- A description of the current situation
- A SWOT analysis (Strengths, Weaknesses, Opportunities and Threats)
- Main issues facing the business
- Main assumptions about the future

CURRENT SITUATION. The planning process begins with an objective assessment of the product's current situation. That will be portrayed by a statistical picture of the last (say) five years of the products sales, market share, prices, costs, and profits, along with the main competitors' performances. Major driving forces in the marketing environment will also be assessed.

SWOT ANALYSIS. Here the manager prepares two lists, an SW list describing the company and the product's main strengths and weaknesses, and an OT list describing the chief opportunities and threats. SW describes factors internal to the company; OT describes forces external to the company. An example of an SW list is shown in Exhibit 9–1.

The manager should begin with the OT list. What, indeed, are the attractive opportunities facing this firm? If he cannot list any, then one can question why he is managing the product. There is no such thing as a mature product without opportunities; there are only managers lacking in imagination. One company CEO expects every plan to contain at least five substantial opportunities, opportunities that promise a high return and a high probability of success.

Likewise, the plan should detail (say) five significant threats facing the business. A company that doesn't see any trouble ahead is headed for real trouble. The worst thing is for the company to be hit by threats that were not foreseen in the plan. The manager's list of five threats leaves a trail that testifies to his foresight in preparing proper contingencies.

The reason to examine the OT list first is that it provides clues as to which company and product strengths and weaknesses require attention. For example, if competitors have set up effective Internet web pages for selling their product and this company has not yet created its own web page, that is not only a weakness, but one requiring quick action. Every company must decide which strengths need to be further improved, and which weaknesses must be corrected, based on the looming opportunities and threats.

MAIN ISSUES FACING THE BUSINESS. Here the manager summarizes the business's main issues. Most CEOs want their managers to present an honest list of the problems and choices facing the business. After all, the CEO's job is to lend help where needed. Exhibit 9–2 presents a sample list of the issues facing one company.

MAIN ASSUMPTIONS. Here the manager brings together the main assumptions about the future. Exhibit 9–3 shows assumptions in one manager's plan.

Setting Objectives and Goals

At this point, the manager moves from analysis to decision-making. Given the current and forecast situation, what should the company aim for? The manager must address two components in this section of the plan.

- Objectives
- Goals

OBJECTIVES. The manager needs to set the broad objectives to be achieved in the coming period. Among them might be:

- increase the margin
- increase the market share
- increase customer satisfaction

The chosen objectives must be feasible and internally compatible. Otherwise the objectives will fail to provide much help in shaping strategy.

GOALS. The objectives must be recast in terms of measurable goals if they are to provide guidance and control. A goal requires stating a *magnitude* and a *target date of achievement*. Thus the objective "increase the market share" can be turned into the goal "move market share from 20 percent to 25 percent by the end of the current fiscal year."

The manager must heed the goals set by senior management. For example, a corporation may want to increase its return on equity from 10 percent to 12 percent, and making further calculations, this might require this product to increase its sales by 10 percent and profits by at least 6 percent.

EXHIBIT 9–1

Checklist for Performing Strengths/Weaknesses Analysis

Marketing

	Performance					Importance		
	Major Strength	Minor Strength	Neutral	Minor Weakness	Major Weakness	Hi	Med	Low
1. Company reputation	—	—	—	—	—	—	—	—
2. Market share	—	—	—	—	—	—	—	—
3. Product quality	—	—	—	—	—	—	—	—
4. Service quality	—	—	—	—	—	—	—	—
5. Pricing effectiveness	—	—	—	—	—	—	—	—
6. Distribution effectiveness	—	—	—	—	—	—	—	—
7. Promotion effectiveness	—	—	—	—	—	—	—	—
8. Sales force effectiveness	—	—	—	—	—	—	—	—
9. Innovation effectiveness	—	—	—	—	—	—	—	—
10. Geographical coverage	—	—	—	—	—	—	—	—

Finance

11. Cost/availability of capital _____ | _____ | _____
12. Cash flow _____ | _____ | _____
13. Financial stability _____ | _____ | _____

Manufacturing

14. Facilities _____ | _____ | _____
15. Economies of scale _____ | _____ | _____
16. Capacity _____ | _____ | _____
17. Able, dedicated work force _____ | _____ | _____
18. Ability to produce on time _____ | _____ | _____
19. Technical manufacturing skill _____ | _____ | _____

Organization

20. Visionary capable leadership _____ | _____ | _____
21. Dedicated employees _____ | _____ | _____
22. Entrepreneurial orientation _____ | _____ | _____
23. Flexible/responsive _____ | _____ | _____

Source: Philip Kotler, *Marketing Management*, 9th ed. (Upper Saddle River, N.J.: Prentice-Hall, 1997), p. 83.

EXHIBIT 9–2

Issues Facing One Company

1. Our main competitor's costs are 15 percent lower than ours. How can we reduce the cost gap?

2. Our current competitive advantage has evaporated. What new competitive advantage can we pursue? Speed? Features? Guarantees?

3. We have a better customer database than our competitor, but it is very costly to maintain and we are not using it fully. How can we get more value out of our customer database?

4. Our dealers are asking for more allowances, which would leave us very little. Is it time to consider dropping our dealers and selling direct to the customers?

5. We are experiencing a high level of customer turnover. What policies should we install to increase customer satisfaction and retention?

EXHIBIT 9–3

Main Assumptions Underlying the Business Plan

1. The economic climate will remain approximately the same. Unemployment will remain at 6 percent and inflation at 2 percent. Consumer real purchasing power will rise by about 1 percent.

2. Unit sales in our market will increase 5 percent this year.

3. Our current market share of 20 percent can be increased to 25 percent.

4. Competitors will cut their prices by 2 percent, and we will match them.

5. Our main competitor will probably launch a frequency award program, the first in our industry. We have a plan ready to match his if he makes the move.

6. No new legislation will be passed this year that will help or hurt our industry.

Choosing the Strategy

The manager now hammers out a strategy to achieve the company's goals. The strategy is describable along six lines:

- The target market
- The core positioning
- The price positioning
- The total value proposition
- The distribution strategy
- The communication strategy

THE TARGET MARKET (TM). Managers do not always define the target market carefully. We still find managers who say their TM is "everybody." Maybe Coca Cola can say that, but even they do not include infants and can recognize that certain adult groups don't or won't drink Coca Cola. As another example, the great retailer Sears used to think everyone was their target market since everyone would visit a Sears store occasionally. But there is a vast difference in visiting rates to Sears between working-class families and professional families.

In specifying the target market, the manager should distinguish between primary, secondary, and tertiary levels of the target market. The primary TM comprises buyers who are highly ready, able, and willing to buy. The firm's main challenge is to identify and reach the primary TM. The secondary TM may be able to buy but is less ready and willing. The tertiary TM may not be able to buy now but should be monitored for a possible growing readiness to buy.

Sometimes a company can be extremely specific about its target market, down to the names of individual prospects and customers. Grohmann Engineering, a German maker of machines for assembling electronic products, drew up a list of thirty companies that it sought as long-term customers. By patiently pursuing them, Grohmann eventually won many of them as customers.

The TM's characteristics should be described in the plan. In the case of consumer products, the description would include demographic characteristics (age, gender, income, education, location) and relevant psychographics (attitudes, interests, opinions). It would also be useful to specify the TM's media and store preferences and habits. Finally, the description should include where members of the target market cluster residentially.

For business target markets, the TM description should specify the industries, size of companies, product applications, and locations the company aims to reach with its products. The business TM can be further defined in terms of business purchase motivations (e.g., price, quality, service), firms that buy on a centralized vs. decentralized basis, and other characteristics.[1]

CORE POSITIONING. A company's offering should center on a core idea or benefit. Volvo centers its offerings on safety; IBM claims to offer the best service. Other companies may center on benefits like best quality, best performance, most reliable, most durable, safest, fastest, best value for the money, least expensive, most prestigious, best designed or styled, or easiest to use.

Although normally a brand positions on one core benefit, some brands will advertise two or three benefits that together make up its core positioning.

PRICE POSITIONING. The firm's strategy also includes charging a certain price in relation to its core benefit. The company should choose one of the following price/performance positionings: More for More, More for the Same, The Same for Less, Less for Much Less, More for Less (see pp. 59–61).

TOTAL VALUE PROPOSITION. The plan should state the firm's total value proposition. It should be a persuasive answer to the buyer's question: "Why should I buy from you?" Therefore it should describe the core benefit and all the other features and benefits, and why, given the price, the offering provides superior total value to the customer. A consumer should perceive superior satisfaction; a business should perceive superior profitability.

DISTRIBUTION STRATEGY. This section describes the business's distribution strategy for reaching its target market. In considering the next few years, a bank CEO may decide to continue to build branches and add ATMs (automatic teller machines) or add direct home banking services using the telephone or computer.

COMMUNICATION STRATEGY. Here the manager sets the product's communication strategy. Specifically, how much money should be allocated to advertising, sales promotion, public relations, sales force, and direct marketing? For each tool, what is the strategic objective? For example, is the advertising geared to building the company image or to selling specific products; in the latter case, should the advertising be largely rational or emotional in its appeal?

The manager should review the plan and make sure there is consistency among the chosen target market, the core positioning, the price positioning, the value proposition, the distribution strategy, and the communication strategy.

Action Plan

The manager must now translate the goals and strategies into concrete actions to take place in calendar time. All plans must "degenerate" into work. That means setting the dates for the company's advertising campaigns, sales promotions, trade show participations, and new product launches. It also means assigning individuals to tasks and monitoring performance. It means communicating the action plans to all the important players so they know what to expect and when to expect it.

Control

The plan must include a mechanism for reviewing whether or not the plan's actions are accomplishing the plan's goals. Plans typically include monthly or quarterly benchmarks against which performance can be measured. When the goals are not being reached, the manager must take corrective steps to change some actions, strategies, target markets(s), or subgoals. For example, managers will often cancel planned advertising in the last quarter when the profit target is not being met. The manager might assume that advertising doesn't have much effect in the short run and therefore he can save money and increase current period earnings. This, of course, can lead to long-run suboptimization, but it is a common practice.

Judging Whether the Marketing Plan Is Sound

How can the company tell whether a particular marketing plan deserves the requested funds or if it must first be modified? Senior management people will have to review and approve a lot of plans submitted by company divisions, businesses, product lines, and brands. How can they assess plans

EXHIBIT 9–4

What Questions Should a Senior Manager Ask About
a Business Plan?

---

1. Does the plan list some exciting new opportunities? Has it also considered major threats?

2. Is the plan clear in defining target market segments and their relative potential?

3. Will the customers in each target segment see our offering as superior?

4. Do the strategies seem coherent? Are the right tools being used?

5. What is the probability that the plan will achieve its stated objectives?

6. What would the manager eliminate if we gave him only 80 percent of his request?

7. What would the manager do in addition if we gave him 120 percent of his request?

---

prepared by subordinates who have more knowledge of each business than they have and decide which plans to approve?

One way to facilitate the task is to make sure that all plans use a common planning framework so that cross-comparisons can be made. The company should create a computer-based planning software program to be used throughout the company. The plan format would require managers to describe the chief components that belong in a marketing plan.

Beyond this, senior managers can use the list of questions in Exhibit 9–4. When the plan fails on a number of questions, the plan should be sent back and modified. Over time, more plans will satisfy the criteria and will need less modification.

Building an Effective Marketing Organization

It is hard to believe that there was a time when companies didn't have *marketing departments*. They had *sales departments*, of course. But they didn't have product managers, brand managers, key account managers, market segment managers, customer service managers, and an assortment of other job positions found in today's marketing departments.

The fact is that marketing began as an appendage to the sales department of companies. Salespeople needed some formal market research; hence the need for a *market researcher*. Salespeople also wanted some advertising; hence the need for an *advertising manager*. Someone needed to dream up eye-catching promotions—hence the need for a *sales promotion* manager.

Even then, those were single appointments. Most of the work of market research, advertising, and promotion was contracted out to market research firms, advertising agencies, and sales promotion agencies.

The Current Proliferation of Marketing Jobs

What, then, gave such a boost to the development of marketing departments, that it reached the point where, ironically, the sales department in some cases became an appendage to the marketing department?

Briefly, it was the growing size and complexity of Big Business. We'll take the example of Procter & Gamble. As a company producing scores of mass consumer products—detergents, toothpaste, cosmetics, coffee, baking ingredients, etc.—P&G inevitably had to appoint *product managers*. Product managers were responsible for charting the course of their products.

Within one of P&G's product categories, soap, was found its original brand, Ivory. P&G began to recognize the value of creating second and third brands. It needed a *brand manager* to launch and manage each brand. Today, in detergents alone, P&G has nine brands and nine brand managers. In fact, each brand manager has at least two other people assisting full time, an associate and an assistant brand manager. That makes twenty-seven brand people running P&G's detergent business.

P&G sells its detergents to large retail chains. Each large chain is so important to P&G that it assigns a *customer account manager* to manage relations with each chain. The customer account managers need the assistance of various specialists in logistics, finance, and customer service to act as a *customer service team*.

But detergents are sold not only through supermarkets, mass merchandisers, and warehouse clubs; they are also sold to laundries, hospitals, and restaurants. The larger markets justify the appointment of *market segment managers*. So if there are six large markets for detergents, P&G might appoint six market segment managers, along with some assistants.

Of course, P&G products are sold throughout the world. This requires the appointment of *country managers* to supervise P&G's product range in each country. But each country manager needs to plan in the context of what is happening in neighboring countries. For the orderly development of the region, say, Western Europe or South America, it is necessary to appoint *regional managers* to whom the country managers report.

Other quaint things have occurred. One of P&G's strong shampoo brands is called Pert, and there is a brand manager taking care of this product. But the identical product is found in other countries under different names: Vidal Sassoon in France and Rejoy in Japan. Therefore it is necessary to have a brand manager for Vidal Sassoon in France who not only lays plans for the product but even thinks of other products that might be launched under the highly respected name of Vidal Sassoon. In fact, such a person is not managing a shampoo so much as a brand asset called Vidal Sassoon. He is called a *brand equity manager*.

Within a country, especially a large one, many consumer differences can be found. In the United States, Californians might like a stronger-tasting coffee or a spicier tomato soup than New Englanders. Companies have appointed a *market area manager* for California, given that it is larger than most countries. Companies have also appointed *ethnic group managers* because the tastes of Afro-Americans, Hispanics, or Asians may differ from mainstream tastes.

The other quaint thing is that two or more brands in the same product category may compete or cannibalize each other. *Category managers* are appointed to introduce order in the category.

Current Issues in Marketing Department Organization

Observers agree today that marketing departments need to be streamlined, if not simplified. Companies must deal with a number of thorny issues.

How can companies get their various marketing managers to start making sound long-term decisions? Marketers are often criticized for being short-run thinkers and doers. That is not surprising, because after all marketing people are responsible for forecasting a sales level and are rewarded for achieving it. There are lots of ways in which a brand manager, facing the possibility of not achieving planned sales, might take actions not in the best long-run interest of the brand. The brand manager, in the last quarter of the fiscal year, may switch funds from advertising to sales promotion because the latter has a much stronger sales impact in the short run. He might lower the price and cancel some R&D and new packaging work; all in the interest of meeting the current period's profit goals. The result might be that the brand is seen on sale too often, its packaging becomes out of date, and its quality declines.

Fortunately, a company can take several measures to counter the short-term perspective of brand managers. The brand manager's performance should be judged on several performance measures, not just current profit performance. Weight should be given to how much the brand manager is spending on R&D, consumer research, and competitor research. Some companies may require their brand managers to commission one new consumer research study each year or to launch a packaging redesign every three years. Another approach is to slow down the rate at which brand managers are promoted to new brands. A brand manager who runs a brand for only two years can milk it and look good. He will manage it differently if he is going to manage the brand for five years.

Should power reside in product managers or market managers? Many companies sell several products to several markets; therefore they appoint both product managers and market managers. AT&T, for example, has product managers for network, call waiting, call forwarding, and caller ID; it has market managers for residential, small business, large business, and national accounts. DuPont has product managers for nylon, dacron, and orlon; and market managers for men's wear, women's wear, industrial markets, and furniture.

Typically each product manager contacts each market manager whose market uses the product, and they estimate together how much of the product can be sold in that market at the planned price. The product manager then subtracts the cost of producing the total volume going to all the company's markets and arrives at a profit forecast. Too often, however, a market manager comes back later to the product manager and says that his market estimate has to be revised; for example, a competitor might have slashed the price. If the product manager refuses to lower his price in that market, then volume will drop; if he lowers the price, then his margin drops; in either case, the product manager will fail to achieve his planned profit. The question becomes where to place the power between product and market managers, especially since their interests may clash.

My opinion is that the company should place the power in the hands of the market managers. The company will do best in the long run if it gives the market what it wants. The company's aim should be to "own" a market. Product is more of a supply function, and product managers must serve the needs of the market as interpreted by the market managers. In a growing number of companies, the market manager may even buy supplies from an outside vendor if the terms are more favorable than buying from the company's own supply system.

This is part of the larger issue of *matrix management*. Matrix management exists when employees report to more than one boss. An example would be the French market manager of Vidal Sassoon shampoo, who is supposed to carry out certain strategies called for by the U.S. headquarters shampoo product manager but also must accede to the wishes of the French country manager, who may not want to devote that much effort to the shampoo product.

Should companies replace country and regional brands with global brands? Many multinational companies would like to replace country and regional brand names for the same product with a global brand name. For example, Mars calls its Snickers candy bar Marathon in England, and its M&M's go by the name Tweets. The products were essentially the same except for the name and packaging. Mars took the bold step of replacing the English names with the U.S. names. It slowly phased in the new names so that consumers would know about the change. The move to global brand names offered several advantages: There would be savings in advertising and packaging; the manufacturing and inventory management process would be simplified; and the corporate brand manager could exercise more central direction on the brand's global development.

How can companies judge the performance of market segment managers? A market segment manager's performance is typically judged by the degree to which the company has increased its market share and profits in that segment. The two performance criteria, however, often are at odds. A hotel manager responsible for increasing the number of business meetings at his hotel can often succeed by reducing the price; here market share will grow and profits will fall. Similarly, a bank manager responsible for increasing the bank's penetration in the superaffluent market might succeed by spending a great deal of money cultivating that market, maybe more than the additional customers are worth. Clearly the company needs to define the weights on different performance goals carefully so that the market segment manager knows whether to emphasize growth or profitability. The company may add some additional criteria, such as performance on customer retention and customer satisfaction.

How can a seamless web be formed among product, sales, and service? Many customers complain that the salesperson has made them a promise but the company's operational units have failed to deliver. The salesperson might have exaggerated the company's capabilities; the product manager may have exaggerated the product availability to the salesperson; or the company's distribution people may have failed in their responsibilities. Whatever the cause, the problem could lose a valued customer. Frank V. Cespedes of the Harvard Business School recently published *Concurrent Marketing: Integrating Product, Sales, and Service*, in which he shows the need for, and the different methods of, forging tighter linkages among those three critical customer-impinging functions.[2]

How can better relations be formed between marketing and other functions, such as R&D, purchasing, manufacturing, and finance? Each company department works on a different logic and seeks to protect that logic. R&D may want to develop the best-engineered products, but marketing may not see sufficient demand for that quality level and price. Purchasing may want to substitute a lower-cost ingredient, but marketing may see that as leading to more repair problems and customer dissatisfaction. Manufacturing people may resist smaller batch manufacturing, but marketing may see it as the next golden opportunity. Finance may want to reduce product support services to save money, but marketing may see this as increasing customer discontent. The point is not that one group is right and the other is wrong. The point is that departments must work more closely together, must dialogue about their conflicts, and must seek team-based solutions that serve the long-run interests of the company.

How can companies do a better job of integrating their marketing communications? Most companies have an Advertising Vice President. They may also have a Sales Promotion manager, a Direct Marketing manager, and a Public Relations marketing manager. It is not likely that those communication specialists actively work together. In consumer companies, most of the budget, which formerly went to advertising, now goes to sales promotion, while the other communication tools receive even less. Don Schultz and his colleagues at Northwestern University have been imploring companies to integrate those functions and tap their synergies. The movement is called Integrated Marketing Communications and covers more than the conventional communication and promotion tools.[3] Every brand contact must deliver the same coherent message. Companies are urged to appoint a CCO, a chief communications officer, just as they might have a CIO, a chief information officer. The CCO would supervise all the communication specialists and create, with their help, a unified communication strategy and set of tactics.

Does a company need a marketing department as it moves from functional departments to process teams? Many companies have soured lately on functional departments, having seen them operate as silos maximizing only their own interests. Thus a purchasing department will try to minimize purchasing costs, which sometimes comes at the expense of product quality. A transportation department may favor rail over air because it keeps down shipping costs, even though the customer has to wait longer for the merchandise.

The influential book *Reengineering the Corporation* urged companies to shift their attention from functions to processes, where processes integrate major blocks of work that the company must perform to deliver on company promises to customers.[4] For example, one major process, order fulfillment and payment, involves several departments: billing, warehousing, inventory, and transportation. Too often, they don't work smoothly together and time is lost. Some companies are appointing process managers whose job is to forge more integration of the separate activities involved in fulfilling a process's goals. The process manager works with a multidisciplinary team. For example, the team managing the new product development process would include a scientist, engineer, manufacturing person, marketer, salesperson, purchasing agent, and finance person.

As process and project teams multiply, marketing personnel may find themselves spending less time in their department and more time as team members carrying out projects. That may decrease the visible size of the marketing department. Each marketer would have a solid-line reporting relation to the project or process team and a dotted-line reporting relation to the marketing department. The head of the marketing department would be responsible for hiring good marketing people, assigning them to teams, getting feedback on their project performance, and making promotion decisions.

How large does a marketing department need to be when all of the company employees start making the customer number one? One traditional function of a marketing department has been to advocate the customers' interests to all the other functions. Many companies today have undergone a transition from being product-driven to being market-driven and customer-driven. Nordstrom, USAA, and the Ritz-Carlton have effectively built a culture where all employees think of the customer as number one. Those companies research and understand the customer's entire purchase and use experience. "Owning" the customer is a companywide function, not just a marketing department function. In such companies, the marketing department may play a smaller role, since every function and process is impregnated with the mission to make the customer number one.

Is marketing properly the lead function in the company in defining product and market strategy? No single function can take total responsibility for defining a company's product and market strategy. Various departments must participate in developing a product or market strategy, since they all will be involved in supporting it.

At the same time, the marketing department is normally more skilled in identifying new market opportunities. Marketers have tools for understanding customer needs and behavior and evaluating and testing the attractiveness of different product concepts. Therefore marketers in many companies may play a disproportionate leading role in proposing and influencing the company's product and market strategies.

Questions to Consider

Marketing is constantly undergoing redefinition and new responsibilities. At one time marketing would have been defined as the art of selling products; later as the science and art of finding and keeping customers; and still later as the science and art of finding, keeping, and growing profitable customers. The changing perspectives on marketing are accompanied by changing perspectives on the nature, structure, and role of the marketing department. It is conceivable that the future marketing department will metamorphose into a different department, perhaps called the Customer Department; or it might break into two or more departments, such as a Marketing Research and Information Department and a Marketing Communications Department. The question is not so much what marketing will look like in the distant future but what improvements can be made in its functioning today. I hope these reflections will stimulate fresh company thinking on the subject.

Here are some things that your company should consider.

1. Do managers in your company see planning as a useful tool or mostly as a corporate ritual and waste of time? If the latter, what can the company do to increase the perceived value of marketing planning to the managers?

2. Does the company's plan format contain clear sections on situation analysis, marketing objectives and goals, marketing strategy, marketing actions, and marketing controls? If not, what improvements can be made? Is the planning format fairly standardized and computer-based so that different levels of management can access specific plans?

3. Is the brand management system working effectively in your company? Are brand managers paying sufficient attention to long-term strategy? Do you think product category management should gain more power relative to brand management?

4. Has your company established a suffficient number of market segment managers and area managers to respond to the differences that exist in the market?

5. Do you see enough seamless cooperation among product management, sales management, and customer service? If not, recommend how to improve the situation.

6. How smooth and respectful are the relations between marketing functions and other departments, such as R&D, purchasing, manufacturing, and finance? What improvements can be made?

10

Evaluating and Controlling Marketing Performance

"I have bad news and good news," says the pilot over the loud-speaker, "we lost our direction, but we are getting there very fast."

After losing each battle, he redoubled his effort (said of Marshall Foch).

Your most important assets—your people, your reputation, your brands, and your customers—are not on the books.—*Ted Levitt*

MARKETING IS A learning game. You make a decision. You watch the results. You learn from the results. Then you make better decisions.

In principle, those who have been doing marketing longer and learning more from their mistakes are the best marketers.

All kinds of things can go wrong in a launched marketing program. The target group might be wrong, the basic offering might be wrong, the price, distribution, or communication might be wrong. Even if those were correctly chosen, the implementation may be poor. When one is disappointed with marketing results, it is important to figure out what went wrong in order to operate more successfully in the future.

We believe the effective marketing organizations are those who develop and apply sound marketing evaluation and control procedures. Two procedures are particularly important:

- Evaluating and interpreting current results and taking corrective action
- Auditing marketing effectiveness and developing a plan to improve weak but important components.

Evaluating and Interpreting Current Results and Taking Corrective Action

Companies set performance goals not only for the year but for smaller periods, such as each quarter or month. The company collects results and checks how close they come to the goals that were set. They celebrate when the results exceed the goals and commiserate or panic when they fall short. But is the company setting the right goals and using the right metrics? One of the worst mistakes a company can make is to set and review financial goals to the neglect of other measures of company health and performance. We would propose that a company should be examining its annual results using three different scorecards. They are a *financial scorecard*, a *marketing scorecard*, and a *stakeholder scorecard*.

Financial Scorecard

The most senior levels of an organization focus their attention on the financial scorecard, particularly the income statement. They know that outside financial analysts will comment on their earnings performance. If their earnings are down or below expectation, the bad news will lead investors to sell their stock. A lower stock price will make capital more costly, with the result that the company will find it harder to achieve the desired rate of return on its assets or equity.

Of course, if the earnings exceed expectations, then the company will find it easier and cheaper to attract new funds for investment and expansion. But they will also have to meet higher expectations.

Exhibit 10–1 presents a company's income statement. It shows quite a good performance. Sales have risen for five years; they almost doubled since the base year. The company's profits tripled over the five-year period. The company's return on sales moved from 6.3 to 12.1 percent, while its return on assets rose from 11.3 percent in the base year to 26.7 percent.

The company's financial performance should be a cause for management and stockholder celebration. Yet a second look at the numbers

EXHIBIT 10–1

A Company's Financial Scorecard

Performance ($ Million)	Base Year	1	2	3	4	5
Sale revenue	$254	$293	$318	$387	$431	$454
Cost of goods sold	135	152	167	201	224	236
Gross contribution	$119	$141	$151	$186	$207	$218
Manufacturing overhead	48	58	63	82	90	95
Marketing and sales	18	23	24	26	27	28
Research and development	22	23	23	25	24	24
Administrative overhead	15	15	15	16	16	16
Net profit	$16	$22	$26	$37	$50	$55
Return on sales (%)	6.3	7.5	8.2	9.6	11.6	12.1
Assets	$141	$162	$167	$194	$205	$206
Assets (% of sales)	56	55	53	50	48	45
Return of assets (%)	11.3	13.6	15.6	19.1	24.4	26.7

Source: Roger J. Best, *Market-Based Management* (Prentice-Hall, 1997), p. 30.

might raise a few sobering questions. The company has kept its R&D expenditures fairly constant during the five years in spite of the sales growth. That means that its R& D expenditures have fallen substantially as a percentage of sales. The question is: Has the company been coasting on some past product patents that are about to expire? Has the company been spending enough on research to build a strong future pipeline of products?

Marketing expenditures, too, have been relatively stable. Of course, there is no reason to increase marketing expenditures for their own sake. In fact, one can conclude that the company's *marketing productivity* has increased since marketing costs have fallen as a percentage of sales. However, the nagging question is whether larger marketing expenditures might have led sales to triple instead of only approach doubling during the period.

At this point one should raise questions that go beyond the financial numbers. One can question whether the financial income statement is an adequate tool for appraising the company's recent performance and

EXHIBIT 10–2

A Company's Marketing Scorecard

Market-Based Performance	Base Year	1	2	3	4	5
Market growth (units)	18.3%	23.4%	17.6%	34.4%	24.0%	17.9%
CommTech sales growth	12.8%	17.8%	13.3%	24.9%	18.2%	7.7%
Market share	20.3%	19.1%	18.4%	17.1%	16.3%	14.9%
Customer retention	88.2%	87.1%	85.0%	82.2%	80.9%	80.0%
New customers	11.7%	12.9%	14.9%	24.1%	22.5%	29.2%
Dissatisfied customers	13.6%	14.3%	16.1%	17.3%	18.9%	19.6%
Relative product quality	+19	+20	+17	+12	+9	+7
Relative service quality	+0	+0	–2	–3	–5	–8
Relative new product sales	+8	+8	+7	+5	+1	–4

Source: Roger J. Best, *Market-Based Management* (Prentice-Hall, 1997), p. 31.

future prospects. Needed is a set of market-based numbers that would reveal more about the fundamental health of the company. Senior management needs to examine a marketing scorecard as well.

Marketing Scorecard

Exhibit 10–2 shows a marketing scorecard for the same company. It features several marketing indicators that might trigger some concern about future prospects. Let's examine each marketing indicator.

MARKET SHARE. Although the company steadily increased its sales, its market share declined from 20.3 to 14.9 percent. The company's impressive sales growth now appears less impressive. The company's sales probably grew because the whole market was growing. In fact, this company failed to increase its sales at the same rate, which means that some other competitors were growing faster.

Market share can, of course, be measured in different ways. The most common way, and the least useful, is to measure the company's sales as a percentage of total industry sales. But since the company's products probably are not aimed at the whole market, that is not a meaningful measure. The proper market share measure is the company's sales as a percentage of the sales in its target market. We need to compare the company's performance with that of its close competitors, i.e., those companies pursuing the same customers with approximately the same offering. By measuring this company's share of its target market, we can tell whether it is the market leader, the second strongest firm, or a minor player. And even if the company started out as the market leader, we want to know whether it is holding, gaining, or losing share. In this case, the company's share is declining. The only possible defense is that the company might be trading share for margin, that is, it may have raised its prices, lost some share, but made up for it in higher total profits.

CUSTOMER RETENTION. Senior management should also be concerned that the customer retention rate has slipped from 88.2 percent in the base year to only 80 percent in the latest year. That will ultimately hurt long-term profits. Companies make most of their money from existing, not new customers. When they lose a customer, they lose a future income stream. IBM, for example, gets deeply upset when it loses a customer. Think of all the computers, printers, modems, software, and services this customer will continue to buy, now from someone else. IBM makes every effort to find out why the customer was lost, so it can avoid losing other customers from similar causes. Interviewing the lost customer might even give IBM a chance to win back this customer upon discovering why he defected.

It makes a difference, of course, which customers defect. If some unprofitable customers defect, it may be good news, not bad news. In fact, companies should consider "firing" their bad customers, or at least raising their charges to make them into profitable customers if they stay.

The worst situation is when the company loses its long-term customers. Customer profitability tends to grow with the length of customer tenure. Longer-term customers tend to buy more, recommend the company more, cost the company less to serve, and accept price increases more graciously. So companies must work hard to retain their best customers and in general must achieve a high customer retention rate. Some of the most profitable companies have customer retention rates above 90 percent.

CUSTOMER SATISFACTION. A declining customer retention rate usually indicates a declining customer satisfaction rate. Indeed, Exhibit 10–2 shows that this company's percentage of dissatisfied customers has increased over the last five years from 13.6 to 19.6 percent. It behooves the company to ferret out the causes behind the increasing dissatisfaction, for if it worsens further, profits will begin to fall.

Most companies track customer satisfaction using a five-point scale: very dissatisfied, somewhat dissatisfied, indifferent, satisfied, and very satisfied. The level of satisfaction is measured not only on an overall basis but for each component of the company's offerings. There may be a great difference between those who report being very dissatisfied and those only somewhat dissatisfied. The company may find that it loses 80 percent of the very dissatisfied customers and only 40 percent of the somewhat dissatisfied customers. In both cases, of course, the company must learn the causes of the dissatisfaction.

Similarly, there can be a great difference between the customers who are satisfied and those very satisfied. Companies can lose anywhere between 10 and 30 percent of their satisfied customers. When asked, such customers might say they were satisfied but found another supplier who could satisfy them more. Smart companies therefore aim not only to satisfy their customers but to delight them. That calls for exceeding customer expectations, not just meeting them.

RELATIVE PRODUCT QUALITY. A company will be more favored when its product quality is high relative to its competitors' product quality. In Exhibit 10–2, we see that the company enjoyed a relative product quality advantage of 19 percent in the base year. In principle, this company in the base year could charge more than its competitors, maybe up to 19 percent more, all else being the same. Even if it charged a premium of, say, 15 percent more, the offer would seem better, because buyers would be getting 19 percent more quality but paying only 15 percent more.

However, we note that five years later, the company's relative product quality has sunk to 7 percent. Either the competitors improved their product quality or this company let its product quality slip. In either case, the company cannot keep charging the premium prices it charged in the past. Buyers would see themselves as being asked to overpay for the product quality difference. The company must either rebuild its quality advantage or adjust its relative prices downward.

RELATIVE SERVICE QUALITY. Customers will respond to the company's service quality as well as its product quality. Exhibit 10–2 shows that the company started with no service quality advantage, and five years later its service quality was 8 percent poorer than its competitors'. Either the competitors have improved their service quality or this company let its service quality slip. This company's service quality disadvantage offsets its product quality advantage and restrains its price premium range.

OTHER INDICATORS. Management may want to add other marketing indicators to the marketing scorecard, including percentages showing the cost of salespeople to sales, sales closings to sales contacts, and so on. The main point is that senior management should not confine its scrutiny to the financial scorecard. Behind good financial results may lurk some impending marketing weaknesses.

Stakeholder Scorecard

An increasing number of companies are adding a stakeholder scorecard in their evaluation of performance. Professor Robert Kaplan of Harvard calls it a *balanced scorecard*.[1] The essential argument is that a company must please not only its stockholders but also its stakeholders—its employees, suppliers, distributors, dealers, and the community. In fact, the interests of the company's stockholders and stakeholders may be at odds if the company isn't careful. One way to increase stockholder profits is to pay less to employees, suppliers, and distributors. Profits will go up in the short run but in the long run the company may lose its good employees, suppliers, and distributors. The argument is therefore made that the company must balance its rewards to its various stakeholders.

The balanced scorecard tracks the level of satisfaction that important stakeholder groups derive from the company's activities and policies. If, for example, the balanced scorecard reveals increased employee dissatisfaction, that may warrant company intervention and correction. If the company starts losing some of its best suppliers, that will result later in lower product quality and slower delivery times. The stakeholder scorecard provides a basis for creating win-win relations with all the company's *partners*. Versions of it have been implemented by Hewlett-Packard, IBM, Xerox, and several other companies.

Improving Marketing Effectiveness Through a Marketing Audit

The three scorecards help a company assess its recent performance and prepare new plans to sustain and improve its future performance. Companies that seek to improve their performance continuously have another task, which is periodically to examine its main functions—marketing, finance, purchasing, R&D, and others—to make sure that each function is appropriately organized for the changing times. Each function should be periodically audited in a systematic manner and reengineered if this is warranted.

Marketing is one of those functions that must be periodically reviewed. Companies today are reconsidering such marketing questions as keeping, expanding, or contracting brand management; replacing field sales with telephone selling; shifting more of the advertising budget into such other communication tools as public relations and Internet advertising; and so on. The best way to review, evaluate, and improve the marketing function is to undertake a *marketing audit*.

Originally the marketing audit comprised a miscellaneous set of questions designed to elicit a picture of how the company's marketing activities are organized and conducted and with what effect. Marketing auditing was a service available from consulting firms, and it varied considerably in form and content. This author developed an early marketing audit instrument that examined seven marketing components: the *macro environment, task environment, marketing strategy, marketing organization, marketing systems, marketing productivity,* and *specific marketing functions*.[2] The audit questions are shown in Exhibit 10–3.

While the question set is comprehensive, users of the instrument should know that not all questions are relevant to a particular company. The auditor has to choose those questions which would be key to understanding and evaluating the company's marketing operations. The goal is to use the information gained in the audit to lead to important findings and recommendations for improving the company's marketing performance. The following definition summarizes the meaning and intention of the marketing audit:

> A marketing audit is a comprehensive, systematic, independent, and periodic examination of a company's—or business unit's—marketing environment, objectives, strategies, and activities with a view to determining problem areas and opportunities and recommending a plan of action to improve the company's marketing performance.

EXHIBIT 10–3

The Components of a Marketing Audit

Part I. Marketing Environment Audit

Macroenvironment

A. Demographic	What major demographic developments and trends pose opportunities or threats to this company? What actions has the company taken in response to these developments and trends?
B. Economic	What major developments in income, prices, savings, and credit will affect the company? What actions has the company been taking in response to these developments and trends?
C. Environmental	What is the outlook for the cost and availability of natural resources and energy needed by the company? What concerns have been expressed about the company's role in pollution and conservation, and what steps has the company taken?
D. Technological	What major changes are occurring in product and process technology? What is the company's position in these technologies? What major generic substitutes might replace this product?
E. Political	What changes in laws and regulations might affect marketing strategy and tactics? What is happening in the areas of pollution control, equal employment opportunity, product safety, advertising, price control, and so forth, that affects marketing strategy?
F. Cultural	What is the public's attitude toward business and toward the company's products? What changes in customer lifestyles and values might affect the company?

Task Environment

A. Markets	What is happening to market size, growth, geographical distribution, and profits? What are the major market segments?
B. Customers	What are the customers' needs and buying processes? How do customers and prospects rate

EXHIBIT 10–3 *(continued)*

	the company and its competitors on reputation, product quality, service, sales force, and price? How do different customer segments make their buying decisions?
C. Competitors	Who are the major competitors? What are their objectives, strategies, strengths, weaknesses, sizes, and market shares? What trends will affect future competition and substitutes for the company's products?
D. Distribution and Dealers	What are the main trade channels for bringing products to customers? What are the efficiency levels and growth potentials of the different trade channels?
E. Suppliers	What is the outlook for the availability of key resources used in production? What trends are occurring among suppliers?
F. Facilitators and Marketing Firms	What is the cost and availability outlook for transportation services, warehousing facilities, and financial resources? How effective are the company's advertising agencies and marketing research firms?
G. Publics	Which publics represent particular opportunities or problems for the company? What steps has the company taken to deal effectively with each public?

Part II. Marketing Strategy Audit

A. Business Mission	Is the business mission clearly stated in market-oriented terms? Is it feasible?
B. Marketing Objectives and Goals	Are the company and marketing objectives and goals stated clearly enough to guide marketing planning and performance measurement? Are the marketing objectives appropriate, given the company's competitive position, resources, and opportunities?
C. Strategy	Has the management articulated a clear marketing strategy for achieving its marketing objectives? Is the strategy convincing? Is the strategy appropriate to the stage of the product life cycle, competitors' strategies, and the state of the economy? Is the company using the best

basis for market segmentation? Does it have clear criteria for rating the segments and choosing the best ones? Has it developed accurate profiles of each target segment? Has the company developed an effective positioning and marketing mix for each target segment? Are marketing resources allocated optimally to the major elements of the marketing mix? Are enough resources or too many resources budgeted to accomplish the marketing objectives?

Part III. Marketing Organization Audit

A. Formal Structure	Does the marketing vice-president have adequate authority and responsibility for company activities that affect customers' satisfaction? Are the marketing activities optimally structured along functional, product, segment, end-user, and geographical lines?
B. Functional Efficiency	Are there good communication and working relations between marketing and sales? Is the product management system working effectively? Are product managers able to plan profits or only sales volume? Are there any groups in marketing that need more training, motivation, supervision, or evaluation?
C. Interface Efficiency	Are there any problems between marketing and manufacturing, R&D, purchasing, finance, accounting, and/or legal that need attention?

Part IV. Marketing Systems Audit

A. Marketing Information System	Is the marketing intelligence system producing accurate, sufficient, and timely information about marketplace developments with respect to customers, prospects, distributors, and dealers, competitors, suppliers, and various publics? Are company decision makers asking for enough marketing research, and are they using the results? Is the company employing the best methods for market measurement and sales forecasting?
B. Marketing Planning Systems	Is the marketing planning system well conceived and effectively used? Do marketers have decision

EXHIBIT 10–3 *(continued)*

	support systems available? Does the planning system result in acceptable sales targets and quotas?
C. Marketing Control System	Are the control procedures adequate to ensure that the annual-plan objectives are being achieved? Does management periodically analyze the profitability of products, markets, territories, and channels of distribution? Are marketing costs and productivity periodically examined?
D. New-Product Development System	Is the company well organized to gather, generate, and screen new product ideas? Does the company do adequate concept research and business analysis before investing in new ideas? Does the company carry out adequate product and market testing before launching new products?

Part V. Marketing Productivity Audit

A. Profitability Analysis	What is the profitability of the company's different products, markets, territories, and channels of distribution? Should the company enter, expand, contract, or withdraw from any business segments?
B. Cost-Effectiveness Analysis	Do any marketing activities seem to have excessive costs? Can cost-reducing steps be taken?

Part VI. Marketing Function Audits

A. Products	What are the company's product line objectives? Are they sound? Is the current product line meeting the objectives? Should the product line be stretched or contracted upward, downward, or both ways? Which products should be phased out? Which products should be added? What are the buyers' knowledge and attitudes toward the company's and competitors' product quality, features, styling, brand names, and so on? What areas of product and brand strategy need improvement?
B. Price	What are the company's pricing objectives, policies,

strategies, and procedures? To what extent are prices set on cost, demand, and competitive criteria? Do the customers see the company's prices as being in line with the value of its offer? What does management know about the price elasticity of demand, experience curve effects, and competitors' prices and pricing policies? To what extent are price policies compatible with the needs of distributors and dealers, suppliers, and government regulation?

C. Distribution

What are the company's distribution objectives and strategies? Is there adequate market coverage and service? How effective are distributors, dealers, manufacturers' representatives, brokers, agents, and others? Should the company consider changing its distribution channels?

D. Advertising, Sales Promotion, Publicity, and Direct Marketing

What are the organization's advertising objectives? Are they sound? Is the right amount being spent on advertising? Are the ad themes and copy effective? What do customers and the public think about the advertising? Are the advertising media well chosen? Is the internal advertising staff adequate? Is the sales promotion budget adequate? Is there effective and sufficient use of sales promotion tools such as samples, coupons, displays, and sales contests? Is the public-relations staff competent and creative? Is the company making enough use of direct, online, and database marketing?

E. Sales Force

What are the sales force's objectives? Is the sales force large enough to accomplish the company's objectives? Is the sales force organized along the proper principles of specialization (territory, market, product)? Are there enough (or too many) sales managers to guide the field sales representatives? Do the sales-compensation level and structure provide adequate incentive and reward? Does the sales force show high morale, ability, and effort? Are the procedures adequate for setting quotas and evaluating performance? How does the company's sales force compare to competitors' sales forces?

Source: Philip Kotler, *Marketing Management*, 9th ed. (Upper Saddle River, NJ: Prentice-Hall, 1997), pp. 780ff.

Many people have worked on improving the marketing audit instrument and procedure, in the interest of making it more scientific and objective. Here I shall outline the approach used by a prestigious consulting firm, Copernicus, because I believe it is one of the best-thought-out marketing audit processes I have seen.[3]

The marketing audit begins with a classification of all marketing activities into twenty-one broad types (see Exhibit 10–4). The aim is to score a company's performance on each of the twenty-one activities on a scale ranging from 0 to 100. The next step is to assess which of the twenty-one activities are the most important for the particular company to perform well, which are of medium importance, and which are of minor importance. As an example, a company's pricing skill may be highly important to a company and yet receive a low score. Clearly that company would need to improve its pricing skill. By evaluating all twenty-one activities on their importance and the company's level of performance, it becomes clear which marketing activities need early improvement and which can wait for improvement at a later date. The company then sets an "improvement calendar," which spells out the order in which marketing activities will be improved over time. Finally, two company people are assigned joint responsibility for improving each activity according to the timetable.

This is the broad picture of the logic of the Copernicus marketing auditing process. Here we fill in further details:

1. Each of the twenty-one marketing activities is judged by a set of questions that will be posed to management. The auditor, however, does not rely solely on management's opinions. The auditor will ask for hard data in the form of documents, plans, and transcripts. For example, if management claims that it has a good knowledge of current customer buying needs but can produce only a market research study that was done five years ago, clearly management deserves a low score on its level of understanding current customer needs.

2. The scoring procedure is based on distinguishing five performance levels of a marketing activity, namely: critical (0–15 points); troubling (16–35); average (36–65); pleasing (66–85); and amazing (86–100). For example, a company's new product success rate can fall into five classes: critical (0% success); troubling (5%); average (10%); pleasing (25%); and amazing (40%+). The auditor, after examining the available evidence, assigns a company performance class and score for each of the twenty-one activities.

EXHIBIT 10–4

Twenty-one Key Marketing Decision Areas

1. Marketing Objectives and Strategies	12. Customer Service Excellence
2. Marketing Climate Analysis	13. Integrated Marketing
3. Segmentation and Targeting	Communications
4. Differentiation and Positioning	14. Distribution/Channel Management
5. Pricing	15. Trade Customer Marketing
6. Product Management	16. New Product Development
7. Advertising Management	17. Marketing Intelligence Systems
8. Public Relations	18. Brand Equity Benchmarks
9. Promotions Management	19. Sales Management
10. Direct Response Marketing	20. Marketing Performance
11. Relational Marketing Management	21. Marketing Organization

Source: Gary R. Morris, Copernican Decision Navigator, 1997 (Tel.: 617-630-8750).

3. Determining which of the twenty-one activities are of high importance, medium importance, and low importance is a more judgmental process worked out between the auditor and management. The decision will influence the order in which various marketing activities are scheduled for improvement.

Exhibit 10–5 shows an elevator company's standings on the twenty-one activities. Clearly the company's marketing performance is very average: Only a few activities are performed above average (for example, customer service is excellent), and a number are performed below average (such as public relations).

Exhibit 10–6 shows the timetable of improvement activities that the elevator company will undertake to increase its marketing effectiveness. A primary person and a secondary person are assigned responsibility for carrying out each improvement at the scheduled time.

The Copernicus approach may be too comprehensive and time-consuming for smaller companies. Still, the central ideas can be adapted. Instead of examining twenty-one activities, the audit can focus on say six to eight activities thought to be important. Each activity can be graded. The gap between the level at which an activity should be performed and the level where it is being performed should be noted. The company should determine the cost and impact of improving each key

EXHIBIT 10–5

Boston Elevators Best Practices Scores

Distribution of Boston Elevators Best Practices Scores

Best Practices Scores

0-15   16-35   36-50   51-65   66-85   86-100

Selected Marketing Decision Areas	Critical	Troubling	Average	Pleasing	Amazing
1) Mktg. Obj. & Strategies			★		
2) Mktg. Climate Analysis			★		
3) Segmentation & Targeting			★		
4) Diff. & Positioning			★		
5) Pricing			★		
6) Product Management			★		
7) Advertising Mgmt.			★		
8) Public Relations		★			
9) Promotions Mgmt.				★	
10) Direct Response Mktg.		★			
11) Relational Mktg. Mgmt.		★			
12) Customer Svc. Excellence				★	
13) IMC			★		
14) Dist/Channel Mgmt.				★	
15) Trade Cust. Marketing				★	
16) New Product Dev.		★			
17) Mktg. Intelligence Sys.			★		
18) Brand Equity Mgmt.			★		
19) Sales Management				★	
20) Marketing Performance			★		
21) Marketing Organization			★		
Overall Best Practices Score			47		

EXHIBIT 10–6

Boston Elevators Three-year Implementation Plan

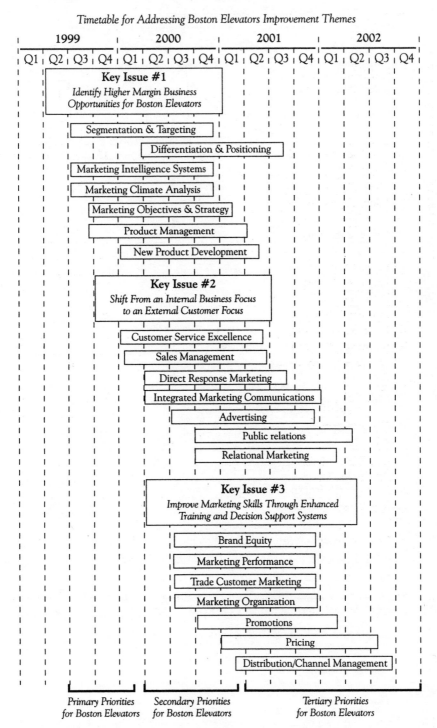

Timetable for Addressing Boston Elevators Improvement Themes

	1999	2000	2001	2002
	Q1 Q2 Q3 Q4	Q1 Q2 Q3 Q4	Q1 Q2 Q3 Q4	Q1 Q2 Q3 Q4

Key Issue #1
Identify Higher Margin Business Opportunities for Boston Elevators

Segmentation & Targeting
Differentiation & Positioning
Marketing Intelligence Systems
Marketing Climate Analysis
Marketing Objectives & Strategy
Product Management
New Product Development

Key Issue #2
Shift From an Internal Business Focus to an External Customer Focus

Customer Service Excellence
Sales Management
Direct Response Marketing
Integrated Marketing Communications
Advertising
Public relations
Relational Marketing

Key Issue #3
Improve Marketing Skills Through Enhanced Training and Decision Support Systems

Brand Equity
Marketing Performance
Trade Customer Marketing
Marketing Organization
Promotions
Pricing
Distribution/Channel Management

Primary Priorities for Boston Elevators   *Secondary Priorities for Boston Elevators*   *Tertiary Priorities for Boston Elevators*

201

activity. Then a "marketing improvement timetable" should be set and responsibilities assigned to specific people.

Marketing audit procedures and forms will probably evolve further as time goes on. The Copernicus system, however, outlines a very useful program that can be implemented at the present time.

Questions to Consider

Marketing is a learned art with some scientific supporting tools. Smart companies install systems so they can learn from their actions. A company's analysis, planning, and implementation must be followed by evaluation and control steps. In particular, management must prepare and analyze three scorecards, namely a financial scorecard, a marketing scorecard, and a stakeholder (balanced) scorecard. Judging performance only by the financial results is not enough.

Because technology and marketplaces are changing rapidly, companies must reexamine from time to time their marketing activities and performance. If their marketing skills fall behind those of their competitors, the next sign will be declining market shares and profitability. The marketing audit instrument offers a systematic way to assess company marketing performance and to uncover new opportunities for improvement.

Here are some questions for your company:

1. Does your company use marketing scorecards in judging performance? What marketing measures are included in your marketing scorecard? What measures should be added?
2. Does your company track the satisfaction levels of major stakeholder groups? Which groups should be tracked, and what sampling procedures can be used?
3. Do you measure your relative product and service quality? Are you pricing higher, the same, or lower than your relative quality advantage will support?
4. Do you see value in conducting a marketing audit? Do you believe that it has value only in troubled times, or would it also have value in prosperous periods?

PART FOUR

TRANSFORMATIONAL MARKETING

11

Adapting to the New Age of
Electronic Marketing

*It is useless to tell a river to stop running; the best thing is to learn
how to swim in the direction it is flowing.—Anonymous*

*When the rate of change inside the company is exceeded by the
rate of change outside the company, the end is near.—Jack Welch,
Chairman of GE*

IN THE COMING decade marketing will be reengineered from A to Z.
There is little doubt that markets and marketing will operate on quite
different principles in the early years of the twenty-first century. The
successor to the Industrial Society—the Information Economy—will
penetrate and change almost every aspect of daily life. The Digital Revolution has fundamentally altered our concepts of space, time, and
mass. A company need not occupy much space; it can be virtual and
anywhere. Messages can be sent and received simultaneously. And such
objects as books, music, and film can be shipped in the form of "bits"
rather than mass.[1]

Today there are more than 100 million people worldwide who can
connect to the Internet. More than 1.5 million domain names are registered on the Internet. Traffic is estimated to double every hundred
days. E-commerce was $20 billion in 1998 and is expected to rise to
$327 billion by A.D. 2002.

Cyberspace will usher in an age when buying and selling will become more automated and convenient. Businesses will be connected to each other and to their customers in a seamless virtual network. Information on the Internet will flow across the globe in an instant and at no cost. Sellers will find it easier to identify potential buyers; and buyers will find it easier to identify the best sellers and products. Time and distance, which acted as great cost and trade barriers in the past, will shrink immeasurably. Merchants who continue to sell in the old ways will slowly vanish from the scene.

The Digital Revolution has opened the door for new startup and niche companies with little capital to reach a worldwide market. As an example, *Clos La Chance Wines* opened its business as a virtual vineyard. The owner buys grapes from other vineyards; leases wine production space and warehouse space; outsources winemaking talent, labels, bottles, and corks; and sells only on the Internet. As a virtual company, it hopes to compete with Mondavi and other well-financed and established winemakers.

Marketers will need to rethink fundamentally the processes by which they identify, communicate, and deliver customer value. They will need to improve their skills in managing individual customers and allies. They will need to involve their customers in the act of codesigning their desired products.

Here we shall look at how the continuously unfolding possibilities unleashed by the digital revolution will change the buying behavior of consumers and businesses. Then we shall tease out the implications of these changed behaviors for the way sellers should operate in the twenty-first century.

How Consumer Buying Behavior Will Change

There are many cool scenarios offered on how our lives will change when computers and ground and satellite-linked networks become commonplace in the home. Here is a recent one:

> Imagine that your house knows you. Imagine it knows you like to listen to Billie Holiday's "Ill Wind" when it's raining outside and "Pump It Up" by Elvis Costello when you're on the StairMaster. Imagine it knows what you have in the fridge and what to order to prepare for Friday evening's formal dinner for four. Imagine it knows to light your path through its halls, interpret your E-mail, and display digital reproductions of Judy Chicago works

on flat-panel monitors when your feminist grandmother visits, Hole posters when your multipierced niece arrives.[2]

What might be found today in the home of billionaire Bill Gates will become commonplace in middle class households within a decade:

- Intelligent security systems will turn lights on and off at different times, detect window breakage or unexpected motion in another room, be able to take a video of any intruders. The front door will house a miniature video camera with face-recognition software that would allow entrance only to recognized persons.
- The computer, television, and telephone will be linked in large-screen video entertainment centers which can instantly download any movie on demand or be used to order an unlimited number of products/services. This center can also be used for videoconferencing where a person(s) in one household can view and talk to a person(s) in one or more other households. These developments will depend upon the speed at which copper wiring into the home is replaced by digital fiber-optic cable or other broadband transmission media.
- There will be several computers throughout the house used by the children to scan encyclopedias or play games and used by the adults for entertainment and to conduct their business and financial affairs.
- A flat-panel screen and computer in the kitchen can be used to scan favorite recipes, view products and "specials"available at the local su-permarket, and order groceries to be delivered within a few hours.
- Much activity in the home will be voice-activated, from entering the front door by saying a password, turning on the lights by saying "Lights on," and dictating letters to the computer instead of using a keyboard.

Households will find it much easier to make product choices and place orders for goods and services. They can look up product descriptions on web sites or monitor comments or carry on conversations in chat rooms. They will visit the sites of information middlemen providers for product information and comparisons. They will use *intelligent agents* who will learn their preferences in music and film and will make new suggestions, and who will review their e-mail and eliminate junk mail. They will be able to obtain advertising and programming on demand. They will use *push technology* to keep them informed of various interests.

Exhibit 11–1 describes how today's consumers can use cyberspace to choose and purchase typical goods and services.

EXHIBIT 11–1

How Cyberbuying Will Change the Way Consumers Obtain Goods and Services

---

Books, Music, Videos, and Software

Today consumers can browse cybermerchants such as *Amazon*, *Barnes & Noble* or *CDnow* to search for specific books, music, videos, and software. These are essentially information products. Consumers can learn what is hot and even get automated recommendations based on their past purchases, or interest profile, or what others with similar purchase profiles have been ordering. The prices are normally lower than those charged by book and music stores, since these cybermerchants don't carry much inventory or rent retail space. Furthermore, retail store personnel are scarcer and more ill-informed, while better information about such products is now available on the Internet. However, consumers will have to add the cost of mail delivery when they don't pick up the goods themselves. Tomorrow, however, many books, music, videos, and software won't be produced in physical form but will simply be downloaded on demand to the customer's computer or TV. Instead of producing, packaging and shipping "atoms," suppliers will download "bits" at a substantially low cost (see Nicholas Negroponte, *Being Digital* [New York: Knopf, 1995]).

Flowers and Gifts

Today consumers can view different flower arrangements on their computer screen and order an arrangement from *1-800-FLOWERS* or dozens of other cybervendors (including cyberdiscounters). They can also enter various cybermalls such as *MarketplaceMCI* or *IQVC* offering gifts and other goods and make their choices.

Clothing

More clothing vendors are appearing on the Internet, such as the *Gap* and *Limited*, from which household members can order their clothing items. In the future many clothiers will offer to "mass customize" items of clothing based on customer supplied sizes and color and fabric preferences.

Automobiles

Today auto buyers can browse the web pages of different automobile manufacturers to see detailed descriptions of their cars or can browse a web site such as *Edmunds* to find new and used car features and prices. From the *Edmund's* site, they can click on *Auto-By-Tel* to search for best dealer and price. They can click on other sites for such car-related purchases as *GEICO* for car insurance, *Warranty* for an extended warranty, and *J.C. Whitney* for auto accessories. In the last year, more than 2 million people bought their cars without shopping in an automobile showroom.

Wine

Wine buyers can turn to Virtual Vineyards, which provides wine education and distribution for more than sixty-five small California vineyards. The web site provides detailed information about each wine, the winery, and the winemaker, along with a tasting chart. The site visitor can order the wine online shipped to his home. The site has added specialty food products that complement the wine selections. It also has translated its offerings into Japanese and has received large orders from Japan. Virtual Vineyards reminds regular customers via e-mail of new wine arrivals and offers prepackaged food and wine gift baskets. It also asks customers to publish their reactions to the wines they purchased.

Newspapers and News

A growing number of consumers are getting their news from such online newspapers as *CNN*, the *Wall Street Journal*, and *The New York Times*.

Stock buying and selling

Many consumers are now getting instantaneous stock market quotes and other financial information from such web sites as E*TRADE and OneSource. They can enter buy and sell orders from their home or office or wherever they have their laptop and modem.

Electronic Money

Consumers will be able to download electronic money (sometimes called Ecash) from their bank account into their hard drive. They will be able to transfer Ecash to vendors for purchases, even for microtransactions, such as payment of 10 cents for a downloaded newspaper article.

How Business Buying and Selling Behavior Will Change

Businesses have traditionally done their purchasing through professional buyers, who would scan catalogs, would phone suppliers, and would try to negotiate better terms. Modern purchasing agents are now adding cybertools to enhance their purchasing capabilities. The Internet offers them much more information than they ever had. They can more easily hunt for the best suppliers and check their credit rating and history. *Information middlemen providers* ("metamediaries") will emerge on the Internet who will assemble and offer evaluations of different suppliers for a small charge.

Exhibit 11–2 shows some ways in which certain businesses are conducting their buying and selling on the Internet.

How Companies Can Win in Cyberspace

We believe the Information Revolution and Cyberspace will substantially alter the marketing landscape and realign the fortunes of various players in the value-delivery process.

Today's consumers face more ways to obtain a good or service than at any time in history. The competition between sales channels is growing more intense. We believe electronic channels will get the upper hand over retail store channels. Let us begin by examining the range of sales channels available to a shopper seeking to purchase a laptop computer. Here are the five principal channel alternatives:

1. *Retail store channel.* The shopper can visit a retail store, such as Circuit City or CompUSA, which carries one or more laptop brands. This channel offers the advantage of letting the shopper see and touch each brand and obtain information and advice from the salesperson. It has the disadvantage of imposing travel and time costs on the shopper and normally charging a higher price than might be available through other channels.

2. *Catalog channel.* The shopper can examine catalogs from some electronics catalog houses, such as Microcomputers Warehouse or J&R Computer World. The catalogs describe and price different laptops. The shopper can make a toll-free phone call and place an order. Catalog marketers sold over $51 billion worth of goods in 1992. The catalog channel has several advantages: ease of ordering; phone service twenty-four hours a day, seven days a week; choice of loaded software; and typically a lower price than buying the same laptop in a retail store. The lower price results from the fact that the catalog house does not rent a retail facility, carry much inventory, or charge a sales tax for out-of-state orders.

3. *Home shopping TV channel.* The shopper may view a laptop offering on home shopping TV and place an order. This channel offers ease of

EXHIBIT 11–2

How Cyberbuying Is Changing the Way Businesses Buy and Sell Goods and Services

---

General Electric (GE)

GE has created the *Trading Process Network* (TPN) where GE, along with other subscribers to GE's service, can request quotes, negotiate terms, and place orders with global suppliers. Suppliers regularly visit this page to put in bids for requested items. GE buyers claim 10–15 percent in cost savings through lower order processing costs.

Cisco Systems

Cisco Systems makes products that help the Internet function, such as multi-protocol routers, digital switching devices, frame relays, and Internet software. Over 13 percent of its 1997 orders come via the Internet. On its web site — *www.cisco.com* — Cisco receives more than 400,000 hits a month. Its web site provides different levels of access to browsers, registered customers, reseller partners, and suppliers. For example, registered customers can do all of their business with Cisco online, such as buying products, checking order status, inspecting prices, downloading software updates, and so on. Cisco now handles over 75 percent of customer service requests over the Internet. Cisco can deliver products ordered online about three days earlier than those ordered by other methods. Cisco claims that its web site is saving $360 million a year in operating costs while simultaneously improving customer/partner satisfaction.

Cisco put together a Knowledge Base of Frequently Asked Questions (FAQ's). A customer can usually get an answer without talking to anyone in the company. That eliminates a lot of phone time and cuts down the phone personnel needed by Cisco. Cisco reduced 70 percent of the calls it was receiving, or 50,000 calls a month. The calls cost Cisco $200 a call (cost is high because of complicated products), thus saving Cisco $10,000,000 a month. Now they have 700 people answering calls instead of 1,000 people. Their call-center people like their work better because it is more challenging. Each new call and solution goes to a tech writer (Polish & Publish) to be entered into the Knowledge Base, thus reducing the number of future calls.

TechData

TechData is a full-line national distributor of PC products, peripherals, and software, servicing 55,000 value-added resellers and retailers with more than 45,000 products from 900 manufacturers. Its site provides an electronic catalog, product searches, pricing, availability, order entry and inquiry options, an index of manufacturers' web sites, and order tracking linked to UPS and FedEx. New

EXHIBIT 11–2 (*continued*)

feature includes Private Label Delivery so that products can be drop-shipped directly to customers' end users.

Egghead.com's Auction

This site provides an auction setting for bidding for various surplus manufactured goods, particularly computer hardware and software, as well as cameras, tools, and TV. The bidding is done in real time at normally great savings to the successful bidder.

Jewelry

A customer may ask a retail jeweler to search for a pear-shaped diamond of four carats with the highest grade of clarity. If the jeweler has joined a certain web site (by paying an annual fee of $100), he can broadcast a request for such a diamond and receive various responses from other jewelers along with their proffered prices. The jeweler can tell his customer what is available and can place an order if the customer wants to proceed.

Travel

A company routinely buys air travel packages for its sales force and convention attendees. It can send messages on the Internet to the major airlines indicating what it wants to buy and can seek the best offers.

---

demonstrating and ordering the product and possibly a lower price. It has the disadvantage of showing only one brand and a price that must be accepted at that moment, leaving no time for comparison shopping.

4. *Direct manufacturer channel.* The shopper may visit the web page of a direct marketer like Dell Computer and order a model equipped with the shopper's desired software. Dell Computer is now selling over $3 million worth of Dell computers a day over the Internet, not counting its sales over the telephone. This direct channel offers a lower computer price than brands sold mainly through retailers, as well as customer-chosen and loaded software. It has the disadvantage that the shopper sees the brand of only one manufacturer at a time.

5. *Electronic intermediary channel.* The shopper can go to the web page of an information middleman who presents and compares the features and prices of all the available brands and indicates where they can be bought for the best price. The electronic middleman may receive income from advertisers, a subscription, or a charge per view. The effect of the electronic middleman is to lower the prices of manufacturers, increase customer welfare, and make middleman profit in the process.

There is a strong opinion that electronic channels will attract business away from store-based channels in many goods and services categories. Store-based channels are growing at the normal population rate of, say, 2 percent, while non–store-based channels are growing at a double-digit rate. Electronic markets offer a lot of advantages to the buyer that are absent from store-based buying. The primary ones are:

- Availability seven days a week, twenty-four hours a day
- No need to drive, park, and shop in a store, and a consequent saving of cost and time
- Potentially a lower price

The main disadvantages of electronic channels are:

- The wait to receive the ordered item(s) might be as little as a day or much longer.
- One cannot touch and feel the merchandise before ordering.

Benjamin and Wigand offer several predictions about electronic markets:[3]

1. As information costs decline, markets characterized by high information and coordination costs will be more highly favored by buyers.
2. Highly familiar or standardized products will increasingly be handled in electronic markets insofar as the customer doesn't need to see or feel them.
3. Products that can be well-supported with "help desks" will have a good chance of being sold on electronic markets.
4. Electronic markets will evolve from single-brand web sales sponsors (such as a Ford automobile web site) to multibrand web page sponsors.
5. Companies with a successful nonelectronic sales channel will also try to set up an electronic sales channel if they foresee an increase in total profits.

6. Electronic linkages between firms will be most likely to increase in the following situations:

    a. Where large purchasers like Wal-Mart see large savings from centralized purchasing and inventory management and require their suppliers to link electronically with them

    b. Where production savings would be substantial from "just-in-time supply" arrangements that require close electronic linkages between the producer and its suppliers

    c. Where companies see large savings from having fewer but larger suppliers who are more closely tied to them

Prediction 2 above makes the point that familiar standardized products would be favored by electronic channels. For example, there is a web page called *NetGrocer* where a shopper can order such standard brands as Campbell's soup, Tide detergent, and other grocery products. And of course, one can order books, music, videos, and other well-known products on the Internet. But the argument has also been made that electronic channels will favor the purchase of "high involvement, information rich" products, such as automobiles and electronic equipment.[4] Suppose one wants to buy a high-quality stereo set. One needs a lot of information about different available brands, their features, and the opinions of experts. The Internet can provide rich information on features and prices and allows easy ordering of the final choice.

In describing electronic channels, we refer to the use of electronic media for information, discussion, and ordering, specifically the telephone, computer, and TV. The telephone was the first electronic medium for obtaining information and placing orders. The arrival of the Internet made it possible to gather information and place orders through the computer. With the imminent emergence of interactive TV, still another electronic medium will become available. What has yet to be determined is the future relative popularity of each medium. Banks, for example, face this problem when they want to supply home-based banking and have to determine whether to base it on the telephone, the computer, or interactive TV. Ultimately, of course, the three electronic media will converge into one appliance capturing the characteristics of all three media.

In the light of the foregoing, what should today's businesses do to ensure winning in the New Electronic Age? Here are four principles:

1. BUILD AND ACTIVELY MANAGE A CUSTOMER DATABASE. In this era of scarce customers, companies need to capture the names of and as much useful information as possible about potentially valuable prospects and customers. A rich customer database can provide the company with a strong competitive advantage. The company can search and rate different groups and individuals for their probability of responding to a given offer or highly tailored offers. A database permits a company's targeting to be superefficient.

2. DEVELOP A CLEAR CONCEPT ON HOW THE COMPANY SHOULD TAKE ADVANTAGE OF THE INTERNET. A company can develop a presence on the Internet in at least seven ways. The company can use the Internet to do research, provide information, run discussion forums, provide training, carry on online buying and selling (i.e., e-commerce), provide online auctioning or exchanging, and even deliver "bits" to customers. These possibilities are listed in Exhibit 11–3. A company should place checks indicating how it is currently using the Internet, and then speculate on additional desirable uses to add in the next year, in two to five years, or never.

The company's web page must be appealing, relevant, and current if it is to attract repeat visits. Companies should consider using state-of-the-art graphics, sound, and video. They should add weekly news or features ("coming next week: John Jones suggests the stock picks of the week"). The site can be developed to provide valuable help, as has been done by *Federal Express* (the ability to trace the location of a package), *Virtual Vineyard* (provides product expertise and a personal connoisseur to recommend choice wines), *Holiday Inn* (booking rooms over the Internet), or *Visa* (telling where its cash machines are located). The site can also try to establish editorial leadership: for example, *Edmund's* is considered the best site for researching automobile features and prices. Editorial authority would enable the site to attract the banners of related companies who may pay a fee to advertise on the company's web page.

The company must view its web page critically and ask a number of questions: Why would someone want to surf to our site? What is interesting about our page? Why would someone want to return to our page? Why would someone want to advertise on our page? (See Exhibit 11–4 for a description of two creatively conceived web sites).

3. PUT YOUR COMPANY BANNER ON RELATED WEB SITES. The company should consider what web sites their target customers are likely to visit and con-

EXHIBIT 11–3

Seven Ways to Use the Internet

1. *Do research*

2. *Provide information*

    — Information about company products, services, locations, history (Coca-Cola)

    — Customer service support (PalmPilot)

    — Customer advice (Clinique, Amazon)

    — Audio and/or video clips for sampling music, books, videos

    — Employee and sales force information (Intranet)

    — Reseller information system (Ford)

    — Provide meta-information (Edmund's)

3. *Provide discussion forums*

4. *Provide training*

5. *Provide online buying and selling*

    — Supplementary ordering channel (Dell)

    — Only ordering channel (CDnow, Amazon)

6. *Provide online auctioning or exchanging*

7. *Provide online "bits" delivery*

1=Now, 2=Next year, 3=2–5 years, 4=Never

sider putting advertising banners on those sites. If the target customers are financial investors, the company may want to place its banners on Schwab's *OneSource* and other sources of financial information. If the target audience is broader, the company might put a banner on one of the popular web sites, such as *Hot Wired, Pathfinder, ESPNET SportsZone,* or *Playboy.* However, the company might have to pay to a popular site between $30,000 and $100,000 for a three-month placement the size of a postage stamp. Companies should negotiate, including offering only to pay for "hits," not exposures (P&G insists on this arrangement).

EXHIBIT 11–4

Two Creative Web Sites

Lexus Automobile Web Page

This page welcomes the visitor to the "Lexus Center of Performing Arts" with a personal concierge, Alex, who offers several different halls to explore:

Model Gallery: information on vehicle performance, luxury, safety, accessories, and specifications

Dealer Grande Hall: provides dealer information by area code, state, and links to dealership's web site

Tech Center: provides a glimpse of technical innovations

Events Center: lists Lexus-sponsored sports, cultural, and automotive events

Reading Room: provides up-to-date information including awards, articles, and reviews

Patrons' Circle: a room reserved exclusively for Lexus owners which offers special privileges available only to such owners

Financial District: helps customer decide whether to buy or lease a vehicle through Lexus Financial Services

E-Mailbox: offers brochures and direct communications with Lexus

Wishing Well: describes Lexus's commitment to various charities

Clinique Web Page

Provides excellent information about cosmetics to consumers

Provides a wide range of personal consultation and beauty tips, new product announcements, and pricing information

Offers a tool to help consumers evaluate their own skin type to help select appropriate products

Offers information about special workshops and store locations

(Does not offer online purchasing, however. This would jeopardize relations with current sales channels)

As an example of a creative banner approach, Toyota USA places its banner on *Yahoo*'s home page showing a small graphic of the 1997 Camry with copy reading: "Want to win a new Camry? Click here." A person could enter the sweepstakes by providing his or her name, address, phone number, e-mail, type of car currently driven, year, make, model, and whether it is leased or owned. The viewer could also request information about the Camry. And if he would visit a Toyota dealer, he could get a coupon that could be redeemed for a sixty-minute long-distance MCI calling card.

Even when a company is disappointed in the number of hits on its web page, there is some evidence that the banner produced a positive ad exposure effect that elevated the viewer's brand awareness. Not surprisingly, more marketers are adding web advertising as a line item in their ad budget. "Of the 100 Leading National Advertisers . . . 46 have purchased Web advertising . . . and nearly all have corporate Web sites."[5]

4. BE EASILY ACCESSIBLE AND QUICK IN RESPONDING TO CUSTOMER CALLS. Customers have high and rising expectations about how quickly and adequately they should receive answers to questions and complaints sent in by phone or e-mail. America Online received terrible word-of-mouth in 1997 when its subscribers couldn't get on line or reach the provider for help. Computer and software companies do a good job of selling their products but tend to do a poor job of providing sufficient customer support service to answer the myriad questions that purchasers have about high-tech products.

Sony is an exception. It has addressed this problem by selling its laptop computer with SOS (Sony Online Service). Their ad reads:

> Computers have come a long way. Getting help with them hasn't. That is, until we developed S.O.S. (Sony Online Support). Simply put, if you have a problem, we'll help you solve it. In fact, we can even do it without your assistance. . . . With your permission, we can actually get into your computer, have a look around, and correct whatever the problem is. (And we can do it from thousands of miles away.) All you have to do is click on our little icon and your computer will call our service center. We'll take it from there.

Setting up an e-mail option on a web page could backfire if the company is not prepared to provide efficient customer response. Volvo's U.S. headquarters was one of the first to provide e-mail access on its web page. However, it received occasional messages like this: "Nice web site, but the sun roof on my 850 leaks." Volvo didn't set up a sufficient staff to respond to such problems and decided instead to terminate its e-mail feature.[6]

Exhibit 11–5 summarizes the ways in which traditional marketing practice will change as a result of electronic marketing.

EXHIBIT 11–5

How Marketing Will Change With Cybermarketing

Marketing Activity	Traditional Marketing	Cybermarketing
Advertising	Prepare print, video or voice copy and use standard media vehicles such as television, radio, newspapers and magazines. Usually only very limited information can be presented	Design extensive information and put it on the company's Webpage and buy banners on other sites
Customer service	Provide service five days a week, eight hours a day in the store or over the phone in response to customer calls; provide on-site visits to maintain or repair	Provide 7-day, 24-hour service response; send phone, fax or e-mail solutions; carry on online dialogue; repair problems from a distance through computer diagnostics
Selling	Phoning or visiting prospects and customers and demonstrating product physically or by projective equipment	Videoconferencing with prospect and demonstrating product on computer screen
Marketing research	Use of individual interviews, focus groups, and mailed or phoned surveys	Use of newsgroups for conversation and interviewing and e-mail questionnaires

Questions to Consider

The rapid pace of change in the Information Age makes it imperative that each company sets aside serious time to peer into the future and ask what adaptations it must make now to survive and prosper. Companies need to answer the following questions as they compete to shape their future in the twenty-first century.

1. Has your company prepared a scenario of how your business will probably look in five years? Which players in the task environment will be helped or hurt by the Information Revolution? Where will profits be made in the value chain?
2. Has your company prepared a web site(s) providing information about your products and company? Does your web site offer some additional attractions or benefits that will bring repeated viewing?
3. Has your company maximized the ease with which prospects and customers can reach you with inquiries, suggestions, or complaints? How fast is your company able to respond to these messages?
4. Is your company building a rich database of the names and profiles of prospects/customers, dealers, and suppliers?
5. Has your company set up an Intranet for company personnel to communicate electronically with each other and with the company's central data banks?
6. Has your company set up Extranets linking to its major customers, distributors, and suppliers?

Appendix

Characteristics, Success Strategies, and Marketing Department Roles in Different Types of Industrial Businesses

ALTHOUGH THE MARKETING mindset and marketing processes are universal, each business and market brings into play specific features. A talented marketer selling heavy equipment would need new knowledge and thought processes if he or she were to switch to selling a commodity. Here we list, for several business markets, their specific characteristics, strategic success factors, and the role played by the marketing department in each case.

I. Project Selling

A. Examples: selling defense systems, power plants, major bridges, large-scale computer systems
B. Characteristics:
  1. Requires a long selling cycle (6 months to 2 years) and a lot of patience
  2. Usually requires a multifunctional sales team (sales, engineering, operations, finance, senior management, safety)
  3. Can involve a bidding situation or request for proposal
  4. Buying decision made by a high-level buying group
  5. Often involves political as well as economic considerations
C. Success strategies:
  1. Relationship and trust are critical to success.
  2. Vendor people get very close to many of the buying company people; relationship marketing.
  3. Team needs ability to influence its own company people up and down the line to deliver fast response time.

4. It helps for the company president to be part of the selling team.
5. Bid price should be set in context of what total follow-on business may be worth over the customer lifetime; aim at multiyear contracts; still there is a lot of short-run project selling needed to meet this year's goals.
6. Team must carefully study customer buying criteria and must determine which competitors will bid and their respective strengths and weaknesses.
7. Need to understand the customer's business and their customers' business
8. Need to do consultative selling and solution selling
9. The solution should show how feature/function/benefit translates to value for the customer.

D. Marketing department role
1. Cost and pricing analysis and creative value-based pricing models
2. Know how to use counter-trade and be on top of exchange rate fluctuations
3. Supplying marketing research and competitive information
4. Assessing customer buying behavior and influence
5. A limited marketing department and a strong commercial unit concerned with tactical marketing; commercial people need information system helping them formulate a profitable offer and facilitating continuous team communication; simulations to look at multiple "what-ifs" to develop designed solutions with the customer
6. Building brand and corporate identity
7. Determining strategic implications to the business

II. *Heavy Equipment Selling*

A. Examples: selling trucks, tractors, printing machines, mainframes
B. Characteristics: depends on whether sale is one-time or repeat
C. Success strategies:
1. Segmenting the market into different types of buyers and equipment requirements
2. Choosing the target segments to satisfy and not spreading too thin over too broad a product line
3. Designing the right product and value proposition
4. Developing a strong aftermarket (parts and service) operation,

because downtime is costly and capital equipment lasts long and needs a strong aftermarket

5. Deciding on pricing as it affects whether to make money on the equipment sale or the aftermarket parts and service
6. Developing a good dealer training program and a strong and loyal dealer network
7. Developing a strong guarantee that meets industry standards and that goes along with a real reputation for dependability and durability
8. Developing a strong sales force to serve dealers but also developing information technology infrastructure to support dealers, create confidence that the dealers are technically competent, and reduce direct sales force costs
9. Develop a system of incentives for dealers to give time to your products and evaluate their performance
10. The ability to build a strong brand positioning and personality
11. Good equipment installation and debugging programs
12. Good customer training programs
13. Willingness to adapt product and service to large customer requirements

D. Marketing department role
 1. To develop good segmentation, targeting, and positioning strategies
 2. Strong marketing communications programs to dealers and end users
 3. Strong dealer and customer feedback programs to know whether objectives are being met

III. *Industrial Commodity Selling*

A. Examples: selling raw materials, screws, component parts, paper, shipping containers, cleaning fluids.
B. Success factors:
 1. Must build a sufficient product range and availability of supply to meet customer demand requirements
 2. Must strive to be a low-cost producer
 3. Important to achieve operational excellence (high reliability of on-time delivery and product quality and performance)
 4. Brand building around technological leadership
 5. Training in the use of the products and application support

6. Continuous improvement in the product—lighter, faster, cheaper, better, louder, brighter, etc.
7. Must build a strong network of distributors and dealers and get them to pay a lot of attention to recommending the company's product
8. Distributor sales force works to get contract, which may be a bid situation; automatic reordering thereafter, so salespeople spend most of their time in customer acquisition rather than in customer maintenance
9. Be good at identifying value impact on customer's bottom line

C. Marketing department role
1. Coordinating R&D activities to support the customer
2. Setting a price range for sales to manage
3. Selling to the sales force and designing launch and advertising material and trade show participation
4. Needs product managers, application segment managers, and a strong sales force
5. Develop feedback mechanisms for measuring customer needs and satisfaction
6. Two structures may be needed: a project-type structure to win (say) an automobile manufacturer's business for a continuously supplied product such as paint, and a salesperson structure to meet the normal needs of the customer and to make sure the customer is satisfied

IV. *Continuous direct supplier marketing*

A. Examples: Continuous supply to an OEM; P&G supplying Wal-Mart.
B. Success strategies:
1. Locate near the customer or at least provide good distribution and availability
2. Adapt the plant and delivery system to the customer's requirements
3. Secure a long-term contract or a good working relationship
4. Supplier must have the ability to improve productivity continuously while reducing costs and prices over time
5. Supplier must anticipate customer needs, use automatic replenishment without customer needing to place orders
6. Sell direct to large customers and use distributors to reach

smaller customers. Supply both with good marketing information and support

C. Marketing department role: similar to role of department in project marketing

V. *Job shop marketing*

A. Examples: contract manufacturing, repair shops
B. Success strategies:
   1. Ability to customize
   2. A manufacturing system that is flexible
C. Marketing department role
   1. Minor; most of the business comes from a technical sales force
   2. Provide "sales tools": data sheets, etc.

VI. *Industrial services*

A. Examples: selling plant cleaning services, payroll services, staff canteen, night security patrols
B. Success strategies:
   1. Service reliability and accuracy designed to exceed customer expectations
   2. Price and time should be less than if customer performed his own service
   3. Flexibility of service availability (7 days a week)
C. Marketing department role
   1. Develop a brand for the service to build credibility
   2. Inform customers of their actual costs of providing their own service

VII. *Professional services*

A. Examples: selling banking services, insurance services
B. Success strategies:
   1. Technical expertise
   2. Speed of solution and reporting
   3. Competitive prices
   4. Relationship management with customers and other significant parties

C. Marketing department role
    1. Must define best segments to target and help develop the strategic portfolio of services
    2. Help develop expertise databases
    3. Promote the firm's distinctiveness

VIII. *Telecommunications service*

A. Example: selling communications services to hospitality market
B. Success strategies:
    1. Knowledge of market, applications, and problems
    2. Support organization dedicated to target market
    3. Packaged solutions (not just products and price)
C. Marketing department role
    1. Package management and delivery
    2. Customer events to build relationships
    3. Enhance visibility in the marketplace

IX. *Wholesale financial services*

A. Examples: credit card processing, credit insurance, warrant providers, private pension plan administrators
B. Characteristics
    1. High-volume, low-cost processing
    2. Systems/technology intensive
    3. Sophisticated buyer (may involve RFP)
    4. Ease of administration critical to retailer
C. Success strategies
    1. Important to achieve operational excellence
    2. Increase market share to maintain low cost position
    3. Innovative product line and extensions
    4. Processing systems that are flexible and somewhat customizable
    5. Understand retailer's business well enough to develop/conduct training programs for retail sales force
D. Marketing department role
    1. Supply program expertise and support for value-adding through relationship management
    2. Negotiate price and contracting parameters
    3. Coordinate new account/product installations
    4. Coordinate account relationships/profitability management

X. *Specification selling*

A. Example: selling individual products to large construction projects
B. Characteristics:
   1. Long selling cycle (6 months to 2 years)
   2. Decision-maker is not the final purchaser
C. Success strategies
   1. Understand and get close to the specifying/consulting engineers who have the initial influence and final veto
   2. Having achieved a specification at early design stages, follow it through the chain to contractors/end users to make sure it sticks
   3. Become a part of the project design team
D. Marketing department role
   1. Research, tracking of major projects
   2. Intensive marketing communications in the project chain
   3. Value-based pricing, cost vs. labor savings
   4. Evaluating and increasing customer service levels

NOTES

1. Building Profitable Businesses Through World-Class Marketing

1. Adrian J. Slywotzky, *Value Migration: How to Think Several Moves Ahead of Competition* (Boston: Harvard Business School Press, 1996).

2. Marshall McLuhan, *Understanding Media: The Extensions of Man* (London: Routledge and Kegan Paul, 1964).

3. Nicholas Negroponte, *Being Digital* (New York: Knopf, 1995).

4. Peter M. Senge, *The Fifth Discipline: The Art and Practice of the Learning Organization* (New York: Doubleday/Currency, 1990).

5. Michael E. Porter, "What Is Strategy?" *Harvard Business Review*, November–December 1996, pp. 61–78.

6. See Robert E. Wayland and Paul M. Cole, *Customer Connections: New Strategies for Growth* (Boston: Harvard Business School Press, 1997).

2. Using Marketing to . . . Deliver Value

1. Akio Morita, *Made in Japan*, (New York: Dutton, 1986).

2. Peter Clothier, *Multi-level Marketing: A Practical Guide to Successful Network Selling* (London: Koan Page, 1990).

3. Wendell R. Smith, "Product Differentiation and Market Segmentation as Alternative Marketing Strategies," *Journal of Marketing*, July 1956, pp. 3–8.

4. Robert Blattberg and John Deighton, "Interactive Marketing: Exploiting the Age of Addressibility" *Sloan Management Review*, 33, no. 1 (1991):5–14.

5. Robert E. Linneman and John L. Stanton, Jr., *Making Niche Marketing Work: How to Grow Bigger by Acting Smaller* (New York: McGraw-Hill, 1991).

6. Hermann Simon, *Hidden Champions* (Boston: Harvard Business School Press, 1996).

7. B. Joseph Pine II, *Mass Customization* (Boston: Harvard Business School Press, 1993). Also see Marc H. Meyer and Alvin P. Lehnerd, *The Power of Product Platforms* (New York: The Free Press, 1997).

8. Thomas V. Bonoma, *The Marketing Edge: Making Strategies Work* (New York: The Free Press, 1985).

9. Frank V. Cespedes, *Concurrent Marketing: Integrating Product, Sales, and Service* (Boston: Harvard Business School Press, 1995); and *idem, Managing Marketing Linkages: Text, Cases, and Readings* (Upper Saddle River, NJ.: Prentice-Hall, 1996).

10. Michael J. Lanning, *Delivering Profitable Value* (Oxford, UK: Capstone, 1998).

11. Simon Knox and Stan Maklan, *Competing on Value: Bridging the Gap Between Brand and Customer Value* (London: Financial Times, 1998).

3. *Identifying Market Opportunities* . . .

1. See the Ikea case in Robert D. Buzzell, John A. Quelch, and Christopher Bartlett, *Global Marketing Management: Cases and Readings*, 3d ed. (Reading, MA.: Addison-Wesley, 1995), pp. 69–95.

2. Sandra Vandermerwe, *From Tin Soldiers to Russian Dolls: Creating Added Value Through Services* (Oxford, UK: Butterworth Heinemann, 1994).

3. Igor Ansoff, "Strategies For Diversification," *Harvard Business Review*, September–October, 1957, p. 114.

4. Modesto A. Madique and Billie Jo Zirger, "A Study of Success and Failure in Product Innovation: The Case of the U.S. Electronics Industry," *IEEE Transactions on Engineering Management*, November 1984, pp. 192–203.

5. For more detail, see Evan I. Schwartz, *Webonomics: Nine Essential Principles for Growing Your Business on the World Wide Web* (New York: Broadway Books, 1997), pp. 98–101.

6. Madique and Zirger, "Study of Success and Failure in Product Innovation."

4. *Developing Value Propositions* . . .

1. Michael Porter, *Competitive Strategy* (New York: Free Press, 1980).

2. Michael Treacy and Fred Wiersema, *The Disciplines of Marketing Leaders* (Reading, MA.: Addison-Wesley, 1994).

3. Jean-Noel Kapferer, *Strategic Brand Management: New Approaches to Creating and Evaluating Brand Equity* (New York: Free Press, 1994).

4. Robert Spector and Patrick D. McCarthy, *The Nordstrom Way: The Inside Story of America's #1 Customer Service Company* (New York: John Wiley & Sons, 1997).

5. Jan Carlzon, *Moments of Truth* (New York: HarperCollins, 1989).

5. *Developing and Using Market Intelligence*

1. See Christina Del Valle, "They Know Where You Live—and How You Buy," *Business Week*, February 7, 1994, p. 89.

2. Faith Popcorn and Lys Marigold, *The Popcorn Report* (New York: HarperBusiness, 1992), and *Clicking: 16 Trends to Future Fit Your Life, Your Work, Your Business* (New York: HarperCollins, 1996).

3. Steven P. Schnaars, *Managing Imitation Strategies* (New York: Free Press, 1994).

4. Michael R. Leenders and David L. Blenkhorn, *Reverse Marketing: The New Buyer-Supplier Relationship* (New York: Free Press, 1988).

5. See Jeffrey H. Dyer, "How Chrysler Created an American Keiretsu," *Harvard Business Review*, July–August 1996, pp. 42–56.

6. See George W. Columbo, *Sales Force Automation* (New York: McGraw-Hill, 1994) and Thomas Siebel and Michael Malone, *Virtual Selling: Going Beyond the Automated Sales Force to Achieve Total Sales Quality* (New York: The Free Press, 1996).

7. See Eric von Hippel, *The Sources of Information* (New York: Oxford University Press, 1988).

8. Philip Kotler, "A Design for the Firm's Marketing Nerve Center," *Business Horizons*, Fall 1966, pp. 63–74.

9. See Gilbert A. Churchill, Jr., *Marketing Research: Methodological Foundations*, 6th ed. (Fort Worth, TX: Dryden, 1994).

10. See Gary L. Lilien and Arvind Rangaswamy, *Marketing Engineering: Computer-assisted Marketing Analysis and Planning* (Reading, MA.: Addison-Wesley, 1997).

11. Bradley T. Gale, *Managing Customer Value* (New York: Free Press, 1994).

6. Designing the Marketing Mix

1. Neil H. Borden, "The Concept of the Marketing Mix," *Journal of Advertising Research,* June 1964, pp. 197–208.

2. Philip Kotler, "Megamarketing," *Harvard Business Review,* March–April 1986, pp. 117–24

3. Robert Lautenborn, "New Marketing Litany: 4 P's Passé; C-Words Take Over," *Advertising Age,* October 1, 1990, p. 26.

4. See Bernd Schmitt and Alex Simonson, *Marketing Aesthetics* (New York: Free Press, 1997).

5. Robert J. Dolan, "Power Pricing Policies," lecture, Harvard Business School, June 17, 1997.

6. See Michael V. Marn and Robert L. Rosiello, "Managing Price, Gaining Profit," *Harvard Business Review,* September–October 1992, pp. 84–94.

7. Ernest Glad and Hugh Becker, *Activity-based Costing and Management* (New York: John Wiley & Sons, 1996).

8. See "Shootout at PC Corral, Texan Computer Giants Dell and Compaq Do Battle," *U.S. News & World Report,* June 23, 1997, pp. 37–38.

9. Actually the Tattered Cover, an independent bookstore in Denver, pioneered the modern hospitality-oriented super bookstore before Barnes & Noble came on the scene. See Leonard Berry, *On Great Service* (New York: Free Press, 1995).

10. See Louis W. Stern and Frederick D. Sturdivant, "Customer-driven Distribution Systems," *Harvard Business Review,* July–August 1987, pp. 34–41.

11. Don E. Schultz and Jeffrey S. Walters, *Measuring Brand Communication* (New York: Association of National Advertisers, 1997).

12. See Robert C. Blattberg and Scott A. Neslin, *Sales Promotion: Concepts, Methods, and Strategies* (Englewood Cliffs, NJ: Prentice-Hall, 1990).

13. See Regis McKenna, *The Regis Touch* (Reading, MA: Addison-Wesley, 1985); and Regis McKenna, *Relationship Marketing* (Reading, MA: Addison-Wesley, 1991).

14. George W. Columbo, *Sales Force Automation* (New York: McGraw-Hill, 1994).

15. For some interesting data and findings on key account management, see Sanjit Sengupta, Robert E. Krapfel, and Michael A. Pusateri, "The Strategic Sales Force," in *Marketing Management,* Summer 1997, pp. 29–34.

16. Peter R. Peacock, "Data Mining in Marketing: Part 1," *Marketing Management,* Winter 1998, pp. 9–18; "Part 2," Spring 1998, pp. 15–25.

7. Acquiring, Retaining, and Growing Customers

1. See John Goodman, "Complaint Handling in America," study by Technical Assistance Research Program (TARP), U.S. Office of Consumer Affairs, 1986.

2. Neil Rackham, *SPIN Selling* (New York: McGraw-Hill, 1988). Also see his *SPIN Selling Fieldbook* (New York: McGraw-Hill, 1996).

3. William A. Sheriden, *Marketing Ownership: The Art and Science of Becoming #1* (New York: Amacom, 1994), and Carl Sewell and Paul Brown, *Customers for Life* (New York: Pocket Books, 1990).

4. Different authors have proposed other customer development stages. See Murray Raphel and Neil Raphel, *Up the Loyalty Ladder: Turning Sometime Customers into Full-time Advocates of Your Business* (New York: HarperBusiness, 1995); and Jill Griffin, *Customer Loyalty: How to Earn It, How to Keep It* (New York: Lexington Books, 1995).

5. See Goodman, "Complaint Handling in America."

6. *Ibid.*

7. Timothy W. Firnstahl, "My Employees Are My Service Guarantee," *Harvard Business Review*, July–August 1989, pp. 29–34.

8. Frederick F. Reichheld, *The Loyalty Effect* (Boston: Harvard Business School Press, 1996).

9. See Kenneth Blanchard, *Raving Fans: A Revolutionary Approach to Customer Service* (New York: William Morrow & Co., 1993).

10. Regis McKenna, *The Regis Touch* (Reading, MA: Addison-Wesley, 1985), and *Relationship Marketing* (Reading, MA: Addison-Wesley, 1991). Also see Jerry R. Wilson, *Word-of-Mouth Marketing* (New York: John Wiley, 1991).

11. See Sherden, *Market Ownership*, p. 77.

8. Designing and Delivering More Customer Value

1. A company using experience curve strategy would increase its size in the existing technology but would be vulnerable to a company that introduced a new, lower-cost technology. Another issue is whether the experience cost curve falls as fast as expected. Finally, the theory won't deliver the expected results if two or more firms decide to compete on an experience curve basis.

2. See "Shootout at PC Corral: Texan Computer Giants Dell and Compaq Do Battle," *U.S. News & World Report*, June 23, 1997, pp. 37–38.

3. The term originally appeared in Stanley M. Davis, *Future Perfect* (Reading, MA.: Addison-Wesley, 1987). Later the topic was researched intensively by B. Joseph Pine, who published his findings in *Mass Customization* (Boston: Harvard Business School Press, 1993).

4. See Hermann Simon, *Hidden Champions* (Boston: Harvard Business School Press, 1996), p. 116.

5. See Fred Wiersema, *Customer Intimacy: Pick Your Partners, Shape Your Culture, Win Together* (Santa Monica, CA.: Knowledge Exchange, 1996).

6. See Christopher W. L. Hart, *Extraordinary Guarantees* (New York: Amacom, 1993).

9. Planning and Organizing for More Effective Marketing

1. See Thomas V. Bonoma and Benson P. Shapiro, *Industrial Market Segmentation: A Nested Approach* (Cambridge, MA: Marketing Science Institute, June 1983).

2. See Frank V. Cespedes, *Concurrent Marketing: Integrating Product, Sales, and Service* (Boston, MA.: Harvard Business School Press, 1995).

3. Don E. Schultz, Stanley I. Tannenbaum, and Robert F. Lauterborn, *Integrated Marketing Communications: Pulling It Together and Making It Work* (Lincolnwood, Il.: NTC Publishing Co., 1993).

4. Michael Hammer and James Champy, *Reengineering the Corporation* (New York: HarperCollins, 1993).

10. Evaluating and Controlling Marketing Performance

1. Robert Kaplan and David P. Norton, *The Balanced Scorecard: Translating Strategy into Action* (Boston: Harvard Business School Press, 1996).

2. See Philip Kotler, William Gregor, and William Rodgers, "The Marketing Audit Comes of Age," *Sloan Management Review*, Winter 1989, pp. 49–62.

3. Copernicus can be contacted at www.copernicusmarketing.com.

11. Adapting to the New Age of Electronic Marketing

1. See Stanley M. Davis, *Future Perfect* (Reading, MA.: Addison-Wesley, 1986).

2. Susan Gregory Thomas, "The Networked," *U.S. News & World Report*, December 1, 1997, p. 66.

3. Robert Benjamin and Rolf Wigand, "Electronic Markets and Virtual Value Chains on the Information Superhighway," *Sloan Management Review*, Winter 1995, pp. 31–41.

4. Evan I. Schwartz, *Webonomics: Nine Essential Principles for Growing Your Business on the World Wide Web* (New York: Broadway Books, 1997), pp. 92–116.

5. Debra Aho Williamson, "Web Ads Mark 2nd Birthday with Decisive Issues Ahead," from *Advertising Age* web page, 5/9/97.

6. Schwartz, *Webonomics*, p. 48.

COMPANY AND BRAND NAME INDEX

SUBJECT INDEX